THE VILLAGE OF BIDDENHAM THROUGH THE AGES

Katherine Fricker
Mary McKeown
Diana Toyn

First published 2012

Published by Biddenham Historical Trust,
Biddenham, Bedford

While we have made every effort to locate sources of illustrations and information, we have not always succeeded. We apologise if any of the information contained herein is inaccurate – we have tried to verify all our sources.

ISBN No 978-0-9551356-2-0

Publisher: Bedfordshire Bugle, 37 Church End, Biddenham, Bedford MK40 4AR, UK.

Printed by Stonebridges Printers Limited, 16 Shuttleworth Road, Elm Farm Industrial Estate, Bedford MK41 0EP.

CONTENTS

Chapter		Page

LIST OF ILLUSTRATIONS
Black and white

Colour Plates

SOURCES OF ILLUSTRATIONS

Black and White

Albion Archaeology – 1, 2.
Jonathan Bean - 31, 42, 59, 65, 66, 76, 77, 78, 83, 84.
Bedfordshire County Council - 43.
Bedfordshire Times and Record - 49, 55, 80, 86, 98.
BLARS - 36, 37, 45, 50, 60, 61.
BLARS community pages - 8, 15.
BLARS – Martin Deacon – 3.
Susan Cordes – 54, 57.
Dick Crisp – 69.
Peter Culverwell – 70.
May Davis – 75, 79.
Roger Day – 95, 96
Heather Eyears – 10, 17, 18.
Thomas Fisher – 19, 40.
Val Fitzhugh – 12, 93.
The Rev Donald Flatt – 32.
Rosemary Harris – 99.
Hilary Hurn – 91.
Mr and Mrs Peter Jones – 41.
Edwin Lambert – 4, 7, 9, 20, 24, 48 (from Beds County
Record Office photo, from painting 1864), 94, 100, 102, 103,
104.
Daphne Lawlor – 85.
David Lewry – 6, 14, 16, 30, 33, 39.
Geraldine Main – 88.
Jill Manning – 44.
A Monk of Turvey – 22.
Ordnance Survey – 92.
Michael Pile – 46. 51, 52, 71, 72, 74.
Private collection – 37.
John Rawlins – 64.
Alastair Reid – 89, 90.

Dorothy Richards – Boteler family tree, Appendix IV.
Pat Robertson – 62.
St James' school – 87.
Steve Sawford – 11, 13, 35.
David Sims – 97.
Diana Toyn – 23, 25, 26, 34.
Victoria History of the County of Bedford – 5, 21.
N Wallace, courtesy of Stuart Antrobus – 63.
Ralph West – 38, 68.

Colour Plates

INTRODUCTION

In 1991 Dorothy Richards published *Biddenham: a Parish History and Guide,* which went out of print some years later. After Dorothy's death in 2007, Mary McKeown, Anthea Slark and Diana Toyn joined together with a view to updating the book, and obtained Dorothy's sister's agreement. Soon work commitments led Anthea to withdraw from the project. Katherine Fricker stepped in to join Diana and Mary to re-draft Dorothy's book, and suggested a complete revision of the original material.

Mary had read an excellent *History of Stevington,* published in 2001, and in the autumn of 2009 two of the authors, Peter Hart and Alan Edwards, very kindly spent a whole morning with the History Team. They gave us much good advice about sources of information, as well as support and encouragement. As a result of that meeting, we could see that Dorothy Richards had given us a very good basis on which to work, and how we could update, expand and develop her book.

We have spent over four years reading, researching and interviewing fellow residents, and we are grateful to the residents, both past and present, of Biddenham for their patience, and for providing so many recollections and illustrations. We hope you will enjoy reading this updated and expanded account of Biddenham's past.

If there are funds left over after publication, they will be shared among village causes. We hope that in due course a Biddenham History Society will be founded, to carry our work forward.

Katherine Fricker, Mary McKeown and Diana Toyn.
November 2012

ACKNOWLEDGEMENTS

We have been helped by many people and organisations in the production of this book. First, two of the authors of the Stevington history (Peter Hart and the late Alan Edwards) put us on the right track, and gave us support. Secondly, Roger Rigby and Roger Gwynne-Jones of Bedford Borough Council, the Parish Council, the Parochial Church Council and the Biddenham Show committee generously gave us funds to help finance the project. Thirdly, we were supported in our researches by the staff at Bedford Library, the Bedford Museum, Bedfordshire and Luton Archives and Records Service and Mike Luke and his colleagues at Albion Archaeology. We also thank Pat McKeown and his team of helpers for organising the talk in the pavilion by Mike Luke about the archaeology of the Biddenham Loop in October 2010, which also raised funds for us.

Many people in the village, and some who have since left or died, kindly gave us their time and their memories, and useful contacts - and ransacked their homes to find photographs and mementoes for us: Jonathan Bean, Richard Church, Peter Culverwell, Daphne Davies, May Davis, Yvonne Fowler, Monica Knight, Daphne Lawlor, Jill Manning, Wendy Musselle, Alastair Reid, Barbara Roberts, Ian and Pat Robertson, Don Sherwood, Anthea Slark and Ralph West. We thank all those who answered the questionnaire that formed the basis for Chapter 13, and Dick Crisp, Derek Frossell, Alan Sims, Jonathan Bean and Jonathan McKeown for their memoirs. Our thanks also go to Michael Pile for making his father's long and detailed memoir available to us.

Martin Whiteley, Pat McKeown, Tony Wood, David George, Christopher Haydn Jones and Peter Applewhite kindly contributed to specific chapters in the book. Steve Williamson researched early 19th century crime in Biddenham and emigrants to Australia for us. NADFAS (the National Association of Decorative and Fine Arts) were of great assistance in allowing us to refer to their survey of St James's church, and Eric Compton provided interesting material about his finds. Edwin Lambert generously gave us permission to use any of his collection of Biddenham material. We also thank Karen Luscombe, the headteacher of St James' school, for searching out documents to help with the chapter covering the recent history of the school.

We are indebted to our proof-readers – Debbi Clifton, Joyce Ellis, Christopher Dawe and Rosemary Harris, to Stuart Antrobus for help with references to the Women's Land Army, and to Rosemary Harris and her daughter Rachel, for work on the cover of the book, and for the production of the beautiful notelets, designed by Rachel. Susan Cordes provided interesting information about the apotropaic marks in the church, and also many photographs, Paul Fricker gave us useful advice, and Jonathan Gambold helped with promotional material. Our thanks too to Thelma Marks for kindly giving us an ISBN number from her stock, and to Jonathan McKeown for helping with the indexing.

Roger Day produced beautiful photographs for the section 'A Walk Round Biddenham' for which we thank him, and David Lewry provided sketches. Jo McKeown and John Howe of Apex Images devoted a glorious afternoon in April 2011 to taking shots of the village from their camera mounted on a telescopic mast 26 metres high, giving us the chance to see the village from a completely new angle: they did not charge for this work.

Finally, our heartfelt thanks go to our supportive husbands, Paul, Pat and Brian, who have endured roomfuls of files, documents and photographs for four years.

Katherine Fricker, Mary McKeown and Diana Toyn

ABBREVIATIONS

BGS	Bedford Girls' School
BHRS	Bedfordshire Historical Record Society
BLARS	Bedfordshire and Luton Archives and Records Service
c	circa
d	died
HER	Bedford Historic Environment Record via www.bedford.gov.uk/archive
m	married
TRE	In the time of Edward (the Confessor)
WI	Women's Institute

CHAPTER 1

THE GEOLOGICAL FOUNDATION OF BIDDENHAM

This chapter was contributed by Dr M Whiteley, Bedfordshire Geology Group

The rocks that lie beneath Biddenham have influenced the way in which the village has developed, in terms of both land use and resources. Biddenham occupies the core of a meander of the river Great Ouse, but the true foundations of the village are the concealed rocks that lie beneath the modern river gravels. These rocks are of Jurassic age, and they formed in a shallow sea that covered most of southern England some 165 million years ago. Giant reptiles swam in the sea, and dinosaurs roamed around the neighbouring land masses – areas that are now recognised as East Anglia and the Pennines.

The rocks that formed in the Jurassic sea were mainly alternating layers of limestone and clay, and it is the limestone, which is known as the Great Oolite, that has imparted its character to Biddenham because it has been used as a local building stone. Historical records indicate that large pits were worked for limestone at Church End, and it is likely that much of it was used for the oldest buildings in the village, including the church. The distinctive honey-coloured stone is full of fossil shell fragments, and is of variable quality, but the best material is described as freestone, and is sufficiently homogeneous to be cut and carved. As a result, the highly prized freestone was used to form the delicate mouldings for doors and windows, whilst the rest was used for walling stone.

The Great Oolite limestones are overlain by a few metres of clay, some thin sandstones, and then more clay. It is this sandwich of rocks that produces the subtle hill on which the village stands. This is most easily detected as you cycle out of

Bedford on the Bromham Road and descend gently from Deep Spinney, which is at an elevation of about 45 metres above sea level, towards the river Great Ouse, which is some 15 metres lower. The Jurassic clays were used for brickmaking in the late 18th century, when a series of pits were worked in the fields to the north of Bromham Road. This area was known as Clay Pit Furlong, but today it is occupied by modern housing and the former golf club. In the centre of the village, the aptly named Clay Farm complex (30-32 Main Road) also reflects the nature of the underlying rock.

We know little about the geological history of the area during the millennia that followed the Jurassic. This is because the rocks that were deposited during that enormous span of time have long since been worn away by water, wind and ice. It is only in the last few hundred thousand years, during the latter phases of the Ice Age, that sand and gravel were deposited by the ancestral river Great Ouse as a thin veneer of unconsolidated sediment on top of the much older Jurassic clays and limestones.

Rather than being a single incised river channel, as is the modern Great Ouse, its Ice Age predecessor was probably a network of very shallow water courses that coalesced and diverged according to the amount of water and debris that it carried. In periods of flood it would have been capable of transporting vast quantities of sediment as it cut its way down through the soft underlying Jurassic rocks and carved out a broad flat-bottomed valley. During phases of reduced water flow the sediment would have been deposited in layers across the valley floor. This process, repeated many times over the course of thousands of years, resulted in a thick sequence of sand and gravels building up all over the flood plain of the river. It is these deposits that have proved to be of enormous commercial value, providing a source of loose aggregate for the construction industry over the last 150 years. Gravel pits were once common throughout the Biddenham area (see Appendix I), particularly in the vicinity of Bromham Road, but extraction has now ceased and there is little remaining evidence of this wholesale exploitation.

Quite apart from providing huge volumes of aggregate, the gravel pits occasionally yielded human artefacts – such as flint scrapers and hand-axes – as well as the fossilised remains of mammoth, rhinoceros and deer. These scientifically valuable objects are probably about 300,000 years old, indicating that Palaeolithic (Old Stone Age) man occupied the lowlands of Biddenham, sustained by water from the river and food from the land and the animals that roamed over it.

It is still possible to visit one of these old gravel pits and examine the ancient sediments that have generated so much scientific interest. Tucked away in a patch of scrubland next to the footpath that connects Fleming Close and Malcote Close is the remnant of a disused pit that once extended over most of the Deep Spinney housing estate. Known as Biddenham Pit, it was designated as a Site of Special Scientific Interest in 1988 because of its geological and archaeological importance. Unfortunately, during the following two decades the small exposure of sand and gravel became progressively overgrown, and the site was effectively lost. However, since 2010 the Bedfordshire Geology Group and Bedfordshire Wildlife Trust have selectively re-exposed the rocks, made the site more accessible and restored its scientific value. It provides a fascinating insight to a long forgotten time when both early Man and woolly mammoths took advantage of a river that flowed through Deep Spinney!

CHAPTER 2

ANCIENT LIFE IN THE BIDDENHAM LOOP
This chapter was contributed by Professor Pat McKeown

'The Biddenham Loop is famous,' said Mike Luke, project manager of Albion Archaeology, and went on to add, 'amongst archaeologists and pre-historians.' This is how he started his fascinating talk to a meeting in Biddenham pavilion in October 2010, addressing this very topic, 'Ancient life in the Biddenham Loop', ranging from the Old Stone Age through the Bronze, Iron and Romano-British Ages to the Early Saxon.[1]

Biddenham village occupies only a small area in the west of this remarkable, meandering 180° loop of the Great River Ouse. (See map, colour section) It is within not only the larger Loop, but also within the village as it is today, that traces of human activity have been found, dated from the **Palaeolithic** or **Old Stone Age** (widely designated as about 2,000,000 to 12,000 years ago in Europe). This is much older than Stonehenge, which from carbon-14 dating, is said to be about 3,800 years old.

In 1861 about 70 flint implements dating from this era were found on the north side of Bromham Road, and are now preserved in the British Museum. In 1867 many worked flints, including axe-heads, also Palaeolithic, were found in the gravel pit now officially designated as Biddenham Pit (part of which was formerly known as Jarvis Pit) in Deep Spinney, as described in chapter 1. This and other adjacent pits 'Have the distinction of being the first prolific Palaeolithic sites to have been discovered in England', said Wymer.[2] The fossilised remains of mammoth, rhinoceros, cave bear, aurochs and reindeer, amongst others, were also found.

Undoubtedly, the prime artefact find of this era was a flint axe-head deemed to be more than 50,000 years old. This was the last glacial period when an ice sheet covered northern Europe, and in Britain, reached south to a line that stretches today from London to the coast of South Wales.

1 – Hand axe from the Palaeolithic era found in the Biddenham Loop. Albion Archaeology, copyright reserved.

In recent years, substantial geophysical surveys and open area excavations have been carried out by Albion Archaeology: 18 hectares in 1996 on behalf of Bovis Homes Ltd.; then 9 hectares in advance of the western bypass (The Branston Way), and in 2007 over 66 hectares for David Wilson Homes. The latter involved some 40 investigators, took just over a year and covered the area of the Loop that is now Great Denham.

Among many significant findings, 'Eight flint concentrations found within the plough soil' were identified as **Mesolithic** or **Middle Stone Age** (12,000 to 7,500 years ago), the location of which suggested that human activity was concentrated along the edge of the river terrace. Luke says, 'The surrounding forest would have provided timber, fruit and a variety of game, with the river being a source of plants, fish, waterfowl and aquatic mammals'[3] for the itinerant hunter-gatherers of this period.

Evidence based primarily on the finding of shallow pits containing pottery chips, struck flint, charred wood and animal bone was also recovered for nomadic and possibly longer-term 'occupation' during the **Neolithic** or **New Stone Age** (7,500 to 5,500 years ago). This is supported by the identification of *mortuary enclosures* and *monuments* which probably served funerary or ceremonial functions. The number and types of monuments and burials found in the Loop from the Neolithic to the early Bronze Age show that it had progressively become a 'ritual landscape comparable to that around Stonehenge'. One monument contained two inhumations or burials; radio-carbon processing dated them as early Neolithic, making them among the very earliest of this type in Britain. It was in another similar monument that a superb polished axe-head was found. Analysis shows that this beautiful and awe-inspiring example of ancient (Neolithic) technology originated in the Langdale Valley of the Lake District, indicating that tribal movements for trade or survival could cover large distances, even through the heavily forested and swampy terrain typical of the time.

2 – Artist's impression of hunter gatherers in the Biddenham Loop.
Albion Archaeology, copyright reserved

Moving into the **Bronze Age** (4,500 to 2,700 years ago), and for the early part of this era, evidence was found 'for the introduction of mixed farming , alongside the continued exploitation of wild resources' but lack of evidence of 'substantial houses, storage buildings and enclosures suggests the continuation of transient life-styles rather than settled agriculture at this time' says Luke[4]. However, the landscape started to change later in the middle Bronze Age, from one dominated by monuments to one divided up into parcels of land which eventually became fields. Farming rather more as we know it today was arriving, with extensive settlements and cemeteries. One building positively identified to the late Bronze Age 'by a partial ring of post-holes and an apparent entrance porch to the south-west' was a roundhouse,[5] probably like one reconstructed at Flag Fen, Cambridgeshire, in October 2011.

3 – A reconstruction of a Bronze Age round house
at Flag Fen, Cambridgeshire, October 2011

Five farmsteads relating to the **Middle Iron Age** (2,700 to 2,000 years ago) were also identified, characterised primarily by large pits, some lined with clay, and used to store grain. Other pits were found, one of which contained a human skeleton, another an iron spearhead tip, and others filled with domestic debris including pottery. Celtic migrants, especially the Belgae from Gaul, settled in the locality of Bedford. They were the Catavellauni tribe. (Much later, in 51 AD, a famous chief of this tribe, Caractacus, was captured by the Romans and sent to Rome in chains).

Towards the end of this era, the late Iron Age, some six farmsteads were established over the whole area,[6] with associated kilns and cemeteries. Away from the farmsteads, a shrine complex was built which, up to now, is unique in Britain but shows similarities to some found in continental Europe. An Iron Age coin was found in the Bromham Road area dating from 15 to 10 BC, and four Iron Age Belgic vessels, also found, are now in the Bedford Museum.

The same type of farmstead continued through the **Romano-British period** (1,960 to 1,600 years ago). Track ways between the farmsteads and boundary ditches were established. Animal bones found and analysed show that during this period, they raised cattle, sheep and/or goats, pigs and horses. The main cereals grown were spelt, wheat and barley.[7] A small number of burials associated with the farmsteads have been found, but at one there was a cemetery containing as many as thirty graves.

The Romans invaded in 43 AD, and quickly subdued the British tribes, including the Catavellauni. Initially they built forts, and later cities at Verulanium (St Albans), Camulodunum (Colchester) and Londinium (London), establishing the latter as the capital of Roman Britain. Their engineers quickly built major roads fanning out from London for rapid deployment of their legions, in order to maintain pacification of the natives. Watling Street went north-westerly, well to the west of Biddenham, and Ermine Street ran directly north to Lincoln, with one of many staging posts on a loop of the road at Sandy – only about 11 miles to the east of Bedford. It is estimated that the total population of Britain at that time was only two to three million, the Romans being a very small proportion of this total. However, they exercised firm control through sound military-backed administration, giving loyal tribes considerable autonomy, and working with them to develop agriculture, especially wheat production – some for export to Roman Europe.

Two Roman sites have been identified in the village of Biddenham. One was a well,[8] probably on the site of a villa north of Bromham Road. It was stone-lined and 12 metres deep.[9] Found during quarrying in 1857, it contained a human skeleton, pottery, animal bones and the sole of a shoe, but most significantly, a sculpture of a bird, thought to be an owl, and a much eroded limestone male torso said to be Dionysus. Later,

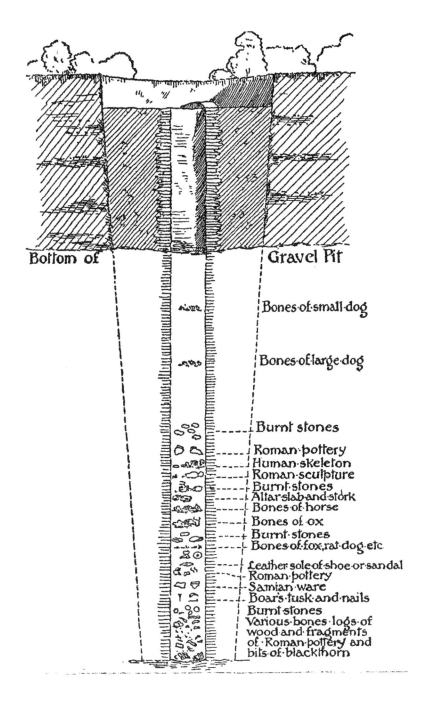

Bottom of   Gravel Pit

Bones of small dog

Bones of large dog

Burnt stones
Roman pottery
Human skeleton
Roman sculpture
Burnt stones
Altar slab and stork
Bones of horse
Bones of ox
Burnt stones
Bones of fox, rat, dog etc.
Leather sole of shoe or sandal
Roman pottery
Samian ware
Boar's tusk and nails
Burnt stones
Various bones, logs of
wood and fragments
of Roman pottery and
bits of blackthorn

4 – Cross-section of 12m deep well
on site of small Romano-British settlement, Biddenham

9

they were built into an exterior wall of Bromham Hall, where the current owner, Mr Chris Whittaker, thinks the sculpture is more likely to be of the Roman god Mithras.

The other Roman site[10] is north of St James's church, where Roman pottery, coins and metalwork have been found. At Church Farm two bronze coins[11] were found; one a dupondius of Antonia (41-54 AD), the other a follis of Constantius (337-340 AD).

Perhaps the most impressive find of the Roman era was made in 1980 by Eric Compton of Queen's Park, using a metal detector in the Loop at Honey Hill Farm – a very rare type of gold ring, found under about 150 mm of earth. He washed it in a nearby puddle to reveal beautifully preserved lettering, 'EVSEBIO VITA' – 'Long life to Eusebius'. Mr Compton wrote[12] that only three rings of this type have been found in Britain, indicating that it had probably been specially commissioned by a very wealthy person. The coins and the ring are now in the British Museum. (Mr Compton went on to find other artefacts, including a silver penny of the time of Henry III, a Mesolithic axe-head, a Neolithic arrow-head and a Roman quern stone).

As their empire declined under attacks by the Huns, Goths and Slavs, the Romans progressively withdrew their legions from Britain between 370 AD and 410 AD, leaving the country open to invasion and settlement by Angles and Saxons, some of whom had previously enlisted as auxiliaries with the Romans. The term **Anglo-Saxon period** (410 AD to 1066) is relatively modern, and refers to the time when settlers arrived from the German regions of Angeln and Saxony. The invading Anglo-Saxons would almost certainly have reached the Bedford area by river, coming up the Ouse from the Wash. The Albion Archaeology investigations for David Wilson Homes in 2007-8 located an early Saxon settlement in the Honey Hill part of the Loop. An Anglo-Saxon settlement in Biddenham is even mentioned in the Domesday Book (see chapter 3). Scrolls and mirrors of this period, previously found near Honey Hill are now in the British Museum.

It was, of course, the Anglo-Saxons who brought and established the 'Old English' language to 'Engla land'. Place names ending in 'ham' are Anglo-Saxon in origin, and are said to mean 'cultivated land'. So Biddenham was, at an early Anglo-Saxon stage, probably known as 'Bydaham'[13] – 'cultivated land belonging to Byda' but the name has changed many times over the centuries, due to the changing pronunciation of the villagers:

Bideham: 1086 - 1347	Bidenham: 1086 – 1316
Beydenham: 1240	Budeham: 1247
Bydenham: 1276 – 1428	Bydyngham: 1428
Bydnam: 1512 – 1535	Byddyngham: 1535
	and Bignam: 1550

Going back to the 7th century, our locality became part of the Kingdom of Mercia, under the famous King Offa. Some 60 years after his death in 796, when Offa was buried in Bedford,[14] the even more famous king, Alfred the Great, expanded his kingdom of Wessex to include our region, and dominate most of what is now England.

But in the 10th century there was again almost continuous fighting, this time between the 'English' and the next invaders, the Danes, again using the Ouse valley as an invading highway. Bedford became a Danish stronghold, and its citizens and all those in surrounding villages, including Biddenham, had to pay tribute to a Danish overlord.

Then, of course, in 1066, the Normans triumphed at Hastings, bringing a dramatic change to the governing of the country. Lands were taken from the English and given as a reward to

William the Conqueror's supporters, and twenty years later, Biddenham featured in the Domesday Book.

In compiling this short survey of early life in Biddenham and the Loop in general, I have been very fortunate to be able to call on the recent archaeological reports compiled meticulously by Mike Luke and his colleagues at Albion Archaeology, Bedford. These add enormously to earlier research and historical publications. I am grateful for his warm and enthusiastic personal help. It is now clear that the Biddenham Loop is amongst the oldest known sites of human (*Homo sapiens*) development in Britain.

References:

1   Mike Luke, *Life in the Loop: Investigation of a Prehistoric and Romano-British Landscape at Biddenham Loop, Bedfordshire* (Albion Archaeology, East Anglia Archaeology Report No. 125, 2008).

2   John Wymer, *The Lower Palaeolithic Occupation of Britain* (Trust for Wessex Archaeology, Ltd, 1999), p 123.

3   Mike Luke, op. cit., p 19.

4   Ibid., p 24.

5   Ibid., p 34.

6   Ibid., pp 68.

7   Ibid., pp 245, 246.

8   [HER 330].

9   *The Victoria History of the County of Bedford* (Dawsons of Pall Mall, 1972) vol 2, p 5.

10   [HER 323]

11   [HER 15953]

12   Eric Compton – letter to Dorothy Richards, 16 June 1993.

13   *The Place Names of Bedfordshire and Hampshire,* English Place Name Society, (Cambridge University Press, 1926) vol III.

14   Peter Grey, *The Villages of the Ouse* (Barracuda Books, Ltd, 1980), p 17.

For further reading: Luke *et al, Close to the Biddenham Loop: 6,000 years of landscape evolution within and near the Biddenham Loop, west of Bedford* (working title), forthcoming (East Anglian Archaeology/Albion Archaeology).

CHAPTER 3

BIDDENHAM AT THE TIME OF DOMESDAY, 1086

5 – Domesday Book extract

In 1086 King William I ordered a survey of all the English land he had conquered, and which under him was held by his barons. They became his tenants-in-chief, and in return, were obliged to provide soldiers to defend the country against rebellion and foreign invasion. This survey, the Domesday Book – so called because it was considered as final as the Day of Doom - was therefore both a record of the new feudal hierarchy and a basis for raising taxes. The people didn't like it for this reason – in fact, it was as unpopular as the 'poll tax' was in the 1990s. Taxes were levied annually, normally 10d per hide. A hide was not a precise area, being roughly the land sufficient for cultivation by one plough in one year. Each unit of five hides could be called upon to support a knight for the king for two months each year. If we add up the land listed in Domesday for Biddenham, we come to a total of about two square miles, or 11 hides – approximately 1,320 acres. This meant that Biddenham could be called upon to support one knight for over four months each year. Knights were expensive to run – the medieval equivalent of tanks in the 20th century. They were trained from the age of about seven, and needed horses, and grooms to get them into their armour.

There is nothing to compare with Domesday Book anywhere in the world. It was written by hand in Latin shorthand on parchment, and took about two years to prepare. The principal questions asked were; how much land is there? Who held it in the time of King Edward? Who holds it now?

The village information was given to two French-speaking Norman commissioners by a jury of local farmers and the parish priest, many of whom spoke an Anglo-Saxon dialect, to say whether the answers that had been given were correct. A monk was employed as 'scribe' to write down the answers, for in those days very few people could read or write – not even the king. When the king's clerks had the details, they re-arranged them under the holders of land, starting with the king and the bishops, and naming all the tenants. In addition to Bedford itself, Biddenham was one of the villages in the Bucklow Hundred, the others being Bletsoe, Pavenham, Stevington, Goldington Highfields, Chainhalle (now lost), Bromham, Putnoe and Stagsden.

Here is a short extract from one of the Domesday entries for Biddenham:

In ead uilla ten Vlmar burgenfis de rege.II.partes
Unius uirg.Tra.e.1.boui.

(In the same vill Wulfmær, a burgess, holds of the king 2 parts of 1 virgate. There is land for 1 ox)

The People Recorded in Domesday

Domesday did not record every person living in the land, but only those who worked. For Biddenham, 20 men of working age are recorded – five smallholders, 10 villagers and five slaves.

The villagers were small-scale farmers, able to support their families from the produce of their share in the village lands, and were not necessarily poor. They were, however, 'tied to the soil' unless they paid a tax for permission to move. After the Conquest they could neither inherit land nor pass it on to their children. They usually had a standard share of 10 to 30 acres in the open fields and did week-work for the lord. Villagers made up three-quarters of the population of England (estimated to have been about 1½ million), and Bedfordshire villagers were rich compared with many elsewhere.

The smallholders would each be tenants of about five acres, but not have a full share in the village fields.

The slaves were either unmarried farm and house servants, or married house slaves, living on smallholdings and sometimes liable to work as the lord's ploughmen. Slaves made up about one-eighth of the population at the time of Domesday, some perhaps having been enslaved as punishment, and others because they could not pay fines. Slavery died out during the reign of Henry I, William the Conqueror's second son.

It is usually assumed that each household consisted of about five people, so the total population of the village could have been approximately 100 at that time. By comparison, in 2008 the population of the village was 2,620.

The Value of the Land Recorded in Domesday

The total value of land in the village in 1086 was 118 shillings, which works out at roughly £1 a hide - considered the ideal assessment in the time of Edward the Confessor. It therefore covered only arable land. In Bedfordshire the arable land totalled about 120 acres. The value of land in Biddenham remained constant from Edward's time until 1086, which is good evidence that when William the Conqueror marched north in the autumn of 1066, leaving a trail of destruction in parts of Bedfordshire, he didn't pass through Biddenham.

The Landholders Recorded in Domesday[1]

The holders of land in Biddenham as tenants-in-chief were
Hugh de Beauchamp, William Speke, the Bishop of Lincoln,
the church of St Edmund's (Bury St Edmunds in Suffolk),
St Paul's church in Bedford, and the burgesses[2] of Bedford.
After the king's own estate, Hugh de Beauchamp had the
largest holding in Bedfordshire, and was thus the leading
Norman lord. William I rewarded him with 43 lordships
in Bedfordshire, Buckinghamshire and Hertfordshire, and
he held Bedford Castle. William Speke also held land in
many parts of Bedfordshire, the manor of Biddenham being
part of his holding. This would be the manor at Biddenham
Ford, later known as Ford End. The manor was tenanted by
Ralph and Serlo de Ros, and included a mill, about 415 acres
of land, and another 240 acres which Serlo rented from
Hugh de Beauchamp. The Bishop of Lincoln's land, about
150 acres, including a mill, was tenanted by Ernwin the Priest.
(Biddenham was at that time in the diocese of Lincoln). The
church of St Edmund's had 60 acres in Biddenham, held by
Ordwy of Bedford. St Paul's church, Bedford, held a total of
120 acres, which had been given to the church by Leofgeat the
Priest and Ralph Tallboys. It was tenanted by Canon Osmund
of St Paul's and Canon Asnfrid, and later became known as
Biddenham or Newnham Manor. Finally, the burgesses of
Bedford held a total of 300 acres, tenanted by burgesses Oscar,
Godwin, Ordwy and Wulfmer.

The Buildings Recorded in Domesday

The only buildings in Biddenham recorded by Domesday were
the manor and two mills. The manor (probably the future
Boteler manor) represented the unit of feudal lordship in the
village. It would be a hall, a strong building of wood or stone
in which the lord might or might not reside (in Biddenham he
did not), and which would at least contain offices, a bailiff,
cellars, and storehouses. Before the Norman Conquest the

manor had been held by 11 freemen. It was a symbol of the lord's authority over the men of the village. There was probably a wooden chapel or church on the site of the present church. The oldest surviving part of St James's Church was not begun until the 12th century. One of the mills was on the manor. These mills would be water-powered, and therefore bordering the river. They were valuable, and usually owned by the manor or the church. No private person could grind their own corn; it had to be taken to the lord's mill, and a fee paid for grinding.

Plough Teams and Arable Land, Strips

Biddenham was farmed on the open-field system; three or four large fields sub-divided into many strips. Each tenant had land-holdings scattered throughout these fields. A three-course rotation of crops was practised – fallow, wheat, then beans or barley (to nitrogenise the soil). The ploughs and the oxen were recorded because the commissioners wished to compare the value of one holding with another. They assumed that eight oxen comprised a plough-team, but probably only three or four oxen were used at any one time. The oxen were thus a measure of arable land. The strips of land which the peasants farmed were always long and narrow, because the plough was heavy and cumbersome, and difficult to turn, so the long strip meant that the ploughman had to make only a few turns during his day's work. The plough could manage about an acre a day, and each family needed about 10 acres to support it. (Horses were not used for ploughing until much later). Six ploughs are recorded as actually being in Biddenham. This means that there were three plough teams to the square mile, which is what we would expect on good fertile soil.

Pasture and Meadow

Pasture was land available all the year round for feeding cattle and sheep. None is recorded separately for Biddenham.

Meadow was land bordering a stream, liable to flood, and producing hay. It was recorded in terms of the teams of oxen that its hay could support. The total meadowland recorded in Biddenham comprised one-eighth of the total land, and was enough for 10 ploughs plus two oxen, but since there were only six ploughs recorded in the village, it is probable that this was an over-estimate.

The Peasant's Life

The peasant's house might be a small structure of wood, and wattle and daub, but most likely he and his family lived in a mud hovel of one or two rooms, which housed some of his livestock as well as his family. The furniture and furnishings probably consisted only of a rough bench and table, pots and pans for cooking over a fire (there would be no oven), and the essential tools of a farmer.[3] The staple food of the 11th century peasant was wholemeal bread (usually barley or a mixture of grains such as rye and wheat) and ale. Bread was eaten at breakfast, the mid-day meal, and supper, and with it cheese, onions or leeks, but not many other vegetables, and very little meat. He would gather nuts and hedge-fruits in autumn. At Christmas he would eat a chicken cooked in the lord of the manor's oven.

What Domesday Doesn't Tell Us

Domesday doesn't record exactly where any fields were in the village, nor does it record the families of the workers, or their names. For Biddenham, the only animals recorded are the oxen which drew the ploughs. In other areas of the county pigs are also noted – they were used as a measure of the size of woodland, where the beechmast and acorns supported them. This absence of pigs suggests that there were no woodlands in Biddenham at that time. (For example, in Stagsden there was 'woodland, 40 pigs'). However, the peasants would have their own chickens, and possibly cows or sheep, but these were not recorded because they did not contribute to the value of the manor. The cows were primarily for breeding oxen, and very little cows' milk was drunk. Sheep were valuable for their fleece, and were rarely eaten. Venison, hare, rabbit, pheasant, partridge, geese, swans, pigeons, doves and ducks were the food of the upper classes.

After Domesday

During the Middle Ages life in Biddenham would have continued in much the same way, the seasons of the year dictating the activities in the farming life, and the church to a large extent governing the behaviour of the inhabitants. Between these two strong influences, the individual villager had very little autonomy in his or her way of life.

However, violence was not unknown, and in 1276 four men from Turvey were accused of breaking into a house at night and 'carried away all William's and Richard's goods and cut the sinews of their legs' – no doubt to prevent them from pursuing the criminals.[4] A more serious case was recorded in 1316, when two unknown thieves strangled (with a belt) Sibyl Aldyth in her house in Biddenham, and fled. In spite of the best efforts of Sibyl's neighbours, the perpetrators were never brought to justice.[5]

Violence was not the only problem faced by rural communities in the 14th century. Whereas some villages suffered seriously from the plague known as the Black Death in 1349 and were deserted, Biddenham managed to survive as a self-sufficient village into the late 14th and early 15th centuries. The main casualty of the plague was the Rector, William de Wykewane, but despite death and social dislocation, the village itself survived.

References:

1   A translation of all the Domesday entries for Biddenham can be found in *Domesday Book, a Complete Translation* (Alecto Historical Editions, Penguin Books, 2002) in Bedford Library, pages 565, 567, 573, 577 and 586.

2   Burgesses were members of a privileged class in towns.

3   Christopher Brooke, *From Alfred to Henry III 871 – 1272* (W W Norton and Co, 1969), p 11.

4   BHRS, Vol XLI – *Translations of Medieval Coroners' Rolls for the County*, by R F Hunnisett – 1276 and 1316 (Bedford Borough Council Community Archives at www.bedfordshire.gov.uk)

5   Ibid.

(The above is an edited and updated version of an article by Mary McKeown that appeared in the *Biddenham Bulletin* in the early 1990s.)

6 - St James's Church

7 - Plans of the Church

The Church of

St. James

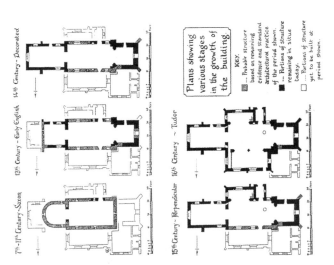

Twentieth Century ~ Modern

14th Century ~ Decorated

13th Century ~ Early English

7th ~ 11th Century ~ Saxon

16th Century ~ Tudor

15th Century ~ Perpendicular

Plans showing various stages in the growth of the building

KEY
⬚ ... Probable structure based on remaining evidence and standard architectural practice of the period shown.
■ ... Portions of structure remaining in situ today.
□ ... Portions of structure yet to be built at period shown.

Drawn by: Linda Lambert 1991

ALTAR
CHANCEL 14th Cent.
SOUTH AISLE 15th Cent. Restored 1959
PORCH 15th Cent.
NAVE 10th or 11th Century
NORTH AISLE 18th Cent.
LOWER BELL TOWER Early 13th Cent.
VESTRY 1975
Font

FEET
METRES

CHAPTER 4

ST JAMES'S CHURCH

Today St James's church stands proudly at the west end of the village in a churchyard enclosed by a stone wall lined on all four sides with lime trees. A stone building has stood here since the 11th or 12th century, but there was undoubtedly a wooden chapel or church even earlier. As was usual in the Middle Ages, the church was placed towards the north of the graveyard and orientated east to west. The south was favoured for burials, the north being associated with the devil.[1] From the roof of the tower you can see four churches – Kempston, Biddenham, Bromham and Oakley - all built from local limestone, standing in a line within easy reach of the river Great Ouse.[2]

The earliest recorded reference to the church is in 1252, when William Passelowe held the advowson.[3] Before this date, in the absence of any written records, the church building itself has to provide evidence of the many alterations and repairs carried out over the centuries.

MAIN FEATURES OF THE EARLY CHURCH

Certain parts of the original small structure can still be seen today. The most striking feature is the large round Norman arch, much restored, separating the nave from the chancel. It

8 – Norman arch

has been suggested that the arch could be Saxon, as there is no typical Norman decoration. The main entrance archway and doorway with a blocked-in window above and to the east are clearly part of the early Norman church.

9 – Main entrance archway with window

Alterations were made in the 13th century. A blocked deeply splayed window and blocked doorway can be seen on the inside of the lower part of the 13th century tower, at the base of which, on the east side, a small part of the west wall of the Norman church has survived.

By the late 14th century, after the ravages of the Black Death, with the increase in population and wealth, church building grew apace.

The chancel was rebuilt and enlarged, and a small, plain chamfered door with painted head was inserted on the south side to give the priest direct access. It is still in use today.

A large east window with stonework in the decorated Gothic style and reticulated tracery was added. The sedilia, a seat below the south window at the east end, was cut into the stonework, for the use of the clergy during mass. A massive six-planked iron-bound chest of hutch construction has survived from the 14th century, and today is kept in the vestry. It was used for storing documents and vestments. The current church registers are kept there. Originally provided with three

10 – The priest's doorway

locks, it could only be opened when the incumbent and both churchwardens were present.

11 – 14th century chest

In the 15th century the south aisle was added and the roof of the nave raised. An altar was installed, indicated by the piscina with cinquefoiled head. It was in this aisle that William Boteler endowed a chantry chapel dedicated to Saint William, to pay for a priest to say prayers and masses for the souls of the founder and his family. The upper part of the tower was built to house the bells. Between 1520 and 1541 various bequests were made for their maintenance.

The fine octagonal font, typical 15th century work, stands on a pedestal with rectangular compartments, each with a plain raised shield. Each face of the drum is ornamented with carved trefoils, quatrefoils and daggers. Three of the faces have a square foliate boss, one with a rose in the centre. The basin is lined with lead, and has a drain hole. From the 13th century a cover was compulsory, as water was blessed on Easter Day, and this holy water had to be protected from dust and dirt, or theft for use in magic rituals. The font stands inside the south main door. It reminds members of the church of the vows made on their behalf at their baptism.

12 – The font

The porch was used for both church and secular business, and was a valuable addition which afforded protection from the weather. Today it retains the original stone bench on the east side, and the wooden plastered barrel roof with vine flowered bosses and stone corbels cut with a cross design. On the stonework to the left of the entrance door a so-called 'mass' or 'scratch' dial can be seen.[4] The inscribed symbols on the stonework on the left as you enter the porch of the church are believed to be 'apotropaic', or ritual protection marks intended to protect the building from evil spirits. The most common marks are scratched and incised letters, crosses and circular daisy wheels. In particular, the double or interlaced V signs are thought to stand for Virgo Virginum (virgin of virgins), invoking the protection of the Virgin Mary. The majority of the marks appear to date from the 16th to 18th centuries.[5]

13 – The mass dial

The parvis, a room over the porch, provided for visiting monks, was possibly used as a sanctuary. There is no evidence that it ever became a school or library, as in so many other medieval churches, such as Bromham.

15 – The Boteler arms

14 – The wyvern   16 – The dove with scroll

A contract dated 16 December 1522 survives for building
the north aisle, between Sir William Boteler, Kt, citizen
and alderman of London, and John Laverock of St Albans,
Freemason. [For the Boteler family tree, see Appendix IV]
The perpendicular arcade separating the nave from the aisle is
of two bays, with a central pillar of four clustered semicircular
shafts supported by semi-octagonal capitals, and standing on
similar bases on ornamental plinths. Three carvings at the top
of the pillars pay tribute to the donors of the aisle: over the
central one, the Boteler coat of arms, to the east a dove carrying
a scroll, and to the west a wyvern (a mythical dragon-like bird).
The wyvern was the crest of the Dyves of Bromham, to whom
the advowson and rectory belonged before 1537. They almost
certainly contributed to the building costs.

17 – Left-hand squint   18 – Right-hand squint

Two squints were cut into the wall either side of the chancel
arch to give a view of the main altar from the new side aisles.

At the east end of the north aisle, there are three small separate brass figures of the Faldo family, William and Agnes (husband and wife) with John Faldo, who died about 1490. They are set into a large slab of Purbeck marble. Part of the inscription reads 'Orate p. aiab' – 'Pray for the souls'. They are shown in their best gowns, with hands folded piously in prayer. William and John are bare-headed, looking straight ahead, and wearing a long belted robe. Agnes, in her long straight v-necked gown with straight sleeves and wide cuffs, looks sideways to show off her butterfly headdress. In addition, a slab to the left shows two effigies of women in shrouds, undated and unnamed, but probably c 1530.

19 – The three Faldo family brasses

THE ESTIMATE OF CHURCH PROPERTY[6]

In about 1345 an estimate of church property at Biddenham was made: 'the church of the parish of Biddenham is taxed at seven marks and ten shillings and no more, with portions of the prior of Newnham and the prior of Cauldwell in the same, plus 30 acres of land, likewise tithe, hay, mortuary oblations and other small tithes'. The tithes, theoretically a tenth part of the income, went towards the upkeep of the incumbent of the church.

Biddenham has two entries in the Newnham roll 1519-20, a document preserved with the Boteler family papers.[7] An account was made by the cellarer, Dom John Salpho:

Biddenham, with the farm of the manor
Rents of assize, besides 1 cock, 2 hens, 40 eggs and
4 boon-days charged under moveable rents; examined
with the parchment rental of 21 Henry VII   48 10¾
Received of Richard Samson for the farm of the
manor and demesne land, demised to him at will this
year; paid at the four terms; late £7 6s 8d a year   7   0   0

                                                         £9 8 10¾

THE ROLE OF THE EARLY CHURCH

The church, the largest and most permanent building in the village, was the focus for all communal activity, either inside or outside in the graveyard. Village life revolved around the seasons, the Christian year (Lent, Easter, the festival of St James, Advent and Christmas). The prime purpose was to provide spiritual guidance, and villagers were expected to attend a service of worship three times each Sunday. The sacraments of baptism, marriage and burial were indispensable. When the churches were enlarged in the 14th century, this gave more room for processions, and sedilia were provided for the officiating priests. Otherwise, the congregation was expected to stand or kneel on the beaten earth floor, perhaps covered in rush mats. Candles or rush lights provided lighting, and charcoal braziers the heating.

By the 13th century the parishioners were responsible for the parish church, apart from the chancel which was owned by the incumbent. The porch, in particular, played a large role in both religious and secular business. Part of the marriage service and the churching of women took place there. The repayment of debts, the signing of contracts and posting of notices must have made it a busy place. Saints' days, processions, rituals, dramas and imagery brought colour, music, light, hope and holidays to lives which would otherwise have been uniformly hard, monotonous and uncertain.

THE IMPACT OF THE REFORMATION

The Reformation transformed the life of the church: when Henry VIII broke away from the Roman Catholic church with his Act of Supremacy of 1534 and closing down of the religious houses, St James's church was granted to John Gostwick, who in the same year sold it to William Boteler, who had to pay £428 2s 5d for the land formerly owned by 'Newnham Priory', 'Harwolde Priory', 'Cauldwell Priory' and 'Warden Abbey'.

Slowly but surely the church was stripped of all statues, saints and the Blessed Virgin Mary, lights, wall paintings and stained glass, and the walls were whitewashed. The liturgy changed too. In 1549 the first English prayer book appeared. In 1550 the stone altars were replaced by wooden communion tables, and in 1559 attendance at church became compulsory. The language used was English – no longer Latin. As far as the evidence goes, the people of Bedfordshire accepted these changes. They settled for a quiet life. Apart from three wall monuments, there would be no serious attempt to beautify the church until the 19th century.

PREPARING FOR DEATH - CHANTRY CHAPEL, WILLS AND CHURCHYARD

The Chantry Chapel and the Bridge

In 1295 the Chantry Chapel to Saints Mary and Katherine was founded at Biddenham bridge in the parish of Biddenham by

Matthew of Dunstable 'for the safety of travellers who were at danger of thieves'. By 1325 the chantry was in need of repair. Simon de Wolston re-founded it, donating houses and land (2 messuages. 4 tofts [homesteads], 50 acres of lands, 12 acres of meadow and 10s in rent in Bromham and Biddenham) for a priest to say a daily mass for the 'souls of Geoffrey le Smyth and all the faithful departed'.

Near Biddenham bridge, in the severe winter of 1281, a woman stayed on a fragment of ice and was swept along as far as Bedford bridge. Then the ice broke and she was seen no more.[8]

Surrounding parishes, which could each benefit from a convenient crossing of the river, were expected to contribute to its upkeep. In 1383 Stagsden, Stevington, Turvey and Biddenham were each charged by the crown for failing to repair the bridge.[9] Grateful individuals made provision for repairs in their wills.

The priest was also expected to collect and spend alms to maintain the bridge. In 1545, when chantries were abolished, the commissioners for Bedfordshire, Sir John St John, Sir Thomas Rotherham and William Smith, made a list of the income and expenditure of Bydenhambridge, closed the chapel in 1553, and pensioned off the incumbent, a naturalized Frenchman, Peter Weaver (or Wegner) with £5 a year.[10] He was said to be 'meanly learned', and the chapel to be 'very ruinouse and in sore decay'. The grammar school, preaching and help for the poor had already lapsed. At that time the Grocers' Company, of which Sir William Boteler was a member, paid the incumbent £6 a year.

Since the 18th century the bridge has been known as Bromham bridge. It is not known why the name was changed. When repairs were necessary, stone was fetched from Bromham. The chantry and a well traditionally associated with it lie firmly on Bromham territory. The well is hidden in a ridge under the wing wall beside the mill entrance.[11] It has probably been there with its healing waters long before the first bridge was built. The chapel site was destroyed during the last alterations to the bridge in 1902. There is little left of the medieval bridge first described as 'the bridge of Bideham' in an entry in the Calendar of Fines for the year 1227-8, and as the 'bridge of Biddenham' in the Pipe Roll of 1224.

SURVIVING WILLS OF THE 15TH AND 16TH CENTURIES

We are fortunate that so many wills of the 15th and early 16th century have been preserved and transcribed. Some were still written in Latin, or even in a mixture of English and French. In many cases, the handwriting is difficult to decipher, and the spelling erratic. Wealthy parishioners would put their affairs in order, often shortly before they died, in order to ensure a comfortable afterlife. Heaven and hell were a reality to them. Debts were to be paid, charitable donations, in particular to the church and for the repair of highways and bridges, were specified, and, not least, bequests to family and friends. The will would be witnessed by several friends, often including a clergyman.

The manner and place of burial were a chief concern. A frequent request was to be buried in the churchyard. William Samson (will proved 1520) wanted 'burial in the parish churchyard of St Jamys, Bydenham'.[12] Richard Boteler (will proved 1411) stipulated modestly 'body to be buried where friends wished'.[13] Alan Kirketon of Bydenhamford (will proved 1399) aimed high – 'buried before the rood if parishioners do not object'. He also wanted 'a light in the window before the Image of the BVM' (Blessed Virgin Mary).[14]

Requests were made for masses to be said for their souls. John Poley – 'To the rector 3s 4d, to be spent for his soul at his burial and to keep his obit in church each year'.[15]

Bequests were not necessarily in cash. John Compton of Stagsden (will proved 1528) left two trees for the repair of Biddenham bridge, and to the bells 3 bushels of barley.[16]

One of the earliest wills is that of the rector, Nicholas Skipwyth MA (will proved 1492/3), in Latin, as befits a clergyman.[17] As a Fellow of Pembroke Hall, Cambridge, MA and Doctor of Theology, he was comparatively wealthy. At his death, he owned a house in Bedford and houses and lands in Biddenham. Medieval priests were unmarried, and generally poor. Their standard of living was often no higher than that of their labouring parishioners. His will emphasises the correctness and dignity of the burial itself:

Half a pound of wax to be burnt round his corpse and not more on pain of anathema, also his body to be buried naked except for his breeches.
(For more of Nicholas Skipwyth's will, see Appendix II).

One other medieval clergyman, John Aylyffe, Rector of Bydenham (1454-1499) is commemorated by a brass plaque on the north wall of the chancel.

Joan Poley, widow (will proved 1510) took infinite pains to assign her possessions to family and friends, household goods and 'gowns' figuring high on the list:[18]
For her principal her best cow; to the high altar for tithes forgotten 6s 8d; for repairs to Biddenham church 3s 4d; to the bells 3s 4d; to mend the rood 40s; to the church of Lincoln 12d; to the friars of Bedford 10s; to the prior and convent of Newnham 20s.
(For more of Joan Poley's will, see Appendix II).

As might be expected, the most detailed will (proved Feb 1533/4) was made by a member of the influential Boteler family.[19] Money was left to various religious foundations for masses to be sung for his soul. He allocated 'a sufficiency' to his wife Agnes and their two sons. To each of his servants 'as well menskynes as womenskynnes' [boys and girls], he left 40s. His house, torches and other lights were 'to be ordered after the manner of the burial of Sir Jas Yarford Kt and alderman late deceased'. His dinner was to be kept at Grocers' Hall, and executors were 'to keep an obit for his soul yearly on the day on which he died, for 7 yrs.' 20s was to be provided at the dinner for officers of the Grocers' Company for 'some convenient drinking'. William Boteler also made bequests to Biddenham; the executors were to distribute every Sunday of the second year after his death 'to 7 honest persons in Biddenham 7d in money.' In addition, within a year of his death they were to distribute among poor persons, especially those in charge of children, £6 13s 4d. To the chapel at the bridge of Biddenham he bequeathed 'an ornament' thought most expedient 'to the value of 20s and to the repair of the bridge £10. To the "ornacon" (ornamentation) of the chapel and altar where his chantry priest shall sing within the said parish church of Biddenham £6 13s 4d.'

20 – The churchyard from the south,
showing the small size of the cedar trees, c 1908

34

St James, Biddenham ~ Window Styles.

SOUTH AISLE, EAST
also
NORTH & SOUTH
CHANCEL
Late 15th Century
Perpendicular Tracery.

EAST WINDOW
14th Century
Retriculated
Tracery.

NORTH AISLE
EAST & NORTH
WINDOWS
16th Century
Tudor Style.

NAVE, SOUTH SIDE
(adjacent to Porch)
Late 14th or Early
15th Century
Geometric Tracery.

SOUTH WINDOW,
SOUTH AISLE
Late 14th or Early
15th Century
Geometric Tracery.

TOWER, WEST END
15th Century
Early Perpendicular
tracery ~ as are the
Belfry apertures.

PORCH
15th Century.

TOWER, RINGING
CHAMBER ~ 19th Century.

Drawn by: Edwin Lambert · April 1991.

21 – St James's, Biddenham
window styles

35

THE CHURCHYARD AND TOMBSTONES

The most striking features of the churchyard when approached through the south main gates are two magnificent cedar trees, one of whose branches overhangs the path and partially obscures the tower. A handwritten note can be found at the back of the baptism register (1813-1875), 'I, Henry Wood, Vicar of Biddenham planted in the Churchyard two Cedars of Lebanon. These two trees were raised from seed out of a cone brought from Lebanon by my brother-in-law Admiral Gardner CB. The trees were about six years old when planted on Wednesday 22 December 1875.

The inside of the surrounding stone wall is delineated on all four sides by fine lime trees.[20] Three yew trees stand at the north-east. In July 2008 the new extension to the churchyard on the north side with land donated by the Pile family was consecrated by Richard Inwood, the Bishop of Bedford. The original churchyard had already been extended by 30 yards in 1897, a gift from E R Wingfield. The cottages and farm to the east of the church were burnt down earlier that year. One of the cottages was the home of the West family. The family grave now occupies that part of the churchyard where their fireplace used to be.

22 – The porch and parvis

After passing through

the main gates,[21] a good view of the exterior of the church may be had by taking the right-hand path. There is the base of an old preaching cross on the left. The tower, porch and south aisle are all castellated. The

23 – The tower clock

spire is of wood covered with lead, and the weather vane is a gilded cockerel. The roofs are clay tiled, with a stone cross at the end of the nave roof. The clock on the church tower was made by William Emmerton of Wootton, and installed in 1787, the year he recast the bells, at the expense of Captain John Brooks, RN, who lived at Ford End Manor House, his family home. A stone plaque on the east side of the tower, hidden from below, could refer to a Robert Leader known to have been a carpenter in the village in 1710. The blocked-up south doorway would have been used when the bells were rung from the lower bell-tower.

The tower buttresses were originally 15th century, but refaced later. There is a plaque on the north-west buttress in memory of John Davis dated 1812.

TOMBSTONES

The earliest burials in the churchyard which have legible inscriptions on the tombstone are:

Thomas Clark 1707   [age and epitaph eroded] and
James Harris 1708   Prepare in youth, no time delay
                            For I in my prime was cald away

Two tombstones with Celtic crosses in the north-east of the churchyard

24 – Tombstones with Celtic crosses

To the left of the main path are several more 18th century
tombstones:

Thomas Adkines   1715   In death how sudding is thy stroke
which no meer man can ere revoke

At least eight incumbents of the parish have been buried in the
churchyard. [See Appendix III for a full list of incumbents].

Two of the notable 20th century tombstones are in the shape
of a Celtic cross:
In memory of Edith Alice Duigan, d 1912, by C E Mallows
Charles Edward Mallows by Edward Landseer Griggs, ARA,
RA.

A fine obelisk (1851) at the north-east corner records the death
of John Mcbride Missing, aged 29, and his father, the Rev John
Missing M.A., of Magdalen Hall Oxford, curate of this parish
'a monument erected by many of his deeply attached friends'.
True to his name, he is not to be found in the church records.

25 – The main south entrance gates,
showing how the large cedar tree obscures the view of the church

CHURCH RECORDS AFTER THE REFORMATION, VISITATIONS AND CHURCHWARDEN'S ACCOUNTS

Glebe Terriers

After the Reformation the ecclesiastical authorities became increasingly aware of the need to keep proper records of church possessions. The documents known as glebe terriers fulfil this purpose, and include terriers (recording property and endowments) and inventories (goods and chattels). The existence of such records helped to prevent the loss and misappropriation of church property.

Visitations

The bishop was bound to follow medieval practice, to investigate the state of the parishes every three years so as to discover and correct any disorders. The two years in between were covered by the archdeacon.[22]

In 1706 Bishop William Wake, Bishop of Lincoln, visited Biddenham and reported that:
Mrs Elizabeth Boteler, widow of William Boteler Esq, was the patron and obliged to allow a stipend of £8 per annum to the Curate, Mr John Towersy. The parish was c 2 miles in length with c 40 families. There is no Lecture, School, Almeshouse or Hospital endowed there. Mrs Boteler had a seat on this parish, which has been long the seat of the antient familie of the Botelers, which will now be extinct.

By 1709 there was no house for the Curate, Mr John Teap of Clopham, who lives a mile off at Stachen [Stagsden]. There is divine service once every Lord's Day, none come to church unbaptised, many are unconfirmed. Catechising is every other Sunday, Communion is three times a year, about 20 received at Easter last. There are no Papists and very few Presbyterians.

These two visitations are a distinct improvement on the archdeaconal one for 1578 when Thomas Wright and Bartholamewe Brytte complained 'We doe present that we had no Communion but once this year'.

Little is known about repairs and alterations to the church between the 17th and early 19th centuries. We do, however, have a hand-written history of St James's by the Rev Henry Tattam (1789-1868), Rector of St Cuthbert's, Bedford, with a description of the church decorations which were removed later in the 19th century:[23]

On the wall over the south door, the commandments are written and also various passages of scripture between the windows. Above the entrance to the chancel, the Creed, the Lord's Prayer and Royal Arms are painted.

In 1847 Mr Wing was paid £4 8s for placing the commandments.

Today all walls are whitewashed.

The conscientious Archdeacon Bonney inspected the church on six occasions, one of 51 Bedfordshire churches he visited and entered in his Visitation notebook.[24] The first time, 1823, several orders were given 'That the font be thoroughly repaired with Parker's Cement, the Pulpit and Desk be Oak grained; the Pews coloured to correspond', among others. The next year the repairs were nearly finished, and after other visits, by 1839, the last time, there were only vestments to be acquired.

It can have come as no surprise to read in 1847 a highly critical article – one in a series which appeared in the *Northampton Mercury,* written under the pseudonym WA – that there was, apart from 'fine old open sittings prevail for the most part', nothing to praise.[25]

'The paving of the floor is most wretched'. A rod and curtain, used to convert the chancel into a robing room, is pronounced 'a contrivance only worthy of a provincial theatre company. The pulpit and reading desk very indifferent.' A large proportion of the north aisle is taken up by 'an enclosure of preposterous size'. His parting shot was reserved for the graveyard – 'The churchyard was locked'. 'WA' was the pseudonym used by John Martin, the librarian to the Duke of Bedford at Woburn. He was 'a man of strong views, he had no fear of controversy'. He drew attention here to the neglect of the church buildings and what he considered vulgar taste. It could be no consolation to the Rev Thomas Grimshawe that 16 years after his death, Sir Stephen Glynne's notes on 6 February 1866 conclude with 'The Church is in very good condition and well cared for'.[26] 'The chancel walls were mantled with ivy'. This was removed in 1936.

The Churchwarden's Accounts[27]

From 1836 to 1853 the churchwarden, John Lavender, kept church accounts in meticulous detail. The regular business included the purchase of communion bread and wine, cleaning of the church, visitations, confirmation expenses, ringing, purchase of candles and coal and Sunday school expenditure.

In 1836/7 5s was paid to Hutchins for keeping boys quiet in the gallery. In 1841 the annual subscription to the infant school commenced. In the disbursements from Easter 1845 to Easter 1846 he notes: 'A man and two horses, gravel carting for two days 10s, archdeacon's fee at parochial visitation 10s 6d, coals for the poor £2 10s, sparrows [these were considered vermin] £4 2s, repair of the parish causeways £2, and the relief of man and woman in want 6d.' In 1852 the bell-ringers were paid for tolling the bell for the Duke of Wellington.

SPECIAL FEATURES - THE BELLS AND BELL-TOWER, THE BOTELER MONUMENT AND STAINED GLASS

Church bells have always played an important part in English country life, and at one time did much more than summon the faithful to worship. They have been rung in times of danger and to celebrate both local and national events. Deaths, too, were announced by tolling one bell. A resident (Rhoda Brooks) remembers walking across the fields and hearing the bell being tolled. It was a shock to find it was for the Rev Eric Gaskell, who had died unexpectedly (1974). Today the bells are rung for church services and regularly at weddings.

The upper part of the bell-tower was built in the 15th century with louvred windows on all four sides. This must have been to house the first peal of bells. At that time, the bells were rung from ground level.

26 The bell-ringers about to start their Thursday night practice, c 2000.
Left to right: Don Glanvill, Brian Toyn, Peter Culverwell,
Margaret Robinson, Ralph West, Robert Robinson

In 1787 the five existing bells were recast into six by William Emmerton of Wootton, with the following inscriptions:

Treble BE LIGHT AND GLAD IN GOD REJOICE
        EMMERTON FECIT 1787
2nd   EMMERTON CAST THIS PEAL 1787
3rd   EMMERTON FECIT 1787
4th   WILLIAM EMMERTON OF WOOTTON FECIT
        1787
5th   FIVE OLD BELLS CAST INTO SIX AT THE
        EXPENSE OF MR JOHN BROOKS
        EMMERTON FECIT 1787

Tenor   BLESSED IS THE NAME OF THE LORD
        EMMERTON OF WOOTTON FECIT 1787

In the summer of 1787 the new bells were opened by the Ampthill ringers.

In 1896 the tenor bell, which was cracked, was recast by Taylor of Loughborough with the following inscription:

WOE UNTO ME IF I PREACH NOT THE GOSPEL
PRESENTED BY WILLIAM CARSON KANE 1896

In the same year the wooden frame dated 1604 was replaced by Taylor with a cast iron H frame and supports, with space on the north wall to add two bells to complete the octave.

In 1986 two bells were presented by churchwarden Cecil Winnington-Ingram; one in memory of his brother, Charles, who died in Africa, and one for himself, with the inscriptions –

Treble CECIL YOUR KINGDOM COME
2nd   CHARLES UKUMBUKO WA NJAA AFRICA
        (The first bell inscription in Swahili –
        "Remembering the hungry in Africa")

27 – The bell with the African inscription about to be installed

The tuning of the bells to match the tower, and the measurements for the pieces to add to the frame, were in the Taylor Job Book for 1896. These two new bells are considerably heavier than the now number 3. The Emmerton bells are typical of the time, lightweight and less able to sustain the vibrations.

In 1994 English Heritage insisted that the cracked No 6 be repaired, rather than recast, to preserve a unique ring of 5 out of 15 Emmerton bells still in existence. The other 10 bells are scattered round the county in ones or twos.

The ringing chamber is reached by climbing a spiral staircase on the north side past a gargoyle and up seven more steps. It is a small room lit by a circular window in the west wall. The bell ropes, with their red, white and blue sallies, hang from a spider hauled to the ceiling. The bells are accessed by a vertical ladder, and a longer ladder from the bell chamber gives access to the tower roof. On opening the inner door of the ringing chamber, a large notice DANGER, BELLS ARE UP catches the eye. The clock mechanism is in the ringing chamber.

There is a set of 14 handbells, acquired in 1903, hanging in a cupboard.

On the east wall hangs a large glazed list of The Church Bells of Bedfordshire 1888, in copperplate writing. It records the number of bells and the weight of the tenor (biggest) bell of every church in the county. A carved stone tablet of 1887 with a raised stippled edge has the names of the ringers inscribed.

28 – William West ringing at Biddenham in the 1920s

Some peal boards are noteworthy:
1884 Association of Change Ringers rang the first 5040 changes (a peal), first in this tower and the first by all the members of the band.
1934 The 50th anniversary of the first peal
1938 The longest peal yet rung in the county (7560 changes)
1987 1st peal rung on the 2 new additional bells.

The West family have provided ringers for over 200 years: James West, for forty years the parish clerk, 1794-1861; William (Billy) West 1848-1938, churchwarden, who could chime four bells at once – three with hands and one with a foot; Reginald (Reg) West, 1885-1956; and Ralph West, who retired at the age of 91 in 2012.

A list of fines must at one time have been an inducement to pay attention:

Fail a come   one pence
Fail a stand   one pence
Crack a stay   two and six
Break a stay   five shillings

Miss Evelyn Steel, one of two unmarried sisters who lived in Kings Close, 11 Main Road, was a founder member of The Ladies Guild of Ringers, and became President of the Bedford Association of Change Ringers. She was a strict tower captain at St James's Church, Biddenham. We understand that she wore her hair in two plaits, rode to hounds, and owned a horse called Sixpence.

29 – The bell-ringers marking the acquisition of their handbells in 1903.
Standing, left to right: Walter West, Tom Green, Harry King,
Dennis Green, Bill Davison.
Front row, left to right: William West, Jack Macksey, Charlie West

Handbell ringing became a musical activity in its own right during the mid 19th century, with teams (mostly male) playing by the 'off table' or 'in hand' methods. After World War I many sets of bells were packed away in towers and vestries and did not see the light of day again until the late 1960s, when the Handbell Ringers' Association of Great Britain (HRGB) was formed.

The team was formed in Biddenham in 1991 by Anthea Slark and Ralph West, using a set of handbells kept in the tower of St James's Church which was originally purchased around 1896. Over the years they have given about 200 performances, and replaced the old bells with a modern three-octave set of Malmark handbells, tuned to concert pitch and costing over £6,000. They also own a set of handchimes. The team belong to HRGB, and attend local and national rallies, giving them the opportunity to play with teams from all over the country.

The Boteler Monument – North Wall of the Chancel:

By far the largest and most striking of the wall monuments is a Jacobean family memorial of the 17th century set within an architectural frame of pink and black. The two principal figures, William Boteler (died 1601) and Ursula Boteler (died 1621) kneel facing one another either side of a prie-dieu. Sir William wears plate body, arm and leg armour with white ruff at neck and cuffs. He is bare-headed, with beard, moustache and shoulder-length hair. His wife is dressed all in black except for her neck and cuff ruffs, with an arched widow's hood and long veil hanging down over her pleated farthingale. Below the parents, the two sons and three daughters, one holding a skull to show that she has already died, kneel in similar fashion. The family crest, above, is surmounted by a boar's head and neck.

Underneath, the epitaph for Sir William ends:
Thus walkt hee here uprightly his dayes ended

30 – The Boteler monument

His soule oulde Jacob's ladder is ascended

And for his wife, Ursula:

Here livd belovd, here lieth, belovd though dead
That hand dispensing still his dayly bread.

The monument was erected by their second son, Oliver Boteler, and Oliver's brother-in-law, Richard Taylor, who married Oliver's sister, Elizabeth.

There are two more noteworthy 17th century memorial brasses:

A memorial brass, 'Helen Boteler, d 1639, wife of William Boteler of Biddenham and daughter of George Nodes of Shephall Esq' is on the north wall of the north aisle. The top of the brass contains the incised half portrait of a lady in a Tudor gown with large puffed and slashed sleeves. Across the wide collar lies a chain necklace and large ornament. The lower section contains a Latin eulogy, the second half of which is a clever play on words.

Alice, wife of Edward Osborne, eldest daughter of William Boteler, departed this life on 12 June 1615. She was honoured with an acrostic epitaph on the north wall of the chancel -

Among the best, above the most admired,
Lovely to all, loving to whom she ought,
In zeale to God and goodness holy-fired,
Charie and chaste in word, and deed, and thought,
Exact in all that in that sexe is dearest,
Of vertue fullest, and of vices cleerest.

Sweet young resemblance of old Sacred Mothers
Blessed example (present and to come)
Of pious pity to her owne and others;
Rare help; rich hap to her deer Pheer at home;
None such as she thinks hee who, still her debtor
Erects her this, but in his heart a better.

Stained Glass Windows

The Charles Howard Memorial Window [see colour section] Various benefactors contributed to the enrichment of the church, and the east window stained glass given in memory of Charles Howard, chairman of the Bedfordshire County Council and churchwarden, who died in 1895, by his grandson, Sir John Howard, is certainly the most arresting, by virtue of its size. The beautiful east window of 1897 was designed by Charles Kempe. Inspired by his study of 15th century medieval glass, he brought a new refreshing interpretation to Victorian stained glass, reflected in the use of mainly green, blue and ruby colours, and the delicate, detailed painting of flowers. Each tracery light has an angel in a white gown. The central figure of Christ the King with a gold crown is seated on a throne. On the left is St Peter, holding a key and a book, with the Archangel Michael and sword behind him. On the right is St Paul, dressed in a sumptuous red gown, seated and holding an open book with the text 'Charitas Xti urget nos' (The love of Christ constraineth us, 2 Corinthians 5:14). Behind him stands St James of Compostela, holding a staff with a bag. The scallop shell on his hat is a symbol of pilgrimage. A ribbon banner unfurls above his head with the inscription, 'Te gloriosus apostolorum' from the *Te Deum*.

The Douglas Carey Memorial Window[28]

The window at the east end of the south aisle was dedicated in 1949 in memory of Douglas Falkland Carey DSO MA, vicar from 1936 to 1946. St Michael stands on the left in a blue tunic and green cloak with gold armour. He has gold wings, and carries a red shield with white cross and a sword. Above is a set of balance scales. To the right St Barnabas wears a green tunic with blue and gold lined cloak. He carries a gold staff in his left hand, and a book in his right, with the words 'A good man and full of holy spirit and faith'. The inscriptions 'ST MICHAEL' and 'ST BARNABAS' stand out below in plain glass scrolls.

The Sir John and Lady Howard Thanksgiving Window[29]

The window on the east side of the chancel was given by Sir John and Lady Howard in 1969 in thanksgiving for the restoration of the chancel.

In the tracery lights are the symbols of the two disciples, the chalice of St John and the sword of the martyrdom of St James. St John the Evangelist stands on the left with an orange and red halo and multicoloured robes with the Transfiguration in gold and white. A white-robed Christ is flanked by Our Lady and St John. St James, patron saint of the church, stands on the right. He has a red halo and holds a staff in his right hand. He has bare feet, and stands over the Agony in the Garden. Our Lord is dressed in gold against a circle of golden light with two disciples asleep underneath.

St James, son of Zebedee, was a fisherman called by Jesus to join him. St James was beheaded by Herod Agrippa. He is the only apostle whose death is recorded in scripture (Acts 12 v2). The Feast of St James is on 25 July.

The Benedicite Window[30]

The window on the east end of the north aisle, the 'John Howard window' or 'Benedicite window', was installed in 1990, and commemorates the life and achievements of Sir John Howard (1901- 1986), churchwarden for 27 years. His 'joy and great happiness found in St James' is marked by a picture of the church in the bottom of the middle light. The three lights are spanned by a suspension bridge, referring to his work as a civil engineer on the Humber and Severn bridges. The left light, headed by the sun, reflects his engineering interests, and the right light, his love of nature, with a tree, birds, deer and butterfly. The arms of the Harpur Trust, of which he was chairman, are at the bottom of the left light. Emblazoned across the middle, over a whale and waves, is the inscription 'O all ye works of the Lord bless ye the Lord'.

The Millennium Window[31] (see colour section)

At the west end of the bell-tower, the Millennium window reflects the village of Biddenham as the villagers saw it at the beginning of the third millennium. The river, which denotes the western boundary of the village, winds from the small central panel at the top through the two main panels, and flows out of the picture at the base of the right-hand one. On its way it sweeps through the date, 2000, symbolising the continuous passage of time. In the top left are two symbols of St James, the crook and the shell. Underneath is the first of the seasonal cameos. The village green with the cedar tree in the vicarage garden and the war memorial depict autumn. A view of the church across a frozen pond is winter. Post Office Row represents spring, and underneath, a game of cricket at the pavilion field, summer. The inscription 'God is our God' is from Psalm 48 v14.

VICTORIAN ADDITIONS, AND MORE RECENT BUILDING AND RESTORATIONS

31 – 1908: the interior of the church, showing gas lighting and the Jacobean screen enclosing the Boteler pew/vestry in the north aisle

Parishioners gave generously to the church, usually in commemoration of a member of the family. Several items of plate have been given, to be added to the three pieces from previous centuries. The oldest piece is a communion cup and paten (1569). Of sterling silver, it has an engraved heraldic boar's head in profile (the crest of William Boteler), with the letter W on one side and B on the other. A silver flagon is engraved 'The gift of Francis Reeve who died July 4th 1689'. Two pewter alms plates are dated 1702.

At some point in the Victorian era unglazed terracotta encaustic tiles were laid in the aisles and sanctuary, now covered in a beige carpet. The tiles have a variety of patterns, including

32 – View through the tower arch to the chancel

fleur-de-lys, lion rampant, birds and foliate designs. The inscriptions 'The Resurrection and the Life' and 'I will not leave you comfortless. I will come to you' are inset in the risers.

The pews, the hexagonal drum-shaped pulpit – from which the sermon is preached – and the altar rails are Victorian. In the 17th century Archbishop Laud had introduced the rails to protect the altar from stray animals. On the walls of the chancel there are two brass plaques, one to Sydney Neal Faulkener OBE (1880 to 1962), and the other to Maria Amelia Whitworth (d 1906), whose parents donated the Victorian altar. Choirstalls and the Bishop's chair were presented later.

Of particular interest are the various fittings designed by C E Mallows, the Arts and Crafts architect who lived in the village. They were made at the J P White Pyghtle Works in Bedford. The lectern (1902), from which the biblical lessons are read each Sunday, is particularly fine. It is a hammered brass bookstand supported on two brass columns, between which a decorative iron tree of life bears copper apples. In addition there are the carved oak vicar's stall

33 – The lectern

(1903), the altar table (1906), an oak board with an inscription

55

(1908) – now in the parvis – and the large wooden cross above the chancel arch (1912). The cross was made from oak grown at Southill Park, Old Warden, Bedfordshire.

The brass cross and candlesticks date from 1891. The churchwardens' staffs can be found at the ends of the two pews where they used to sit. The People's Warden was represented by a crown at the top of the staff, and the Vicar's Warden by a mitre. Today both churchwardens are elected at the annual meeting of parishioners.

A particularly fine pale green embroidered laudian (cover for the main altar) has an eight-pointed star. 16 flowers of the locality have been worked in white, yellow, mauve, pink, red and blue, with a fish – symbol of Christ – in the centre.[32]

34 – The embroidered laudian

A deep blue and gold woven fabric used on the altar in the south aisle is part of a tapestry which adorned the Queen Mother's balcony in Westminster Abbey at the coronation of Queen Elizabeth II on 2 June 1953.[33]

Made of metal and wood, the aumbry and frame on the left-hand wall of the south aisle were given to the church by the Sisters of St Ethelreda's Children's Home when they moved from Bromham Road to Conduit Road in Bedford in 1994.

The Organ

Music has always been part of church worship. A clarinet, now kept in the vestry, was played by James West (1794-1861), a churchwarden for 40 years, before a harmonium was installed. In the 19th century the singing gallery (since demolished) was in the church tower.

In 1898 the organ, built by Bishop and Son of London and Ipswich, was installed. It has two manuals, with ten ranks of pipes, and was worked by bellows. Over the years there have been numerous repairs, including electrification in 1938. In 1965 the organ was rebuilt by Leighton Organs on the extension principle, a mammoth undertaking. Recently there has been another extensive repair.

The Vestry[34]

The vestry at the north-west corner was added in 1974. It was built of good weathered stone collected from cottages and barns in north Bedfordshire. Embedded in the floor are 18th and 19th century tombstones which were originally in the churchyard.

On a stone plaque on the west wall are the initials of the two churchwardens PJK (Peter King), JH (Sir John Howard), EAG (the incumbent, the Rev Eric Gaskell) and RJC (Treasurer, Jeff Cockings). The spiral staircase comes next, leading up to the bell-tower.

On the stonework at the north-east corner, a particularly gruesome gargoyle, swallowing some unfortunate, can be seen. Gargoyles were reputed to keep evil spirits away

35 – A gargoyle at the north-east corner of the nave

from the church, and our five have a more practical purpose in throwing rainwater clear of the wall. Stone roses decorate the drainpipes on this north wall. The position of the original north door, now blocked in, can still be seen.

Restoration

The church was restored and reseated under James Horsford of Bedford at a cost of £842 in 1861/62. The roof was retiled in two colours with diagonal patterns. Further work costing £320 followed under Usher and Anthony of Bedford in 1891 (windows, heating, lighting and ornaments). The repair of the bell chamber and restoration of bells cost £220 in 1896[35].

In 1899 the glebe lands (24 acres and 24 perches) in the Queen's Park area of the village, were sold to the Broadwood Piano Company for £6,600.

The early 20th century heating consisting of a coke furnace with a flue running up the centre of the nave gave way to central heating by oil in 1931, and in 1955 a major restoration of the belltower cost £2,874, and was celebrated with floodlighting. 14 tons of stone were used, and three tons of lead were removed and recast. In 1987 floors and pews infested with dry rot were replaced, and the church was rewired.

Recently the parvis floor was replaced (2008), the organ refurbished (2009) and the clock, which had been wound by hand for over 200 years (for the last 25 by Don Sherwood), was refurbished, and an auto-wind unit fitted (2009/10). The Friends of St James supported the clock project, and raised £10,000 to cover the cost.

The Church Barn[36]

Not until 1978 did the church own a hall which could be used for Sunday school, coffee after services, Parochial Church Council meetings and the youth club. One of the Church Farm buildings was bought from Mr Kilbourn at Church Farm for £5,000. An equal amount was spent on materials, and labour was provided by the government job creation programme. By 1981 the barn was finished and inaugurated. It can be reached from the church by stepping-stones leading to the west gate.

Two Church Treasures

The church contained two interesting treasures; the Flemish tapestry and the medieval lectionary. The tapestry, thought to have been brought from Flanders by Sir William Boteler, is dated 1549. It depicts a Roman Emperor's head and a German baron's crest, and could well have graced the banqueting hall at Kirtons Ford End Manor. It was later given to the church as an altar cloth, and it is said that subsequently the church cleaner used it as a dustsheet, not knowing its value. It was rescued by the Rev William Norman, framed, and hung in the vestry which was then in the bell-tower. It was later taken by the Rev Eric Gaskell to the Victoria and Albert Museum, which offered to buy it for £1,800. This was accepted, and the proceeds put towards the cost of the new vestry.

One would not expect a cupboard marked 'miscellaneous' to contain a medieval document in a Victorian frame. Found in 1994 by the North Bedfordshire Recorders Group, it was authenticated and dated 1280-1300 at the British Museum. It is part of a lectionary or martyrology intended to be read as a daily lesson in a refectory, or in a church service. Saint Wulfstan, 'a good social reformer', is mentioned, and a letter 'E' heading in Tudor blackwork is probably a filing mark. It was later cut down and pasted on a piece of parish register. This piece of vellum, with good pen flourish initials, has survived a long and chequered career until brought to light by Jackie Stubbs, one of the Church Recorders.

VICARS OF THE 19TH CENTURY

The Reverend Thomas Shuttleworth Grimshawe (1778 to 1850)

One of the most interesting vicars about whom we have substantial information is the Reverend Thomas Shuttleworth Grimshawe. In 1808, with an MA from Brasenose College, Oxford, Thomas became vicar of Biddenham, a position he held until his death in 1850. He is buried in the chancel, and commemorated by two family plaques, one on the outside east chancel wall, and another on the inside of the church. From 1809 to 1843 he was also rector of Burton Latimer in Northamptonshire. He merits an entry in the *Dictionary of National Biography,* his most successful publication being *The Life and Works of William Cowper* (1835, 8 volumes, reprinted seven times).

The Bedford Record Office was able to purchase, in about 1988, Mr Grimshawe's receipted household bills, mostly from 1849, which give a fascinating insight into the life of a clergyman in the mid-19th century.[37] The living of Biddenham was valued at £150 a year, yet his known expenses in 1849 amounted to over £370.

36 – Receipt, Charlotte Grimshawe

Subscriptions to 'the Athenaeum Club (£6 6s 0d), the Society of necessitous Clergymen (£1 1s 0d), the Infant School (£5 0s 0d)' and 'the Royal Society of Literature (£2 0s 0d)' were major annual expenses. On a personal note, 'polishing Britshka [an open carriage] body (£4 12s 6d), dress (£0 2s 6d), butcher (£100 0s 0d), 4 bottles of pale brandy (£0 5s 6d each)' show that he needed to make up a deficit of at least £220 from his private income in this one year alone. From the census for 1841 we learn that resident in the vicarage were Thomas, aged 60, his wife Charlotte, aged 45, their daughters Georgiana (16) and Caroline (14). Also resident at the vicarage were two men aged 50 and 30, who were 'independent', a governess, aged 42, three female servants and one manservant.

In the rate account of 3 July 1838, the Rev Thomas Grimshawe held a modest 9 acres 3 rods 3 poles of land in the village, consisting of the parsonage, house and land, with a rateable value of £45 (sixpence in the £). As the only landowner who lived in the village, he took precedence over the Honourable G R Trevor with his farms and cottage and the Misses Trevor, who were the other two landowners. At this time there was a bakehouse, smithy, shop and public house in the village.

In the 42 years of his incumbency, the Rev Thomas Grimshawe was in a strong position. He had no competition from other denominations. Since 1665 the Five Mile Act had prohibited nonconformist ministers from conducting meetings with a radius of five miles of the borough of Bedford. Anyone with nonconformist leanings would need to walk into Bedford or one of the surrounding villages. He certainly took a strict view of his duties, when in the first year of his incumbency, 1808, he noted after the baptisms of the Ward family on 23 November 1808:

I take this opportunity of stating that I solemnly protested to the Father of the above children against his having withheld the rite of Baptism from them so long, contrary to the custom of the Land, against the practice of the established Church & the generally admitted command of the scriptures, & which neglect would have deprived them of Christian burial, had they died.

Mr Grimshawe was survived by one son, Charles Livius, who became High Sheriff of Bedfordshire in 1866. Sadly, another four children did not outlive him - three died in early infancy, and his son, John Barham Grimshawe, died at Trinity College, Cambridge, aged 23.

'He walked in faith, adorning his high and holy calling by a blameless life and liberal mind' was Mr Grimshawe's short and to the point epitaph.

The Biddenham Friendly Society

Two later vicars of the 19th century were actively involved in the benevolent work of the Biddenham Friendly Society (1836-1878). The Rev Chernocke Smith had set up a clothing, and then a shoe club, with an annual payout of between £5 and £6. The next vicar, the Rev Henry Wood, encouraged members to pay in a small sum

37 – The Rev Henry Wood M.A.
Vicar 1865-90

regularly during the year, at the end of which farmers and local gentry were asked for contributions, and the result divided out and spent on shoes and clothes.[38] As president, his annual subscription was £1. Although labourers were very poor, self-help schemes flourished for over 40 years, to avoid the spectre of the workhouse.

The Reverend William Egglesfield Bathurst Norman (Vicar 1890 to 1935)

Admired and feared in equal measure, the Rev William Egglesfield Bathurst Norman was our longest-serving vicar. He lived in the Old Vicarage with his wife, Ellen, and four children – three girls and a boy – Katharine, Margaret, Francis and Helen. He would take them to school in Bedford in a four-wheeled chaise drawn by an elderly pony. The gardener/groom, Percy West, was seated raised up at the back. The pony had a

38 – A village school group with the Rev William Norman, c 1930.
Back row: Miss Haffenden, - , Jack Mayhew, - , - Green,
- , The Rev William Norman.
Middle row: Joyce Shaw (older sister of Lettie), Jim Shaw, - ,
Ralph West, - , - , Eric Green, Roy West, Ralph Chapman, - .
Front row includes Charlie Burrows, Mary Church,
Kath Gudgin and Arthur Gudgin

hard time of it, pulling six people. The village boys, on their way to school in the morning, laughed and shouted at them. The son, Francis, would often start to walk, rather than be seen riding to school, until he was hauled back by his father.[39]

He was something of a scholar, with a collection of documents and fossils. Indeed, about 1920 he gave a lecture to the Bedford Natural History and Archaeological Society about the history of Biddenham, the text of which was deposited by his widow at the Bedford Record Office.

It is generally considered that he was careless in his dress. The older inhabitants who remember his weekly Bible instruction at the village school testify that he wore the same long black

39 – The parclose screen

gown and flat black cap for months, even years, until they were 'green with mould'. The village children, after the initial 'Good morning, sir', knew better than to talk without being spoken to. Behind his back, of course, he was known as 'Billie Norman' or 'the parson'.

He kept a sharp eye on the whole village. He would walk every footpath two or three times a year, and any damaged path, fence, stile or gate would be reported to the Estate carpenter for repair. He was in the habit of taking holidays on his own, walking across the fields to Midland Road Station. He would come home carrying a suitcase with a blackthorn stick over his shoulder, then return on foot to the station to fetch a second suitcase.[40]

The event for which he was chiefly remembered was the Sunday school treat in July. Mr Norman would visit each house and cottage to invite everyone to tea, consisting of bread, butter and slab cake. The games and prizes were enjoyed by all, but the lasting impression was made by 'scrambling for sweets', thrown by the vicar and parents, which resulted in a pocket full of sweets and grass. Even on a festive occasion such as this, the boys, as was their wont, would aggravate the vicar. They took it for granted that he would chase them and give them a blow on the head with the gong stick with which he announced each item.[41] This strong action on his part was not held against him; he was admired by young and old for his devotion to village affairs.

After a long illness, he died at the vicarage. At his memorial service in November 1935, the *Bedford Record* noted that 'the village lost a great friend and a devoted servant'.

The Rev William Norman had already re-opened the parvis (room over the porch), reached through the south aisle, on 9 March 1903.

After his death the parishioners showed their appreciation of his 45 years' service by restoring the south aisle chapel in 1939. The delicately carved 16th century parclose screen which encloses it originally came from the Boteler pew, later used as a vestry at the eastern end of the north aisle.[42] The six bays have a cresting rail surmounting two bands of frieze. The carved panels of the lower stage each carry a different design of urns, stylised foliage and berries.

THE CHURCH TODAY

St James's is now part of a larger parish which includes All Saints' church, Kempston. The present incumbent, the Reverend Stephen Huckle, is assisted by two Readers, Christopher Dawe and Paul Fricker. The main service at St James's on Sunday mornings is the sung Eucharist, and an evensong combined with All Saints' is held on two Sundays a month, as well as the Eucharist on the first Sunday. There is a Communion service at St James's every Thursday morning, and baptisms, weddings and funerals take place at the church on a regular basis. Various study groups are held, especially during Lent. St James's is indebted to the work of the churchwardens, at present Ann Morrish and Laurie Hurn, for the day-to-day running of the church. Hilary Hurn is the verger. The parochial church council, the main administrative body, meets seven times a year.

There is a strong pastoral ministry, especially concerned with visiting the sick. Concerts and flower festivals are frequently held at the church, and a number of activities take place in the church barn. A carol service on Christmas Eve in the churchyard brings families together from Biddenham, Deep Spinney and Great Denham. The church works closely with a number of other churches in the neighbourhood, and is part of the Shalom Group including members from Catholic,

Anglican and Presbyterian churches. It gives encouragement to Christian work abroad.

The Friends of St James, started by Peter Leverkus, is a thriving organisation which includes people from the village and elsewhere who are interested in the church as a historical building, whether they attend church or not.

The vicar and Paul Fricker take assemblies at St James' lower school, and the church is represented on the governing body. The school holds its Christmas carol service at the church, and pupils and teachers participate in one of the Sunday morning Eucharist services each year.

With the development of Great Denham, the church is working hard to ensure that those moving into the area are given a warm welcome at services and other activities. St James's church has existed in recorded references for at least 800 years, and its impact on the village is still strong.

References/Notes:

1   Richard Taylor, *How to Read a Church* (Rider, 2003), p 29.
2   Mark Child, *Discovering Churchyards* (Shire Publications, 1989), p 72.
3   *The Victoria County History of Bedfordshire, Part 26* (1912), p 39. Alternative spellings Passelewe and Passelawe.
4   Brian Harris, *Guide to Churches and Cathedrals* (Ebury Publishing, 2006), p 121.
5   For further information, see www.apotropaios.co.uk or susan.cordes@o2.co.uk
6   Harvey, *History of the Hundred of Willey*, p 16.
7   BHRS vol. 49, p 23.
8   *Bedfordshire Magazine*, vol. 26, p 88.
9   A Simco and P McKeague, *Bridges of Bedfordshire*, p 40.
10   R Rideout, *Bromham in Bedfordshire: a History* (2002) p 27.
11   P McKeague in *Bedfordshire Magazine vol 21*, p 208.
12   BHRS vol 76 p 194.

13   Ibid, vol 58 p 3.

14   TW 148 and 165 at BLARS

15   BHRS vol 45 p 123.

16   Ibid, vol 76 p 210.

17   Ibid, vol 58 p 26.

18   Ibid, vol 45 p 80.

19   Ibid, vol.58 p112.

20   Given by Charles Burton (d 1951 aged 94), buried in Biddenham churchyard.

21   Replaced in 1990, from a design of 1926. Ronald Peatfield had already given similar gates in 1955, in memory of his parents.

22   BHRS vol 81 p116.

23   Rev Henry Tattam, unpublished MS, p 6.

24   BHRS vol 73 p 116.

25   Ibid, p 117.

26   Ibid, p 119.

27   W E Tate, *The Parish Chest* (Phillimore, 1983), p 84.

28   Designed by Alfred Williamson of Barnet.

29   Designed by Alfred Fisher, made by Whitefriars Stained Glass Studios of Wealdstone, Middlesex.

30   Designed by Alfred Fisher, made by Chapel Studios, King's Langley, Herts.

31   Designed by John Lawson of Goddard and Gibbs Studios, consecrated by John, Bishop of Bedford, 21 May 2000. The money was raised by donors in the village.

32   Designed by Joan Freeman, and embroidered by Clarissa Robinson.

33   Gifted by Joan Martin, Biddenham, whose father was one of the clergymen at the ceremony.

34   Built by Marriotts of Northampton, dedicated by the Rt Rev John Hare on 5 May 1974.

35   BHRS vol 73 p 114.

36   Dedication service by John Taylor, Bishop of St Albans, 1981.

37   BLARS Z614.

38   *Bedford Mercury* 8 May 1880.

39   Albert Church, *Recollections of my Life in Biddenham,* p 13.

40   Ibid, p 3.

41   Ibid, p 4.

42   Altered and relocated by Sir Alfred Richardson.

The NADFAS (The National Association of Decorative and Fine Arts) report of 1996 has been an invaluable source of information.

Further reading:
Victoria County History of Bedfordshire (Willey Hundred)
Harvey, *History of the Hundred of Willey.*
John Richardson, *The Local Historian's Encyclopedia* (Historical Publications, 2003)
Pamela Cunnington, *How Old is that Church?* (Blandford, 1990)

CHAPTER 5

BIDDENHAM 1500 TO 1700 - BOTELER/DYVE RIVALRY

Biddenham between 1500 and 1700 was the scene of a clash between the newly rich in the form of the Boteler family, and the traditional landed gentry in the form of the Dyve family. The clash was over land in the late 16th century, but by the time of the Civil War, 1642 to 1649, it was a division over national politics, with the Botelers supporting parliament and the Dyves, the King. [See Appendix IV for the Boteler family tree].

In the Middle Ages there seems to have been no close connection between Biddenham and any great baronial family. There was, however, a manor house at Ford End, called after the Kirtons, who owned it.[1] In the mid-15th century, the Kirton heiress, Grace, married Richard Boteler, a London merchant. The name Boteler is recorded in Biddenham in 1313, through a Thomas Boteler, but it is not recorded in the subsidy rolls for 1309 and 1332.[2] What is clear is that the marriage of Grace Kirton and Richard Boteler was the start of the rise of the Botelers to wealth and prominence.

40 – Ford End (Kirtons), 1912. Demolished 1967

Grace and Richard's son, William, like other 16th century figures, such as William Harpur, made the family fortune in London.[3]   He was a citizen and grocer of London. Between 1508 and 1532 he was eight times master of the Grocers' Company. He was elected alderman of Cheap ward in 1507, and served as sheriff that year. From 1514 to 1515 he was auditor and he became Mayor of London from 1515 to 1516, when he was knighted. His will, which was proved in February 1534, shows that he had built up a substantial London estate in addition to Kirtons. He was able to fund a chantry chapel at St James's, Biddenham, for prayers to be said for the souls of himself, his parents and his late wives, one of whom was Elizabeth, the widow of John Saunders, a merchant of Calais. She had brought shops and cellars in Calais to the Botelers when she married William. William left a widow, Agnes.[4]

William's son, also called William, gained from the religious changes of the 16th century, and especially the dissolution of the monasteries. Much of the land in Biddenham, known as Biddenham Manor, had belonged first to the Canons of St Paul's and then, from the 12th century, to the Augustinian Priory of Newnham. At the dissolution of the monasteries, the land was granted to John Gostwick, but he sold it to William Boteler in 1540.[5]   William was a stapler, a member of the government-sponsored company responsible for wool exports. He married into another great wool family, the Paycocks of Coggeshall in Essex. However, although he had enjoyed commercial success, William seems to have become tired of the City, and eager to acquire more land, sell his staple shares and devote himself to Bedfordshire, hence his purchase in 1540.[6]   By 1543 he possessed at least 633 acres of land and eight houses in Biddenham, and about 90 acres in Bedford and 20 acres in Clapham.[7]   His will, which was proved in 1554, makes it clear that he wished to be thought of as a country gentleman. He was to be buried in the chapel which his father had built in Biddenham church. He instructed that what remained of the London property was to be disposed of, and his executors were told to sell the shops and cellars in Calais. His second son, Robert, was to be apprenticed to his father's friend, Blaise Sanders, citizen and mercer of London, but his eldest son, William, who was only about 10 years old on his father's death, was expected to play a full part as gentry in Bedfordshire. This was not to happen for a few years, as his mother, Anne, remarried to a Thomas Goodwyn and for a time Kirtons seems to have been let. However, William took up residence there when he became of age, and began to consolidate the estates.[8]

William steadily added to his land, so that by the time of his death in 1602, the total estate had increased by about a third. There were 780 acres, three messuages and 15 cottages in Biddenham; the White Hart, six cottages and about 100 acres in Bedford; a messuage, three cottages and 124 acres in Clapham and Oakley, and a house and 17 acres in Knotting. This land acquisition aroused the ill-will of the more ancient and noble family of Dyve, across the river at Bromham. The Dyves looked on William Boteler as an upstart, as his ancestors had obtained their fortune in trade. Moreover, William did not choose to live a quiet life on his estates, but acquired increasing influence in the neighbourhood. In 1588 he became sheriff of Bedfordshire, making him the King's representative in the shire court. If this was not enough, William's second wife, Ursula, was a woman of character who would stand her ground if there was an issue under dispute.[9]   When the character of the Dyves is factored in, the stage was set for trouble between the established gentry and the newly rich.

In the 15th century the Dyves, a traditional landed family with estates in Bedfordshire, Buckinghamshire and Denbighshire, had acquired most of the manor of Bromham. In 1565 Sir Lewis Dyve completed the purchase of the whole Bromham estate. He was a colourful, forthright character who had ransomed himself with a payment of 600 marks after he had been taken prisoner in 1558 on the fall of Calais. In 1574 he had become sheriff of Bedfordshire after the county ceased to share a sheriff with Buckinghamshire.[10]   Sir Lewis was an established member of the local gentry who regarded the Botelers as tradesmen and upstarts, and who could be disregarded where land acquisition was concerned.

In 1588 Sir Lewis bought a piece of land in Biddenham called Dyves Downs Farm, which William Boteler had intended to buy, and for which he had already paid £100. In retaliation, William bought the reversion of parts of the Latimer and Neville estates in Bromham. This was very unfortunate, as Sir Lewis had already incorporated these lands in others included in the parkland.[11]   Sir Lewis is normally blamed for what followed, but R W Rideout maintains that it may well have been his son, John Dyve, who was responsible. Legal documents filed by William's grandson in connection with later attempts to resolve the title to the disputed lands state that in a bill filed in the court of the Star Chamber by the grandfather, against Sir Lewis, it was said that it was Sir John Dyve, who, as heir had 'conceived against your sayde subject most grievous displeasure and deadly hatred'. Forgetting 'both his dutye towards God and obedience towards your majestes laws' he sought to bring William (the grandfather) 'to final perdition and destruction.'[12]

In 1589 William Boteler was challenged to a duel, presumably by John Dyve. William refused to fight, as he was sure that he would have lost, but this demonstrated to the Dyves that he was no gentleman. On 23 December 1589 William ceased to hold the office of sheriff of Bedfordshire which had given him special protection from attack as he was a servant of the crown. On Christmas Eve, William was aware that John and his retainers were lying in wait for him, as they were expecting him to go into Bedford to hear the sermon. He wisely did not go. However, on 26 December 1589 John Dyve issued a challenge, and on the following Sunday he and nine retainers and friends, armed with swords, daggers and staves, ambushed William and four servants on his way home from church. The leader of the assailants was William Broughe 'a man of bad behaviour' who was a particular friend of John Dyve. He said that 'there is noe remedye but we must fight it out.'[13] The other assailants were Lewis Simson, Thomas Smythe (yeoman), Henry Tommes (yeoman), Randolph Walton (yeoman), Brian Inglande (late of Clapham, yeoman), David Faldoe of Biddenham (gentleman), Edward Leader (yeoman) and William Deerye of Biddenham (labourer). In the affray, William Boteler was knocked to the ground and was left bleeding. His servant, Peter Sampson, was run through the throat, Robert Sampson was wounded in the right arm and Andrew Wright lost two fingers from his left hand. John Dyve and his men departed 'in great braverye and jolitye rejoiycinge greatlye of that which they had done.'

The land dispute was ultimately settled by an exchange of lands in Bromham and Biddenham, probably in 1605. There is no record of whether the Star Chamber ever heard the case. Sir Lewis must have realised the gravity of what had happened, as on his deathbed in 1592 he urged his son to end his personal quarrel with the Botelers. Furthermore, in 1599 Dame Ursula deputised for the Countess of Warwick as godparent for John's eldest son, the second Sir Lewis Dyve, who was to become famous at the time of the Civil War in the 17th century, and who was to fight on the opposite side to the Botelers.[14]

The struggle between King and parliament in the 17th century saw a revival of the Boteler/Dyve dispute, but this time it involved national politics rather than just land. The land issue may well have been diffused and not resurrected, because when William Boteler died in 1602 his eldest son, Thomas, was under age. Although young, his father arranged his marriage at Biddenham church to Ann, daughter and heir of Francis Farrar of Harrold on 10 January 1602, a month before his death.

The young couple went to live at a fine new mansion house built by Francis Farrar on a site between Harrold church and the river, Harrold Hall. Sir Thomas and his heir Sir William, who succeeded him in 1625, both lived at Harrold Hall, but about 1650 the family decided to let Harrold Hall and return to Kirtons, perhaps because it was conveniently near to Bedford. This would have suited Sir William, who played a prominent part in public affairs.[15]

William became sheriff in 1637 to 1638, and was responsible for the collection of Charles I's very unpopular tax, ship money. This was particularly hated in Bedfordshire. The inhabitants, living a long way from the sea, resented paying for the navy, which had traditionally been funded by coastal towns. Although some members of the family continued to support the King (his brother-in-law John Keeling, cousin, Richard Taylor of Clapham, and brother, Francis Boteler were royalists), William's sympathies leaned increasingly to parliament. He was an unsuccessful candidate in the disputed election in the town of Bedford in 1640, he was much engaged in quarter-sessions business, and by the time of the outbreak of Civil War in 1642 he was a member of the sequestration committee of the county committee and a close friend of the parliamentary leader in this area, Sir Samuel Luke. He was rewarded with a knighthood in 1654.[16]

On the other hand, the head of the Dyve family in 1642 was John Dyve's son, Lewis. He had had an adventurous youth in Spain, where his stepfather, the Earl of Bristol, had been ambassador, before returning to England and becoming MP for Bridport, and then for Weymouth in 1625 and 1626. By 1641 it was clear that his sympathies were royalist, and he was adjudged by parliament to be a delinquent on 14 February 1641.[17] In 1642 an order for Dyve's arrest was put out. In July 1642 a small party, which included the then sheriff, Sir Thomas Alston of Odell, and Sir Samuel Luke of Cople, rode out to

Bromham Hall to arrest Sir Lewis. At the Hall Lady Dyve and some of the servants said that Sir Lewis was out. Other servants denied this. Randolph Lawrence, one of the parliamentarian party, decided to search the house, but he found that there would be resistance, so he went back to Bedford for more men. Sir Lewis had his chance to escape, but there were injuries to both sides from pistols and muskets. It is not certain how he escaped: some say that he swam the river, but it is more likely that he crossed the river on horseback and rode north to join the Royalists at York.[18]

This was but the start of a colourful and action-packed career for Sir Lewis during the Civil War period. He fought with Charles I's nephew, Prince Rupert, at Edgehill in 1642, and at Turnham Green. In 1643 he was appointed governor of Abingdon, and while he was away, Sir Samuel Luke's parliamentary men took grain worth £31 1s 3d from Bromham Hall, and the residue of Sir Lewis's goods were 'caryed away.'[19] Dyve got his revenge in September 1643 when he plundered Sir Samuel Luke's house at Cople on the way to Bedford and Newport Pagnell. However, Dyve did not have the ammunition or powder to hold on to his advantage: the King at Oxford sent supplies too late. For the rest of the war Dyve was in charge of the garrison at Sherborne Castle in Dorset, until he was taken prisoner in August 1645.[20] Lewis Dyve's adventures between 1645 and the return of the monarchy in 1660 show his resilience and determination. He endured two years in the Tower of London until November 1647, when he was moved to the King's Bench prison as he was being sued for debt by the lieutenant governor of the Tower. In January 1648 he managed to escape, but was arrested again when he joined Charles I's forlorn attempt at a comeback and was captured after the Battle of Preston. He made a spectacular escape while awaiting trial, jumping down the sewage outlet from the Tower into the Thames and boarding the boat his friends had provided that took him to The Hague.[21] Dyve met the diarist John Evelyn at The Hague. He remarked in his diary 'this knight was indeed a valiant gentleman; but a little given to romance.'[22]

Sir Lewis Dyve needed perhaps to emphasise the romantic exploits of his youth by the 1650s, as his lands had been sequestrated in 1651 and sold to his father-in-law in 1652. However, he did retrieve his lands in Bromham, Biddenham, Kempston and Stevington when Charles II returned to England in 1660. He never made up the financial losses he had suffered: Pepys in his diary in 1667 and 1668 estimated that Dyve had lost £164,000 in the King's service.[23] The Dyves do not seem to have recovered financially, and Sir Lewis Dyve's grandson, also Lewis, sold the Bromham estates to Sir Thomas Trevor, the Chief Justice of the Common Pleas, for £21,394 in 1708.[24]

The Botelers, on the contrary, had a less dramatic time during the years 1642 to 1660, and avoided imprisonment and serious financial loss. The letters that they have left behind show a placid family life, disturbed mainly by illnesses and journeys.[25] The sadness for the fifth William Boteler, who succeeded to the estates on his father's death in 1656, and his wife, Elizabeth, daughter of Sir Thomas Hatton, was that neither of their sons survived infancy. Eventually in 1671 the estates were divided between the three surviving daughters and their heirs: Anne, wife of Nicholas Carew of Beddington, Surrey; Helen, wife of Sir Pynsent Chernocke; and Mary, who married her cousin, William Farrar, and had two daughters and coheirs - Margaret, the wife of Robert Chester and Elizabeth, wife of William Hillersdon of Elstow.[26]

Kirtons, the home of the Botelers, is mentioned in documents going back to the 14th century. The parsonage house was also important in the 16th century. It had three warden pear trees in the yard or garden, and the pears were particularly reserved in leases of 1566 and 1574.[27] There was also a dovecote in the parsonage yard in 1574.[28] This was the first known church house in Biddenham where the parson lived, now number 39 Church End. His manservant lived at number 41 Church End.[29]

As well as the Botelers and the parson, there were also comfortably off yeomen farmers in Biddenham in the 16th century. Joan Poley had hangings of red say (fine woollen cloth) in her house.[30] Richard Sampson, a yeoman of Biddenham, entered an account of his land in his notebook in 1540. His total holding in Biddenham was about 76 acres in the common fields and 8½ acres of meadow.[31] Yeomen like Richard had houses built for them, and there seems to have been substantial, surviving building work in Biddenham in the 16th and 17th centuries.

In her 'Walk around Biddenham', Dorothy Richards noted that the part of Ouse Valley Farmhouse that was furthest west, in stone, originated in the 16th century. It was originally four cottages, and then became the old bakehouse and village shop.[32] She also pointed out that the forge, the former blacksmith's cottage on Main Road, Meadow End Cottage and Horseshoe Cottage on Main Road, as well as Groom's Cottage on Main Road and Dawn Cottage on Gold Lane, all date from the 17th century.[33] 55 Church End (Church Cottage) is the only remaining dwelling from a row of four 17th century cottages which burnt down in 1959. The others were wattle and daub, but this cottage has a limestone rubble chimney complex to the east, with a limestone inglenook in a single storey extension, and therefore survived.[34] The barn at the entrance to Church Farm Barns, with its distinctive weatherboarding, has also survived from the 17th century.[35]

The WI scrapbook for 1956 records that at the end of the 16th century it was the custom to bless a house on the completion of the building. We do not know when this custom ceased, but apparently the top was lopped off a small fir tree and bows of white ribbon were tied to it. One bow was for prosperity, one for health, one for long life to its owners, one for happiness, one for fertility and one for charity. When the last bow was in place on top of the tree, the tree was fixed to the roof of the finished house and everyone assembled cried, 'Bless this house.'[36]

Another building of significance in Biddenham during this period was the mill. The will of Thomas Justice of Biddenham, made on 20 June1674, shows that he held the mill. In 1692 William Boteler of Biddenham leased to Thomas Brown, miller, a small piece of ground on which a windmill stood called 'Windmill Hill' and two pieces of land adjoining in Biddenham for 99 years at 6s 8d per year.[37] The parish registers which survive from 1602 reveal that other skilled occupations in the village in the 17th century were the blacksmith, Thomas Newell, and the watchmaker. In 1602 the watchmaker was Thomas Russell, son of Thomas Russell, a bell-founder and clockmaker of Wootton.[38]

Although there were those who were skilled and successful, there were also those who fell upon hard times or found themselves unable to work. From the 16th century onwards the vestry developed from the manor court. It was called the vestry because the meetings were held in the church vestry. The vicar chaired these meetings, as he was educated, respected and considered to be impartial. The vestry addressed day-to-day matters that governed the life of the community. It set the rateable value of property so that the local tax, the annual rate, could be collected. The rate was used to pay for poor relief after the Elizabethan Poor Law of 1601 came into operation. The vestry also supervised the election of the local officials who oversaw the administration of the poor law – the overseers and the parish guardian – as well as those who took care of the highways, the surveyors of the highways, and the churchwardens.[39]

In 1668 the overseers of the poor, Thomas Ballin, Henry Hayne and Henry Woodward, gave Joan Faldo 6d for 44 weeks, William Naylor and his son 3s 6d, and paid four shillings for a load of straw for the thatching of widow Butcher's cottage. William Boteler contributed 3s 6d to these costs.[40] The Botelers did not just contribute to the annual rate; they also gave to charity. The WI scrapbook for 1956 specifically states that the Botelers were remembered for their charity and goodwill. Examples of this were quoted, notably that a barrel was kept in their house. It was always full of table-beer for the free use of the poor, and an iron ladle was attached so that they might help themselves. The inscription on the barrel read 'Drink one and go about your business'. Ursula Boteler, who died in 1621 and whose monument is in Biddenham church, directed the executors of her will to purchase land to the yearly value of 20 shillings to the benefit of the poor of Bedford on Christmas Day. Ursula's son, Sir Thomas, left an annuity of 20 shillings from land at Biddenham, payable on St. James's Day. In addition, on St Thomas's Day £5 was to be paid out of the estate for the purchase of a prime ox, which was to be killed and the flesh distributed amongst the poor of the parish, the bigger families to get the larger portions.[41] We shall see that this tradition lasted until World War II.

The Botelers did not just help the poor. On 6 August 1529 the earliest Biddenham charity appeared under the will of Sir William Boteler. £2 was to be set aside for the repair of the highway.[42] Maintenance of roads and bridges was a constant drain on local resources, and often depended on generous legacies as well as the annual rate. The convenience of Biddenham Bridge to everyone inspired Thomas Howden to leave eight pence in his will for its maintenance. In 1509 Joan Poley, a widow, left 20 pence for maintenance. We have records of further repairs in 1651 and 1685.[43]

Communication with neighbouring towns and villages was

not always advantageous. In 1608 plague reached Biddenham. It was confined to one household, the Wrights, but seven members of the family died of it.[44] The roads themselves could also be dangerous. On 26 March 1605 Gamaliel Ratsey, a notorious highwayman, who had long terrorised the eastern counties, was hanged on Biddenham gallows.[45]

However, for most of the approximately 183 people who lived in Biddenham,[46] life in the years 1500 to 1700 was largely agricultural and confined to the village. They did not react to the religious conformity imposed by the Elizabethan church settlement in 1559 and copy the nonconformity started by the Bunyan Meeting at Bedford in 1650.[47] The villagers grew their own food, kept their animals and hoped that they would have sufficient to provide for themselves and their families. Life was simple, and revolved around the farming seasons of the year.

References:

The Boteler family tree can be found in Appendix IV.

1   Margery Roberts, Biddenham - a sequestered village in *Bedfordshire Magazine,* vol 10 no 80, Spring 1967, p 11.

2   Survey of Biddenham carried out for Conservation Section, 1977, p 4.

3   Joyce Godber, *History of Bedfordshire* (Bedfordshire County Council, 1984). p 195 says that William Harpur, Lord Mayor of London 1561, had some connection with a Green family in Biddenham, but this seemed to be a coincidence.

4   Information from introduction to TW documents, BLARS.

5   Dorothy Richards, *Biddenham – a Parish History and Guide* (New Moon, 1991), p 5.

6   Margery Roberts, op. cit., p 314.

7   Survey of Biddenham carried out for Conservation Section, 1977, p 4.

8   Information from introduction to TW documents, BLARS.

9   Ibid.

10   R W Rideout, *Bromham in Bedfordshire: A History* (R W Rideout, 2002) p 65.

11   Ibid, p 66.

12 Ibid, p 66.

13 Ibid, p 66.

14 Ibid, p 66.

15 Information from introduction to TW documents, BLARS.

16 Ibid.

17 R W Rideout, op. cit., p 68.

18 Dorothy Richards, op. cit., p 5.

19 R W Rideout, op. cit., p 71.

20 Ibid, p 73.

21 Ibid, p 75.

22 Ibid, p 76.

23 Ibid, p 76.

24 Ibid, p 77.

25 Information from introduction to TW documents, BLARS.

26 Ibid.

27 TW 606 and 674, BLARS.

28 TW 674, BLARS.

29 Dorothy Richards, op. cit., Walk round Biddenham section, p 12.

30 Joyce Godber, op. cit., p 165.

31 Ibid, p 211.

32 Dorothy Richards, op. cit., Walk round Biddenham section, p 15.

33 Ibid, pp 7, 10 & 11.

34 Ibid, p 12.

35 Ibid, p 13.

36 W I scrapbook, 1956, p 19, at BLARS.

37 Ibid, p 15.

38 Ibid, p 24.

39 *Stevington: The Village History*
(Stevington Historical Trust, 2001), p 123.

40 W I scrapbook, 1956, p 16, at BLARS.

41 Ibid, p 5.

42 Dorothy Richards, op. cit., p 51.

43 Ibid, p 25.

44 W I scrapbook, 1956, p 24, at BLARS.

45 Dorothy Richards, op. cit., p 19.

46 Ibid, p 15.

47 *Stevington: The Village History,* op. cit., p 104.

CHAPTER 6

BIDDENHAM 1700 to 1850 - SOCIAL CHANGE AND ENCLOSURE

The 18th and early 19th centuries witnessed many changes in the parish of Biddenham, though it remained agrarian in character. When the first census was taken in 1801 there were 57 houses inhabited in Biddenham with a population of 252. It is estimated that the population from 1700 to 800 was about 200.[1] 19th century censuses reveal that the population grew to 310 by 1811 and 393 by 1821, but then dropped to 369 in 1831 and 345 in 1841 because of agricultural depression. It was only by 1851 that there was a recovery to a population of 373 as agriculture became more prosperous again.[2]

During the 18th century the land ownership of Biddenham changed. In 1708 the Trevor family owned the Bromham Manor and the Botelers had returned to Kirtons in the Biddenham estate. However, by 1758 the Boteler property had passed to the Trevor family, ending the long connection the Botelers had had with Biddenham. Kirtons fell into decline, becoming a workhouse and then cottages.[3] The Trevors were ambitious, and keen to pursue their legal and diplomatic careers. They owned Bromham Hall, but George Rice Rice-Trevor, who inherited the Bromham Estate in 1824, was the first to live frequently at Bromham and undertake several local projects, including the restoration of the church.[4] The Trevors did not live in Biddenham: they followed the practice of leasing fields to farmers, who built themselves brick farmhouses or added to old timber framed houses.

A number of substantial houses and cottages were built in Biddenham during the 18th century. Lavender Lodge was the first house in Main Road to be built at this time. It was the farmhouse to Clay Farm and was named after the Huguenot family, Lavender, who also farmed Church Farm.[5] The Old Vicarage, 67 Main Road, was built in 1762 and used as the vicarage until 1935.[6] Biddenham House on the corner of Gold Lane was built in 1766, but there have been significant additions on all four sides.[7] Grove House, 18 Main Road, was originally

41 – Biddenham House before the extension was added
at the turn of the 20th century

two 18th century houses abutting each other. [8] 18th century cottages which survive include 35 Main Road, 37-41 Main Road, 20-28 Main Road, Innkeeper's Cottage, 55 Main Road, Walnut Cottage, Manor Road and 1-3 Day's Lane.[9]

The houses and cottages relied on candles for lighting. Water came from wells. Albert Church remembers going to the Old Vicarage as a boy for carol singing in 1910. He recalls the very large kitchen with a pump inside it to bring water up from the well. He also remembers the toilets were 20 or 30 yards from the house. The pathway went through an avenue of yew trees flanked by hazel trees. 'Yes, a very uncanny place if you had to go there on a winter night'.[10]

The furnishings of the cottages were simple. Robert Leader, a

Biddenham carpenter in 1710, had a table, a form (bench), a few chairs, one or two cupboards, a dresser, a chest of drawers, a warming pan and some pewter.[11] However, there were signs of wealth in 18th century Biddenham. In 1706 Elizabeth Boteler built a dovecote to go along with the carp pond which had been dug in 1700. Dovecotes were very popular in England at this time, as the doves could supply meat and eggs. The Biddenham dovecote was in a field to the west of the carp pond. It was a square timber framed building with bricks in between and plastered over. The roof was tiled with four gabled dormers, whose ridges met at the apex, which was crowned with an ornamental finial.

42 – The dovecote and pond, 1961

The 461 nests inside were built on elm wood boards, some of brick and some of clay, mixed with straw and cow-dung.[12] So impressive was this dovecote that it inspired Sir Thomas Trevor, who had acquired Bromham Hall in 1708, to demolish the dovecote erected by Sir Lewis Dyve in his rabbit warren in 1605 and re-erect it in a field west of Berry Farm House, where it would not obscure the view from the Hall and it could be refurbished. The new tenants of Berry Farm House were to supply the pigeons. [13]

A map of Biddenham drawn as a result of a survey by Thomas Gostelon in 1794 shows the medieval field names still in use.[14] It has been suggested that this was a draft enclosure map, but this is by no means certain.[15] What is for sure is that in 1794 there is evidence of continuity of settlement at Biddenham Green, Church End, Duck End and Ford End.[16] Although the medieval field names North Field, Middle Field and South Field were still in use, Church Field is clearly marked as part of Middle Field, and Windmill Field is named as well as North Field.[17]

The low-lying areas of land by the river were used as meadowland, and in 1794 the main meadows were known as Broad Mead, Midsummer Ground, Ely Meadow, Sunder Mead and King's Mead.[18] Other land was used as a coneygar (rabbit warren).[19] There were stone pits in two parts of the parish of Biddenham, both close to the river and opposite the parish of Kempston.[20] At the north side of the parish, beside the turnpike road, there were gravel and clay pits.[21] Albert Church had heard from the old men of the village that before 1860 clay was dug from the clay pit at the Bromham Road end of Day's Lane. It was used for building farmhouses and buildings and the old thatched cottages, which were made of wattle and daub. He said that Clay Farm was built of this clay, and the nests in the dovecote.[22]

In 1794 most of the land in Biddenham was owned by Viscount Hampden of Bromham Hall. He was Thomas Trevor Hampden, the Second Viscount Hampden, who had succeeded his father, Robert, the first Viscount in 1783. Robert had been British Ambassador to Vienna and The Hague. He was also a considerable classical scholar: he was a Fellow of the Society of Antiquaries and a Fellow of the Royal Society. He wrote a commentary on Horace and a number of poems in Latin.[23] The trend of the late 18th century was towards removing the medieval field system and forming large fields enclosed by hedges. It is understandable that the first Viscount Hampden was perhaps too busy to undertake enclosure. The second Viscount was also very slow to make the change that most landowners were promoting so as to improve crop rotation, introduce new crops and increase yield. Historians are not sure why Biddenham and Stagsden, where he was the main owner, were not enclosed until 1828, when most parishes in Bedfordshire were enclosed between 1794 and 1819. Joyce Godber suggests that there were always some who were indifferent and unwilling to change. When the Carlton enclosure was proposed, Viscount Hampden said that he wasn't desirous of gaining any advantage, nor was he inclined to promote the project, but he would not object 'provided that he is franked from all charge except in the proportion that he may reap of any contingent profit'.[24] He clearly did not want to get too involved or to be the instigator of the change, though he would take the profit!

In 1812 an Act of Parliament for the enclosure of the common fields at Biddenham was passed, but Viscount Hampden was still reluctant to share out the land and put the Act into practice. He died childless in 1824, and was succeeded by his brother, John Trevor Hampden, as third Viscount Hampden, but he also died childless in 1824. John Trevor had been a diplomat serving as British Minister to the Elector Palatine and the Court of Turin. He left the Bromham and Biddenham estates to his relative, George Rice Rice-Trevor, who was due to succeed to the barony of Dynevor. John Trevor Hampden's will specified that when George Rice Rice-Trevor succeeded to the barony, the Bromham and Biddenham estates were to pass to his daughters, a decision that was to have significant consequences for Biddenham in 1852.[25]

George Rice Rice-Trevor frequently stayed at Bromham Hall, and with a local interest, he proceeded to implement the Enclosure Act. Thomas Thorpe was first appointed in 1827 as being a person not interested in the division of the land, to execute the Act. He died before the completion of the work. Thomas Lilbourne of Cardington was then appointed to carry the Act into execution. The document appointing Thomas Lilbourne was signed by Miller Golding, the agent for the Trevors, and witnessed by John Foster:

I, Thomas Lilbourne do swear that I will faithfully and impartially and honestly, according to the best of my skill and ability, execute and perform the several trusts, power and authorities by virtue of an Act for enclosing lands at Biddenham, in the county of Bedford, according to equity and good conscience and without favour or affection, or partiality to any person, or persons, whomsoever. So help me God. Signed Thomas Lilbourne.[26]

The total acreage of the parish by the 1820s was 1,572 acres. Of this, there were 1,240 acres of commonly held land to be enclosed, 319 acres of old enclosures and 13 acres of roads and byways.[27] The notice of the allotment of land was read in the parish church of Biddenham on the morning of Sunday 10 October 1827 immediately after divine service. The greater part of the land went to the Trevors, a small amount went to the vicar (the Rev Shuttleworth Grimshawe) and a small amount to the parish clerk (James West).[28] The land allotted to the vicar was north of the Old Vicarage and into the present green, amounting to one rood and six perches. The village green was not included in the enclosure award, but it was minimized in size.[29] Apart from the old enclosures in the south-east corner of the parish which marked the manor of Kirtons or Ford End, the home of the Botelers, the enclosed fields that now replaced the medieval strips were owned by the Trevors and rented by tenant farmers. In 1838 the rating records reveal that these tenant farmers who rented from the Hon G Rice-Trevor were Miller Golding at East Field, William Golding at South Field, John Lavender at South Field, Matilda Whitworth in the centre of the village, Charles Golding near the church and John Biggs near the turnpike road. Lesser tenant farmers renting grassland or a cottage and land were John Shelton and John Felts at Ford End, James Frost, Chris Robinson, William Fuller near the church and John Burton in the centre of the village. Thomas Wells rented the pub, John Prudden rented the blacksmith's shop and James Felts rented the bakehouse. Other cottagers had to go to work for the tenant farmers in their fields or become domestic servants in their houses: they did not have enough land to support themselves.

The implementation of the Enclosure Act in Biddenham came at a difficult time economically for agrarian areas in England. Despite the Corn Law of 1815, which prevented the import of cheap foreign corn, demand for British corn dropped after the end of the Napoleonic Wars because townspeople suffered unemployment as a result of the change from military to peacetime production. By the 1820s work became scarce for farm labourers, and to add to their troubles, the introduction of new machines - especially for threshing - removed a lot of winter work. The young and the poor left for the towns in the hope of finding work there, as industrial production would hopefully revive.

In some counties in the south and east of England in 1830-1832, there were disturbances in rural areas as a protest against the introduction of machines and low wages. Threshing machines were smashed, farm buildings and ricks were set on fire and farmers received threatening letters. There were fewer than 10 disturbances in Bedfordshire, so it does not seem that villagers here resorted to violence. However, the population of Biddenham dropped from 393 in 1821 to 369 in 1831, and

345 in 1841.[30] It was not until the 1840s that agriculture and population recovered as townspeople started to benefit from European and colonial markets, and could afford to buy more farm produce such as meat, cheese and butter. Farmers who diversified into these products could obtain better prices, and in turn paid better wages.

During the difficult years of the 1820s and 1830s, there was a problem of poverty to be addressed, despite migration to the towns. There had always been paupers in Biddenham: Dorothy Richards listed 'pauper' amongst the 18th century occupations of the village.[31] Up until 1834, when the new Poor Law Act came into force, the parish vestry which was the forerunner of the parish council, set the rateable value of property, collected an annual rate and supervised the operation of the arrangements for dealing with the poor, including the election of the local officials: a parish guardian and overseers. The overseers gave support, a dole, to the poor from the rate, but after 1834, the poor were forced to live in the workhouse if they could not support themselves. The overseers before 1834 had taken a firm but fair stance, but life became tougher for those who fell on hard times after 1834.

Even before 1834 Biddenham was a closed parish: no one could settle there without a job and the overseers made sure that they would not be responsible for helping out migrants to Biddenham if they got into financial trouble. In 1714 the following letter was obtained from the overseers of the poor and churchwardens of Bletsoe in respect of John White:

We the churchwardens and overseers of the poor in the parish of Bletsoe in the said county of Bedford, do hereby acknowledge and own that John White, taylor, and his wife are legal inhabitants of our said parish of Bletsoe, and we do hereby promise for us and our successors to provide for him and his family which he now has, and hereafter shall have, whenever he, they, or any of them shall become chargeable, or likely to become so.[32]

They were equally firm about children born out of wedlock. The father, if known, was required to sign a bond accepting responsibility. In 1741 a bond was made by Richard Tilcock of Ickwell and his father William Tilcock, yeoman, on account of Mary Woodward of Biddenham, a single woman.[33] The tough stance of the overseers meant that the paupers, who received help before 1834, were generally old people without families to look after them. They had their living costs met from the poor rate. After 1834 they suffered the indignity of having to go into the workhouse, the former manor house of Kirtons at Ford End. Outdoor relief had come to an end, especially in rural areas where there was usually space in the workhouse for those who were destitute.

If the poor wished to emigrate, the overseers were prepared to use the poor rate to try to end the problem of a poor family once and for all. In 1846 the Biddenham overseers joined with the Bromham overseers to deal with the problem of Sarah Carrier and her child. They paid £13 as a contribution to the Bromham overseers to arrange the emigration of Sarah and her child to Australia. [34]

For those who were suffering hardship, but who had not reached total destitution, private charities still existed. In Elizabeth Boteler's will of 22 July 1706, £200 was set aside to provide a bull from the Boteler Estate to provide meat to the value of £5 for the poor once a year on 21 December, St. Thomas' Day.[35] The *Bedfordshire Times* reported on 23 October 1847 that:

Mr and Mrs Trevor (Hon George Rice Rice-Trevor and his wife) whose ever watchful eyes are over the comforts and interest of the poor, have not forgotten them in the midst of their liberality, for every poor family in the three parishes of Bromham, Stagsden and Biddenham have received at the hands of this truly benevolent family, gifts of the most useful description, comprising articles of clothing and divers necessary household matters, according to the size and wants of their respective families ..... A packet of tea was one of the gifts presented to nearly, if not all, the families, thus giving an opportunity to every poor old man and woman in the three villages, in their own chimney corner and in their own humble way, of enjoying the favourite beverage.

Most of the other occupations in the village in the 18th and early 19th centuries were to a large extent dependent on the success of farming. The blacksmith shod horses and repaired tools: the innkeeper supplied beer to the farm workers. However, when she listed the 18th century occupations, Dorothy Richards found that there was a watchmaker, Thomas Russell, the son of Thomas Russell of Wootton; a soldier; a glazier; a woollen draper and a basketmaker.[36] She did not find any evidence of lace makers, though as we shall see, there were 76 by 1851. Lacemaking seems to have become an occupation for the poor, particularly in the 18th and 19th centuries, until the advent of machine lace forced the lace makers to make coarser lace which at first could not be copied by the machines. The Overseers of the Poor frequently paid an experienced lace maker to teach the children of the poor. There was concern for these children, as they earned little because of their age, and their general education was neglected in favour of lacemaking.[37] We know that by 1841 Elizabeth Panter and Susanna Newman were established lace makers in Church End, Biddenham.[38]

As well as supervising the arrangements for dealing with the poor, the parish vestry also elected the surveyor of the highways. He was the parish official who was responsible for the maintenance of all the roads in the parish, except for those assigned to the turnpike trusts after the mid-18th century. The surveyor had to collect the rate to do the work, and he had to ensure that it got done: that the parishioners turned out for the required 6 days each year to repair the roads. In the year between 25 March 1839 and 25 March 1840, Charles Golding, the surveyor of Biddenham made the following payments:

To West for three days repairing the Causeway, five shillings. To Hodge for two days breaking stones three shillings and four pence and for one day maintaining the Causeway one shilling and eight pence. To Boy Billing for breaking stones, one shilling and sixpence. To West for two days laying a drain in the school yard three shillings and four pence, and for four days repairing the Causeway six shillings and eight pence and for clearing out the parish ditch five shillings. To Maxey for repairing the Kempston plank four shillings and sixpence.

These accounts were examined and found correct by two of the other major tenant farmers in the village, John Lavender and William Golding.[39]

The Causeway or coffin path was a vital amenity for the village, as it was the shortest way for relatives of the working class to carry the coffin of the deceased to the churchyard for burial. The paths and gates were kept at a certain width to allow the coffin with a man on either side to pass through comfortably.[40] In the 18th century, the Botelers had left £2 per annum to keep the Causeway path six feet wide. This money was sent to the vicar who ensured at parish vestry meetings that maintenance was carried out.[41]

The roads assigned to the turnpike trusts after the mid-18th century were not the responsibility of the surveyor of the highways. In the case of Biddenham, this was the road to Northampton from Bedford, the present Bromham Road, which became a turnpike in 1754. Turnpike trusts came into existence in the early 18th century and their number trebled between 1750 and 1770. They were a response to the problem of constructing and maintaining roads which were not just for local benefit. The turnpike trusts were created with Parliamentary authority to improve and maintain inter-parish road networks used mainly by 'outsiders' and they funded this by charging tolls for passage along them. Acts creating the trusts were instigated by the local initiative of men of property. They petitioned Parliament to designate specific segments of road as a turnpike and themselves, as a trust, its governing body. They met the operating expenses by borrowing against the tolls through the sale of interest-bearing bonds.[42]

The trusts frequently encountered financial problems, as they had few full-time salaried officials, and auditing of books was not required. The original turnpike trust for Bedford to Northampton was not successful, and a new trust was established by Act of Parliament in 1790 for the Biddenham end of Bromham Bridge to the Olney to Wellingborough road. In 1874 the trusts ceased to operate.[43]

The bridge over the River Ouse, which was known as Biddenham Bridge and then for some reason became known as Bromham Bridge in 1728, involved much expensive maintenance.[44] In 1724 100 cartloads of stone from the Biddenham pits to the south of the church was used to repair the bridge after a flood. It was recorded that 'coping stones were gathered up out of the river.'[45] In 1728 Dennis Farrer, a local

43 – The bridge, drawing by Thomas Fisher, 1812

magistrate, allowed a bill for 40 loads of pebbles to 'pave' the bridge, this stone coming from Stagsden, and 44 loads of gravel at 3d per load. In 1752 a carpenter made a wooden support for the construction of a new arch for the bridge. Maintenance then seems to have lapsed, and in 1799 the bridge was reported as ruinous and in decay. However, by 1813 the need to bring carts safely from Bedford to Bromham required more work on the bridge. In particular, to help the carts, the width of the bridge in the section over the flood meadows was increased from six feet to seventeen feet. The work was done by M R Salmon, the surveyor to the Duke of Bedford.[46] Repairs were still required on the bridge almost every year from 1823 until 1855. The structure of the bridge suffered from the flooding, which could be serious. In 1823 between 31 October and 1 November the flood water was so powerful that a conical haystack out of a meadow at Bromham, weighing 14 tons, came to rest in Mr Golding's meadow at Biddenham, standing upright as it was built.[47] Despite these problems, the County Surveyor was moved to report in 1850 that 'a worse constructed bridge and with worse materials could not have been built.'[48] The bridge was an ongoing issue for the future.

One feature of what is now the Bromham Road into Bedford was removed in 1801. This was the gallows that had been on the first corner of Bromham Road as you approach Bedford after Biddenham Turn since at least 1303, judging from records. It was marked on the Jefferies map of Bedford in 1765 and on the map of Biddenham in 1794.[49] Executions were to take place in the recently built Bedford Prison. The records of the gaol state that in 1801 'at the adjourned mid-summer session, it was ordered that the old gallows at Biddenham be taken down as useless.'[50]

Crime was rare in Biddenham in the early 19th century.[51] The lack of serious crime may have been due to the fear of the possible punishments. The execution of the Lilley brothers from Kempston in April 1829 for maliciously shooting Thomas King, a gamekeeper at Bromham, had some local impact. Poverty did not necessarily lead to crime: Steve Williamson found no correlation between the refusal of poor relief and crime. He also found that few could afford to prosecute, and there were no funded public prosecutions by the ratepayers in Biddenham from 1825 to 1835, as 70% of the rate of 6d in the pound came from just four ratepayers, including Joseph Whitworth, a farmer, and John Lavender the overseer of the poor. It had to be in their interest to prosecute, and their main concern was property.

Although the 1820s and early 1830s were difficult years economically and there was rioting in parts of East Anglia, there was no rioting or tumultuous assembly in Biddenham. The nearest to disorder was the case of James Bracket, a 65-year-old widower, who was prosecuted by the parish overseers for misbehaviour in the workhouse and sent down for 21 days. In 1833 William Rose was charged with assaulting an overseer, Henry Staines, and in 1834 with drunkenness.

Most of the cases involved theft of some kind. In 1821 a theft was reported of 13s 6d from the home of Thomas Killingworth, a yeoman. Killingwoth's daughter had set a trap after she became suspicious that money had been stolen. She left two marked half crowns in a drawer while she went out. Next day, she found that they had gone, so her father obtained a search warrant. Three men were found guilty of the theft of two coins to the value of five shillings. One of them was a labourer working for Killingworth, who got one year in gaol. Another, who was a servant in the house, got six months, and a third man was sentenced to one month in gaol and a fine of one shilling.

A more serious issue than the house-breaking were the events of 1827. In September 1827 John Hodgins and Thomas

Allen were charged at the Assizes with feloniously killing a sheep belonging to John Lavender, a major landowner and churchwarden in Biddenham, and then 'carrying away part of the said sheep'. Allen had already served 21 days in prison for a misdemeanour in the poorhouse, and 14 days for destroying a crop of potatoes. At the trial, Lavender's shepherd testified that Allen and some other person were seen running away from the close the sheep was in. Allen made a full confession in gaol, and named Hodgins as his accomplice. The jury found them guilty, and 17-year-old Hodgins and 20-year-old Allen were sentenced to death. This was 'mercifully' commuted to transportation for life. Hodgins left for New South Wales on 29 May 1828 and Allen died in gaol a month later before he could be transported. Steve Williamson has discovered from the New South Wales archives that Hodgins made two applications to marry within six months whilst in New South Wales. We do not know what happened about the first application: maybe the woman died, or one of them changed their minds. The archives also reveal that Hodgins 'absconded' while in an area of coastline that was very dangerous. He died, or disappeared, aged only 43 or 44, after absconding.

The only other Biddenham resident to be transported in this period was John Johnson in 1837. He was well known to the law, and by 1837 the authorities were probably pleased to be getting rid of him. In August 1828 he had been sentenced to six weeks for being a rogue and a vagabond. In October 1829 he was given one month for leaving his family chargeable on the parish. In March 1832 he was found guilty of stealing beans, and sentenced to three months and to be whipped. Finally, in January 1837 he was convicted of stealing wood and given seven years transportation. He was shipped to Tasmania in November 1837.

One other interesting case in Biddenham was ended before it reached the Assizes. In 1832 Thomas Clark's mother-in-law,

Hannah Hatton, died as a result of an injury caused when she became caught in the middle of an argument between Clark and his wife. The case against Clark was not pursued, and it does not seem to have jeopardised the relationship with his wife, as the 1851 census recorded them as still alive and living together.

Most of the other cases involved poaching, but they did not involve shooting of gamekeepers, so did not lead to the terrible outcome of the Lilley case in Kempston in 1829. A few of those fined for poaching were able to pay rather than go to prison. James Hutchins, a labourer of Biddenham, paid the £5 fine to the committing magistrate in 1822, and was discharged from gaol that same day. As the average wage even for married men was under 10 shillings a week, this was a lot of money to have available.

Most of those convicted of poaching went to gaol. James Croot served two terms in gaol for poaching. In 1823 he was sentenced to three months for poaching with snares, and then got another four months in 1824 after being found with a hare in his possession in Bromham. In the three years after the Lilleys were executed, there were no indictments for night poaching recorded at Bedford Assizes. As time went on though, the number of game related prosecutions increased. The only Biddenham case that came to court in 1832 was that of Humphrey Profser who was charged with using a gun to kill game. This charge was withdrawn on the promise not to do it again. In 1834 William Garratt was prosecuted for seeking game with a snare, and pleaded guilty. He had to pay a 10 shillings fine or serve 14 days in gaol. At the same time, Kempston men were featured much more regularly in prosecutions for poaching. They were also prosecuted more frequently for fishing by landowners such as the Marquis of Tavistock. In 1835, two cases involved Biddenham men, James Croot and Thomas Dawson, who were both fined.

In the period 1780–1850 the middle and upper classes sought to deal with the problems of crime and pauperism amongst the working class through organized religion and education. The more affluent families employed their own tutor, and in the Bedford area, they sent their boys to Harpur Trust Schools (girls' education was only available after 1882). The children of the farm labourers had to receive their instruction in the three R's (reading, writing and 'rithmetic) from Sunday school, where the principal aim was to learn to read the Bible, and, if they were fortunate, from a small village school often founded by a benevolent wealthy landowner, as in Bromham,[52] or by families, usually Dissenters, putting up the funds to start a school, as in Stevington.[53] The history of the village school in Biddenham will be discussed in the first chapter on Education, Chapter 9.

The school provided a useful venue for village activities. In addition to 'penny readings' in the school, farm barns were also used for concerts, which included songs, musical performances supplied by local talent and recitations.

Other activities were less peaceful and law-abiding. Prizefighting was forbidden by the Quarter Sessions, but in 1845 a prizefight was held between Robert Goddard and Charles Johnson in Biddenham. The police intervened, and the promoters moved the fight to Fenlake on the other side of the river. The move brought the number of spectators to nearly 1,000. The fight was exciting, and fiercely contested: it went on for 42 rounds. Goddard won, but Johnson was injured and taken to the Infirmary.[54]

Biddenham was still a small rural community in 1850, but the farms were prospering once again, and the population was rising. Life followed the traditional seasonal farming year: spring ploughing, calving and lambing, summer haymaking and corn harvest, autumn ploughing and threshing, and winter repairs and maintenance, as not so much outdoor farm work was available. Within this framework were the excitements like prizefighting, but the excitements were limited to the Biddenham area. The turnpike had opened up communications to Northampton, but it was the railway that was to really open up access to the wider world in the 1850s.

References:
1   Dorothy Richards, *Biddenham. A Parish History and Guide* (New Moon, 1991), p 15.
2   R.W.Rideout, *Bromham in Bedfordshire – A History* (R W Rideout, 2002), p 155.
3   Survey of Biddenham for the Conservation Section, 1977, p 4.
4   R W Rideout, op. cit., p 78.
5   Dorothy Richards, *A Walk around Biddenham* (New Moon, 1991), p 7.
6   Ibid, p 10.
7   Ibid, p 15.
8   Ibid, p 4.
9   Ibid, pages 4, 5, 11 and 16.
10   Albert Church, *Recollections of My Life in Biddenham,* p 19.
11   Joyce Godber, *History of Bedfordshire* (Bedfordshire County Council, 1984), p 381.
12   Dorothy Richards, *Biddenham. A Parish History and Guide* (New Moon, 1991), p 18.
13   R W Rideout, op. cit., p 140.
14   Dorothy Richards, op. cit., p 127.
15   Survey of Biddenham for the Conservation Section, 1977, p 10.
16   Ibid, p 5.
17   Ibid, p 6.
18   Ibid, p 6.
19   Ibid, p 7.
20   Ibid, p 8.
21   Ibid, p 10.
22   Albert Church, op. cit., p 33.
23   R W Rideout, op. cit., p.79.
24   Joyce Godber, op. cit., pages 405-406.
25   R W Rideout, op. cit., p 80.
26   WI scrapbook, 1956, p 14, at BLARS.

27   Survey of Biddenham for the Conservation Section, 1977, p 10.
28   Dorothy Richards, op. cit., p 6.
29   Survey of Biddenham for the Conservation Section, 1977, p 10.
30   R.W Rideout, op. cit., p 155.
31   Dorothy Richards, op. cit., p 22.
32   WI scrapbook, 1956, p 16, at BLARS.
33   Ibid, p 16.
34   Ibid, p 16.
35   Dorothy Richards, op. cit., p 20.
36   Dorothy Richards, op. cit., p 22.
37   *Lace Making in Bedfordshire*,
       pamphlet supported by Bedford Borough Council.
38   Dorothy Richards, op. cit., p 35.
39   WI scrapbook, 1956, p 16, at BLARS.
40   Albert Church, op. cit., p 20.
41   Dorothy Richards, op. cit., p 20.
42   *The Bedfordshire Magazine*, vol 22, p 249.
43   R W Rideout, op. cit., pages 109-110.
44   Dorothy Richards, op. cit., p 24.
45   Ibid, p 25.
46   Ibid, p 25.
47   Ibid, p 26.
48   R W Rideout, op. cit., p 104.
49   Dorothy Richards, op. cit., p 19.
50   Ibid, p 9.
51   We are grateful to Steve Williamson for providing us with information
       about crime in Biddenham 1821 – 1835, obtained largely from his
       research using Petty Sessions and Quarter Sessions records.
52   R W Rideout, op. cit., p 52.
53   *Stevington, the Village History,*
       (Stevington Historical Trust, 2001), p 188.
54   Joyce Godber, op. cit., p 520.

CHAPTER 7

BIDDENHAM 1850 TO 1914
HIGH FARMING, AGRICULTURAL DEPRESSION
AND SOCIAL CHANGE

On 1 May 1848 Frances Emily Rice-Trevor, the oldest daughter of George Rice Rice-Trevor, heir to the 3rd Baron Dynevor, married Edward Ffolliett Wingfield. When her father succeeded to the title of 4th Baron Dynevor in 1852, in accordance with John Trevor's will the Biddenham estate passed to his daughter, and thence to the Wingfield family. This made the Wingfields the largest landowners in Biddenham during the latter part of the 19th century.[1]

Historians have called the years 1850 to 1870 the golden ones for landowners, farmers and some of the skilled labourers. The repeal of the Corn Laws in 1846, which had prevented the import of cheap foreign corn, did not lead to the financial ruin that the farmers had feared. By the 1850s Britain had become the 'workshop of the world'. The workmen employed in the towns, for example in the cotton mills and the iron works, were buying bread, meat, cheese and butter. The railways helped to get these products to the towns, and farmers enjoyed better prices for them. The threat from foreign corn did not materialise between 1850 and 1870, as Europe's growing population used the corn produced in Europe, and it was still too expensive to bring grain from America and Canada in quantity.

By 1851 the population of Biddenham had risen from 345 in 1841 to 373.[2] An analysis of the census reveals that there were five farmers and one farmer and land agent, most of whom were tenants of the Wingfields; one farmer's bailiff and 95 agricultural labourers. The Mannings at Green Farm were not tenants of the Wingfields, but the other farmers were: notably at Church Farm, William Lavender; Manor Farm, Charles

Howard; Grove Farm, Joseph Lavender and Clay Farm, John Lavender.[3]

44 – Manning's Farm, 1965

The tithe award records in 1852 show that most of the farming was arable: there were 1,100 acres of arable land. However, there were already 475 acres 14 perches of meadow and pastureland, an area that was to increase considerably by 1905. The remaining land was used as gravel pits (two acres) and roads, waste or building sites (13 acres).[4] Arable farming prospered until about 1870, the farmers profiting from mechanical inventions such as John Howard's mechanical plough, manufactured at the Britannia works in Bedford. However, mechanisation started to affect the number of jobs available on the farms, and the population of Biddenham declined to 350 in 1861, and declined again to 321 in 1871.

Increasing use of animal husbandry also affected the number of jobs available for farm labourers. Sheep formed a large part of the village income in Biddenham, and with rising demand for milk, meat and butter in the towns, dairy cattle, chickens, goats and pigs were reared by more and more Biddenham farmers by 1900.[5]

Charles Howard at Manor Farm was the most important sheep farmer in Biddenham. Charles was the second son of the manufacturer, John Howard, who had started the Britannia works in Bedford. Charles attended the Commercial School, but he only spent a very short time in the family firm:

From early manhood - one might almost say from youth – Mr Charles Howard followed his natural bent in the study and practice of agriculture ….. In 1842, while only 17, he won a cup in a ploughing match for the farmers' sons. In 1847 the Manor Farm at Biddenham was offered to Mr Howard by the late Lord Dynevor, and in a very few years, Mr Howard had gained for himself a reputation for skill and enterprise, which made him an authority in the land.[6]

The subject on which Howard had gained such a reputation, and which brought 'honour on the county' was the rearing of sheep (Oxford Down rams) and cattle (shorthorns). Howard was following the principles of the educated farmer of the time, trying to improve his stock, visiting agricultural shows both national and local, and reading and acting upon the advice given in farming journals. *The Bedford Bee,* in an article published on 23 July 1879, describes Charles Howard's career as a farmer:

Having devoted special attention to sheep culture while assisting the late Mr William Bennett at Lewsey Farm, Dunstable, Mr Howard at once resolved to found a flock. He had been one of the first to observe the great promise of a cross-bred sheep not at that time recognised by the Royal Society. In 1849, a pen of this sheep won a prize for Mr Howard at the Royal Smithfield Show. With others Mr Howard used great efforts to induce the Society to assign a separate class for this breed, but it was not until 1862 that he succeeded, and when, in that year, the famous Battersea Show was held, the Biddenham flock took the first Royal prize. The Oxfordshire Downs, which name was given to this famous breed, are acknowledged to possess large frames, aptitude to fatten, excellent wool, superior mutton and uniformity of character in a remarkable degree. From the year 1862, Mr Howard has taken enough first prizes to weary one in reading the list. Not only have the Biddenham flock taken prizes, but their descendants have almost without fail achieved similar successes in various parts of the world. In most English shows and at the Great International Exhibitions at Belgium in 1868, Vienna 1873, Bremen 1874 and Paris 1878, Mr Howard has borne off honours after smart competition. Two First and two Second prizes, amounting to 1,600 francs were awarded to the Biddenham flock at the latter Exhibition. Sheep from this flock are annually purchased for France, Belgium, Holland, Germany, Denmark, Sweden, Poland, Russia, Portugal and other countries.

In 1865 Howard started auctioning his rams annually. Generally about 60 rams were auctioned to many different countries in the world. In 1875 the price reached about 17 guineas a ram. In July 1879, however, the price reached by the 55 rams sold was about £14 each on average.[7] The impact of the steamship and foreign competition was beginning to be felt in livestock as well as wheat farming, and farmers had to turn to cheese, butter and milk production to surmount the agricultural depression. Charles Howard was well aware of the depression, and in a speech at the sale he 'took account of some of the prospects before agriculturalists. He reiterated in forcible and temperate terms his well-known opinions upon the remedies for the present stagnation.'[8]

Although sheep were Charles Howard's first interest, he also bred cattle. In 1857 he formed a herd of shorthorns, one of which won the first prize at the Great Leeds meeting in 1861. *The Bedford Bee* mentions that in 1870 the herd was disposed of at high prices 'and a second herd is in the process of formation.'[9]

Howard was praised for his farm management: in 1874 he received the Gold Medal of the Royal Society for special farm management. He took part in national organisations such as the London Farmers' club, to which he read many valuable published papers on practical farming. He was also a member of the council of the Shorthorn Society of Great Britain and Ireland, a trustee and member of the council of the Smithfield Club, a member of council and steward of the Royal Agricultural Society, and a frequent judge of stock at the national and local shows of England. *The Bedford Bee* concluded its article about Charles Howard:

The times are bad, yet they would be worse but for the practical genius of those who have thought, observed and experimented in the various departments of agriculture, and whose developments, whether in crop or cattle culture, have brought honour to their names and increased the wealth of their class and country.[10]

Charles Howard was clearly a distinguished Biddenham farmer, who survived the agricultural problems of the late 1870s and 1880s, to die in 1895 as squire of Biddenham Manor, as the WI scrapbook of 1956 described him. The scrapbook recounts that Howard was a strict disciplinarian: small boys and men were not allowed to whistle or sing when passing his door. The scrapbook contains pictures of Charles Howard's daughter standing at the Manor doorway, and William Goss, Howard's coachman, holding his hunter while standing in his cottage doorway with his dog. A further photograph shows Mr and Mrs Goss with their daughter and son-in-law Mr and Mrs Shorley. They found their way round the agricultural depression by growing vegetables and fruit, and taking them by cart to Bedford to sell.[11]

When wheat prices fell during the 1870s as a result of the availability of, and competition from, cheap wheat from North

45 – W Goss, coachman to Charles Howard, Mrs Goss, and their
daughter and son-in-law, Mr and Mrs Shorley

America, there was a shortage of work for the less skilled labourers, who had to leave for the towns to find work. The population of Biddenham fell from 321 in 1871 to 308 in 1881. It picked up a little from 1881 to 1891, when it was 352, but then it fell again in 1901 to 325. Only after 1901, with the improvements in transport that enabled those working in Bedford to live in Biddenham and the farmers to fulfil the needs of the town, did the population rise to reach 451 by 1911.[12]

The reaction of the Biddenham labourers to agricultural depression was not as strong as that of those in neighbouring Bromham. In Bromham, the Agricultural Labourers' Union had a branch, with Arthur Mayhew as branch secretary.[13] They demanded better wages. However, the union soon ran out of money, and the labourers had either to get work where they could on the farms, preferably looking after animals, as these were the more secure jobs, or they had to leave for the towns or emigrate to America or Australia to get work.

By the beginning of the 20th century the Biddenham farms were mixing grain production with livestock rearing. In 1905 the Board of Agriculture recognised the parish to contain 1,585¾ acres of which 798½ acres were arable, 606¾ acres were permanent grazing, four acres were woodland and 176½ acres were roads, gravel pits, houses and gardens.[14] At Grove Farm Anthony Chibnall in 1900 had 100 cows, some sheep and some pigs.[15] Robert Whitworth at Church Farm also kept sheep, as well as growing wheat and barley.

We are fortunate in having an interesting account of farming at a tenanted farm, Church Farm, from Ted Pile, who started work there in 1913 (it is not until the 1920s that we have an account of working for the Wingfield Estate in Albert Church's memoirs).[16] Ted lived in Biddenham from when his family moved to Day's Lane in 1905 when he was four, until he died in 1992. He left school in 1913 and started work as third horse keeper on Bobby Whitworth's farm, Church Farm. Ted remembered that there were 18 adult men working on the farm at that time: the head horse keeper, other stockmen, the shepherd and extra men to do jobs like hedge trimming and ditching.[17] As well as growing wheat, the farm specialised in barley production for Wells brewery in Bedford, and sheep rearing. It was the wheat and barley harvest, and the fact that horses were still used for the farm work until 1916 that gave Ted his first job. Ted remembered that:

At harvest time Alf Johnson came to me and told me about the job. I went down to the farm and saw Mr Whitworth who said he wanted some boys to lead horses in the harvest field while the carts were being loaded with sheaves. I was to earn 8d per day, which comes to 4s a week! When loaded, the carts were taken across the fields to where the stacks were being built. The stacks were all round ones - sometimes there would be 10 in a row.

There would be four, sometimes five, men at the rick; one man unloading the sheaves from the cart and two men on the rick passing the sheaves to the builder. We used to go on the wheat in the morning, when the sheaves were damp with the dew, and then on to the barley after the sun had dried the stacks, because wheat would dry itself in the stack, but barley would go mouldy.[18]

To keep the men refreshed while they were doing this hard physical work, the farmer supplied them with free beer at breakfast time, 11 am, dinner-time and 4 pm. This beer was not enough for the men. Ted remembers that:

Soon after 6 am the breakfast beer was drunk and I was given the job to take two gallon bottles slung on one of the men's leather belts to the pub, either the Three Tuns at Biddenham or King William at Kempston, whichever was the nearest. Beer was tuppence a pint single, but if you had two gallon bottles on your shoulder, it cost 14 pence a gallon.[19]

Life did not stay the same for Ted on the farm. He was soon promoted, and saw the increasing mechanisation of everyday farming work. In 1915 Ted was made second man to Arthur Burton, the head horse keeper, and when he was taken ill, Ted had to take over responsibility for all the horses. This meant getting up at 4 am to get the horses in to be fed, groomed and harnessed. He also had to break horses in. In about 1916 tractors came to the farm. Before they came, Ted was sent to the Saunderson works for about four weeks to learn how to drive and repair a tractor.[20] He was still only 15, but with many of the men away fighting in World War I, responsibility fell upon the boys. Some of the horses were also in Salonika with the Bedfordshire soldiers, as Ted remembers that the horses were recognised by a soldier who had worked with them on Whitworth's farm.[21] The shortage of horses as well as men may have inspired Mr Whitworth to introduce tractors. The tractors were used to pull binders, which enabled the horses to rest, as it was hard work for three horses to drag a binder for three hours. The tractors were also used to saw wood, grind flour and cart bales of clover to the station and bring goods back to the farm.[22]

46 – Foster Lincoln threshing machine

Horsepower and machines were used after the harvest for the threshing and ploughing. The threshing of the barley took about a month. The grain was put into two hundredweight sacks and taken to Charles Wells brewery in Horne Lane, Bedford to be made into beer. Seven carts went to the brewery, and each man got a pint of beer.[23] At the same time, the fields had to be ploughed ready for the next crop. Ted remembered:

We would start out at 6 am, except in the winter (November to February) when it was 6.45 am, because it was too dark to see what to do. About 8 or 9 teams would all plough, mainly two horses in a team on a single furrow plough. Perhaps another team would be carting water and coal for the steam engines – a big engine at one end of the field and one at the other pulling a cultivator up and down.[24]

Ted also helped to look after the sheep, as Whitworth's farm was a mixed one. On Saturdays he drove the sheep to market, 40 to 50 at a time. Once all the sheep were penned, he could get a drover's ticket from the auctioneer's office. This enabled him to buy a bottle of lemonade and a large lump of bread and cheese from the pub next door. He then walked home.[25]

Although life on the farm was hard in the early 20th century, with long hours and low wages, diversification helped to combat agricultural depression, and provide jobs for men and boys. As Ted recalled, there were celebrations and benefits if the harvest was good.

When the boss had a good harvest, he gave a harvest home supper which was served hot by Mrs Gun and the Three Tuns. The ladies and Mrs Whitworth sang 'Will you give me the keys of your heart.'[26] The 1956 WI scrapbook looked back on the past harvest home suppers, or horkeys, and described the food: cold roast sirloins, hams, pork pies, pasties, pickles and sauces, tarts, jellies, cakes, biscuits and sweetmeats, all washed down with ale, tea and homemade lemonade. The scrapbook mentions speeches as well as singing following the meal. The floor of the barn would also be cleared for dancing. The farmer and his wife danced with their employees in order of seniority. The favourite dances were 'Three Meet' and 'Sir Roger', the music being supplied by fiddles.[27]

Ted Pile also remembered the lardering day after the harvest, when everyone had a day's holiday:

The head horse keeper had to go to all the merchants who supplied goods to the boss such as the saddler, the blacksmith, the corn merchant, the wheelwright to collect money to buy cheese, tomatoes, bread and beer, ginger beer for the boys and tobacco and cigarettes. He also got a nine-gallon barrel from the brewery. They had supper and then sang the old farmer's songs: 'Little Polly Perkins from Paddington Green' and 'Three Cheers for the Red, White and Blue.'[28]

Ted was part of a hard-working culture that could also find enjoyment. Dudley Peacock, the son of Ted's friend, Harry Peacock, described him deservedly in his funeral address at Biddenham church on 21 December 1992 as 'a man who got things done, hard-working, warm-hearted, reliable, of integrity', who loved Biddenham.

The occupational breakdown of the 1851 census showed that there were 76 lace makers in Biddenham. Lacemaking was a very important occupation for poorer women and children in the village up until the end of the 19th century, either to earn their own living or to supplement the family income. Young girls would go to the village school in the morning and to the lacemaking school in the afternoon. It was felt that children's, especially girls', general education was neglected in favour of lacemaking, but economic necessity prevailed. In Bromham, the lace school was in the grounds of Bromham Hall. Miss Rice Trevor continued to run it as an 'industrial school' for older girls after the foundation of her own village school.[29] In Biddenham, the lace school had less grand surroundings and associations. It was held at Mrs Brockett's cottage, 53 Church End. The girls paid two pence a week to attend, provided their own pillows and bobbins, and endured the strict teachers who rapped the girls' knuckles with a ruler when they took the wrong bobbins. They started on a very simple pattern called the spider, a narrow straight lace, and moved on to more complicated patterns such as the Tudor rose and leaf design. This was possibly taught to Bedfordshire women by Catherine of Aragon's ladies-in-waiting when she stayed at Ampthill from 1532 to 1533 during the divorce proceedings with Henry

VIII, or when she was later living at Kimbolton Castle after the divorce.[30]

When lacemaking was still a profitable occupation for women, before the advent of factory-produced lace, women could regularly be seen outside their cottages in Biddenham on sunny afternoons, working with their pillows and lace bobbins. The 1956 WI scrapbook has a picture of Mrs William Goss, who died in about 1900 aged about 80, seated at her cottage door with her pillow and bobbins. She lived in one of the old cottages near the church which have been demolished.[31] However, throughout the 19th century the earnings of Bedfordshire lace makers fell. The complete machine production of lace was possible by the end of the century, and though the lace was not of the highest quality, it was acceptable to the popular market. Bedfordshire lace makers adapted patterns to try to beat the machines, but by the 1891 census, the number of workers had fallen dramatically - not just in Biddenham, but also in the county as a whole. Only a few old ladies competed for the limited work available to the handmade trade from the lace dealers.[32]

In the mid-19th century Biddenham was a self-contained unit: the residents generally found employment in the village. It was later, with mechanisation, agricultural depression and improved communications, that some started to work elsewhere. The farms did not just need labourers; as the 1851 census reveals, the wealthier tenant farmers employed house servants, a housekeeper, housemaids, a governess, gardeners, grooms, a gamekeeper, a footman and cooks. The farms also required services such as those of a wheelwright, who had to build and keep in good repair the many farm and village vehicles that often ran on rutted farm tracks. Alfred Hebbes, who retired at 70 and handed the business over to his son-in-law, was the wheelwright and carpenter in Biddenham for 50 years. He lived in a cottage at Duck End, and had a workshop there.[33]

Just as important as the wheelwright was the blacksmith. Fred Summerlin was blacksmith in 1851, and he employed a journeyman apprentice. He was succeeded by Bill Davison in 1884, who took the smithy into the age of the motor car and the aeroplane.[34] By the early 20th century, his concerns, as we shall see, were not just with repairing agricultural implements and shoeing horses.

In the second half of the 19th century, Biddenham also had a range of shops, so it was not necessary to go into Bedford for everyday needs. Ethelbert Edwards at Ouse Valley Farm on Duck End Lane was the baker and grocer. The butcher on the Main Street in 1851 was John Felts, and from 1876 to 1890 James Bayes. Charles Frossell was a shopkeeper and baker from 1876 to 1890, as was John Bayes. Samuel Green was a boot and shoemaker from 1876 to 1890, as was Mr Greetham of Dawn Cottage. Other useful services were provided by the farrier, the florist and William Johnson, the vermin destroyer.[35] One of the few people who found work outside the village in the early part of this period was Captain Pole. He lived in Biddenham, but was a gentleman-in-waiting to Queen Victoria. The stagecoach went past the top of Gold Lane each morning and stopped to pick him up and take him to London when his presence was required at court.[36]

On 21 April 1880 the first sub-post office was started in Biddenham in the Old School house. The schoolmistress, Adelaide Elizabeth Osborne, was also appointed postmistress. Her husband delivered the mail. In 1886 her salary was £7 4s per annum. By 1890 the post office had moved to number 28 in the Post Office Row of thatched cottages. It was run by Mr Arthur Ingram, who was gardener and handyman to Robert Whitworth at Church Farm, and his daughter Miss Ingram. By 1907 there was a cycle allowance and Sunday pay for deliveries at Biddenham sub-post office. There was plenty of work, as in 1907 only 1% of the British population had a telephone.

The postcard was the means of rapid communication, and for a halfpenny stamp, postcards were delivered the same day. Sometimes a bill would be sent, paid and returned again receipted, all in the same day.[37]

47 – the post office, 1903

The post office and the school provided good job opportunities for men and women. Other workers were at the mercy of more powerful villagers. The Rev Henry Wood closed down the laundry in the outbuildings attached to the Old Vicarage because the laundry-maids persisted in shouting and giggling at the farm hands passing by.[38]

Other villagers, 13 of them in the 1851 census, were paupers, and others probably only avoided the workhouse through careful scavenging from the countryside and charitable donations. The proprietors of Kempston water mill donated a quarter of their malt annually at Whitsuntide. The malt was delivered directly to the overseers of the poor, and brewed by them into ale, which was distributed among all the poor inhabitants of Biddenham on the Tuesday following Whit Sunday.[39] In 1883 the parish decided to amalgamate the ancient village charities such as the Boteler charity and the Butler or causeway money, so that all the money could be used to buy a bullock at the Christmas fat stock show. It would be kept at either Grove Farm or Church Farm for fattening for the week before it was slaughtered for St Thomas' Day. Tables were put up as the meat was cut up. The men had a dinner of liver, kidneys and steak and cooked potatoes, new bread and home-brewed beer. The women collected the joints of beef: 4 lb per adult per head and 2 lb per child.[40] Ted Pile remembered that 'it was a grand sight to see all the women coming up the village with their baskets of beef.'[41] He also remembered that Mr and Mrs Bucknall, when they were living at Manor Farm House, invited all the village people to the house just before Christmas to collect 2 lb of free tea. Mr Bucknall was a retired tea planter, so he would have known how to obtain the tea in quantity and at a reasonable price. At the same time, the vicar, and the Misses Campbell who lived in Biddenham House, gave coal to the very poor folk.[42] It is interesting that despite the poverty, there were no notorious crimes in Biddenham leading to the execution of the offender or to life imprisonment during this period. Crime amounted to minor incidents, which after 1895 were recorded in the register of the Bedford division of the county police force of which Biddenham was still part.[43]

Life was hard for the women - cooking, cleaning and washing in their cramped cottages. As wood became more difficult and expensive to obtain in the late 19th century, as a result of population growth, coal had to be used as fuel for cooking and heating water. This, with all the smuts, made cleaning harder and did not remove the risk of fire: in 1897 the cottages, one of which was the home of the West family, near the church burnt down.[44] Even so, the women did pay attention to their looks, and to feeding their families well. The 1956 WI scrapbook contains an interesting section 'our grandmothers' recipes for cosmetics' and recipes for everyday dishes.

The recipes for cosmetics included advice for making hands soft and white. 'Put a pinch of powdered alum into a basin and break into it the white of an egg. Mix this up and spread over the hands just before retiring.' There were also recipes for a hair tonic containing elderflower water and violet powder which could be scented with a drop or two of an essential oil such as lemon, lavender or attar of roses.[45]

Amongst the food recipes, rook pie was the speciality of early spring. The women were told to:

Take one dozen young rooks, shot from the nest in spring, skin them and cut away the back, leaving only the breasts and legs. Simmer these gently for three hours with a bunch of sweet herbs, salt and two rashers of bacon. When tender, thicken the gravy and put into a pie dish. Cover with pastry and bake for half an hour. A delicious dish.[46]

The first milk taken from the cow after calving was the perquisite of the cowman, and was shared among his family and friends. It was used to make a form of egg custard called beastings pudding or locally, bignings. The milk from the freshly calved cow was mixed with a pint of fresh milk, egg, sugar was added to taste, the pudding sprinkled with grated nutmeg, and baked in a slow oven until it had set.[47]

The classic dish that the Biddenham women made for their families was the clanger. The recipe that was given to the WI scrapbook was to:

Take a pound of plain flour and half a pound of suet, chop the suet and add it to the flour with a pinch of salt. Mix to a stiff dough with cold water and roll out. Cover half of the dough with a mixture of cold meat, chopped onion and a sprinkling of chopped parsley and any other herbs to taste. Cover the other half of the dough with jam or treacle. Roll up in a cloth and tie in the centre and at both ends and boil for three hours.[48]

The end-product was not always edible. An elderly farm worker told one of the compilers of the WI scrapbook this story in 1956:

When he was a boy about 70 years ago, he left school aged 10 and was given a job with a neighbouring farmer driving the plough: this is walking beside the team of horses and turning them round at the end of the furrow and starting them down the field again. He took his clanger wrapped in a red spotted handkerchief when he left home at 6 am and left it in the farm barn for his midday meal at 2 pm. As his mother wasn't very well off, having several other children and a husband to cater for on 18s per week, her cooking was limited. The boy's clanger was composed largely of flour and water and a sprinkling of pork and parsley, so when it was cold it became very hard. Therefore in company with another boy, he had a game of football with their clangers before eating them. They thought that kicking them around tended to soften them.[49]

Extra fillings for the clangers, such as onion or jam, depended on the time of year or the time that a father might have to tend a cottage garden and grow potatoes, onions, turnips, carrots, beans, cabbage and fruit trees and bushes after putting in a long day on the farm.

Before the children went to work on the farms, they attended the village school which, as described in Chapter 9, had been built by voluntary subscription and government grant in 1832. The 1870 Education Act had made school attendance compulsory, but exemption was given when children were needed for farm work. The school logbook for 1873 reflects this; 'a lot of pupils absent when school re-opened in September after a month's holiday in consequence of the gleaning not being finished.'[50] On 6 August 1914 the entry reads 'school closed this afternoon for the Biddenham Flower Show. Harvest holidays: five weeks from 7 August.'[51] However, from January 1883 the school attendance officer had been visiting about once a month, and attendance prizes were awarded by the Bedford education committee from 1913.[52]

By the last part of the 19th century the children seem to have been hired directly by employers on leaving school. However, before about 1870 the Biddenham feast, which was celebrated each year on St James's day in front of the Three Tuns was the occasion for hiring farm workers and domestic help for the coming year. Those with experience of working on the farms wore some token of their calling: horse keepers carried a whip, cowmen wore a straw plait tucked in their hatbands and shepherds carried a crook. There was also a fun and romantic side to the feast. There were stalls, sideshows, roundabouts and swings. In addition, if a girl went to the village feast alone with a young man, it was a sign of a special favour: a fairing given and accepted meant the pair were pledged sweethearts.[53]

It was rare that the village school could lead to educational opportunity and a life outside the village. However, this happened to Joseph Carrier, who was born on 10 March 1850 in Biddenham to a family who for generations had been farm labourers and lace makers. Both his parents were illiterate, and his father died in poverty in the union workhouse. While still young, Joseph met with a shooting accident that resulted in his losing a hand. However, he showed great promise and aptitude at school, and generous local people agreed to sponsor him through a teacher training course. In 1882 the Rice-Trevors appointed him as headmaster of the school they had established in Bromham. However, Carrier was also a talented artist, and in 1896 he left teaching to follow a career as an artist. In 1905 he emigrated to Canada with his wife, Georgina, whom he had married in 1873 at St James's church, Biddenham. He died in Canada in 1939, leaving behind his pictures of Bedfordshire and British Columbia, including his portrait of the Hon Miss Rice-Trevor, which hung in the main school classroom at Bromham.[54]

48 – St James's church and cottages, (destroyed by fire in 1897)

The years 1850 to 1914 saw many traditional village customs continuing, such as the harvest home suppers and the Biddenham feast, but also there were new interests and activities. The 1956 WI scrapbook records that the old May Day celebrations were still taking place at the end of the 19th century. Young people went about the village on Mayday singing and dancing and carrying garlands of flowers. In addition, just as it is recorded as taking place in Dorset in the novels of Thomas Hardy, if anyone misbehaved, the villagers formed a procession at one end of the village equipped with drums, tin cans, whistles and noisy instruments. An effigy was made of the offending person, which was carried in procession and burnt outside the miscreant's door to the 'music' of the band. As much noise as possible was made to highlight the miscreant's offence.[55]

By the second half of the 19th century the village school was being used as a venue for penny readings. Visitors paid one penny entrance fee and were entertained in the village schoolroom to readings of poems and books of interest by the vicar, schoolmistress or some other educated person. Concerts were held in the farm barns. They consisted of recitations, songs and musical performances by local people.[56] James West, the parish clerk for 40 years, who died in 1861, played the clarinet.[57]

Some of the activities reflected the age or were linked to the church. A Church Lads' Fellowship and Girls' Friendly Society met before 1914. The concern about the abuse of alcohol, and the growth of the temperance movement, led to a branch of the Band of Hope meeting in the schoolroom.[58] By the beginning of the 20th century, as Ted Pile remembered, a branch of the Boy Scouts had been started by Major Randall, who had served in the Boer War. Ted recalled that there were two patrols, and the boys learnt scouting, tracking and cooking, and camped out at the weekends.[59]

Besides the Boy Scouts, another new activity for the early 20th century was the cinema. The three picture palaces, the Picturedrome, Palace and Empire, were in Bedford. Ted Pile recorded that in about 1913 when he was first working, he walked into Bedford with friends. He went to the market and bought sweets (one and a half pounds for 1½d) and then went to the pictures for 3d. After the show, he went to the chip shop and bought two half bags of chips, as you got more chips for your money that way. He then walked home to Biddenham.[60]

The number of sporting activities available from 1850 to 1914 increased as time went on, and came to include more and more team games. The river was a traditional source of sport and exercise. Ted Pile remembered learning to swim in the river:[61] before the river was dredged it was slow-moving and shallow, so people could swim, punt and canoe between Bromham and Kempston. Fishing was also a popular and economically useful activity. Many carp, pike, tench, bream and perch were caught, though the prize was on 22 December 1880, when a 9.5 lb salmon was caught in the eel traps of Kempston mill.[62]

Other traditional country pursuits continued. The huntsmen met outside the Three Tuns once a month and rode down to the river,[63] chasing the fox. Mr and Mrs Bucknall at Manor Farm House kept five horses for hunting. Less expensive hunting and shooting involved sparrow-catching to make pies.[64]

49 – Bromham and Biddenham United football team, 1908.
Back row (left to right): H Smithy, C Smith, W Mills,
E Branson, T Smith, G Pool.
Front row: E Lancaster, W Smith, W Branson, A Gudgin,
T Lancaster, J Barford, J Ball

By the early 20th century team games were well established in the village. There was a Biddenham quoits team.[65] Ted Pile became captain of the village football team, Biddenham United. The Biddenham cricket club also flourished. Its members included Biscay Burton, J P White and his brother Charlie and the Rev W E B Norman.[66]

The 1890s saw an improvement in the services available in the village and in local government. In 1892 a cast iron pipe was laid in Main Road. This brought gas from the Bedford gasometers to the village (electricity did not come to Biddenham until 1930). It enabled houses to be lit by means other than candle or oil light.[67] Up until about 1850 lighting was derived from rush lights. Tallow candles, or wax candles in the houses of the well-to-do, were then introduced, followed by oil lamps.[68] It was not until 1934, with the Rural Supplies Act, that piped water from Clapham reservoir came to Biddenham. However, the residents used ponds to obtain water for their livestock, and wells - raising the water by bucket and chain - for themselves. In the field to the north of Church End an old windmill was used to pump water supplies to the villagers. The wells were supplemented by rainwater collected in large wooden water butts by the back doors of the cottages.[69] Until the 1920s septic tanks or cesspits were still used for sewerage. However, there is no record of major public health problems, which is a tribute to the regulation of local affairs by the new parish council, which met for the first time on 4 December 1894 at 6.30 pm in the schoolroom, with seven members present.[70]

The Biddenham that the new parish council administered was still very self-contained, but changes in transport had begun to open up links with the outside world. In 1858 the railway line from Leicester to London, King's Cross, reached Bedford. It speeded up communications with the capital and provided a large market for local produce in London. Truck-loads of horse manure from the large number of London stables, and soot from thousands of London chimneys, both used as fertilisers, came back to the provinces.[71] Rail communication with Northampton via Oakley, Turvey and Olney, with an extension to Stratford-upon-Avon, was possible after 1852. The Bletchley line had been opened in 1846. Bedford was well served by railways until the closures in the 1960s. To reach Bedford station and the town, the ordinary residents of Biddenham, as Ted Pile described, walked across the fields and along Ford End Road. Wealthier residents had horse-drawn transport by the end of the 19th century. Dogcarts were widely used; doctors and farmers had a pony and trap; wagonettes drawn by one or two horses were hired for outings; the Rev William Norman had a landau, and Mr Kane of Biddenham House kept a curricle (a small box seated vehicle) which he drove himself. [72] The adventurous tried the 'penny farthing' bicycle: some were seen in the village. George Roberts of Day's Lane owned a two-seater bicycle with cushion tyres, two large wheels at the back and one small one in front. By 1912 a bicycle cost 7s 6d.[73] Road accidents were not unknown either. In 1913 Amos Turney was badly bruised when he was thrown from his trap at Biddenham Turn when driving home.[74]

The early years of the 20th century were to see the start of a transport revolution that was eventually to make Biddenham very accessible to outsiders, and allow its residents to travel widely for work and leisure. Motorised transport came to the village in the years preceding World War I. In 1905 a man had to walk in front of the new motor cars with a red warning flag. In 1912 a car turned into Biddenham Turn at the speed of ten miles an hour carrying two men with deerstalker hats, gloves and goggles. It was certainly noticed! A few Biddenham residents bought cars, notably Mr Campbell at Biddenham House, the Rev William Norman, Miss Evelyn Steel and Percy Shurety, who became the village taxi driver. [75] To have a ride in a car in the early years of the 20th century was very exciting, as Ted Pile recalled in his memoirs. The blacksmith, Bill Davison, had a brother who was chauffeur to a maharajah. He came to Bedford to visit relations, and stayed for two weeks. 'The children were very thrilled to see a fine car come to our village, and while staying, he would give many of us kids a ride in this lovely car. I am now going back to around 1909 and to have a ride in this car was very exciting.'[76] The rest of the time, Ted had to walk, as there were no buses into Bedford when he started work in 1913, and it was not until the 1920s that he could afford to buy a motor bike for £19 and take his future wife out for rides.[77]

According to Ted Pile, Bill Davison and his brother started to build a car with the help of Claude Graham-White, but they never got very far with it.[78] Graham-White had become friendly with Bill Davison while he was a pupil at Bedford School from 1892 to 1906. Davison allowed him to tinker about in the forge. He did eventually make a car, and he made bicycles, many of which survived in the 1950s, which were inscribed with his name and proprietary 'Cable' brand.[79] However, Graham-White was most famous for his interest in early aviation: he qualified as a pilot in 1909, one of the first Englishmen to do so, and in 1911 he established a teaching school at Hendon. In 1911 he flew his plane to Biddenham to display it at a function arranged by the Primrose League, which was held in the meadow below the church. There is a vivid account of this exciting event in the 1956 WI scrapbook:

White was due to arrive at 11 30 am, but he did not arrive until 2.30 pm, because of trouble with the plane, as he had flown to France the day before. We believe that this was the first occasion when a plane landed in any village in Bedfordshire. Never before or since have so many people congregated in Biddenham. They came by pony and trap, on cycles, and on foot (some villagers made money by storing the bicycles). The crowd was so large and curious that a guard had to be put round the plane to prevent souvenir hunters demolishing it in their efforts to obtain pieces of the plane as souvenirs.[80]

By 1914 Biddenham had had a taste of new methods of transport. Motorisation in particular was to make Biddenham much more accessible to Bedford, and the railway linked Bedford to London and several other important towns. Diversification helped the farmers through the years of foreign competition and agricultural depression at the end of the 19th century, and they could send their produce to Bedford, London and several other important towns with rail connections to Bedford. Accessibility to Bedford and the availability of high quality education in the town encouraged well-to-do people to build houses in Biddenham and settle there. Between 1901 and 1911 the census reveals that the population of Biddenham grew from 325 to 451, whereas the population of villages that lacked Biddenham's advantages either declined or only grew very slightly. In Stevington the population declined from 536 in 1901 to 479 in 1911. In Bromham the population grew slightly from 321 in 1901 to 350 in 1911.[81]

Maps of the time show that the west of the village was not greatly affected by the new building: this was an area of estate cottages, established large houses such as Biddenham House, farm houses such as Manor Farm House, and services such as the school, the Three Tuns public house and the post office.[82] However, the character of the village green was changing. In 1869 the Rev Henry Wood's brother-in-law, Admiral Gardner, had brought back seeds from the Lebanon in a cone. Six seeds were planted in the Old Vicarage greenhouse. Four of them germinated, and six years later (in 1875) two of these were planted in the churchyard and two in the Old Vicarage garden. Only one cedar tree now survives, in the Old Vicarage garden, giving great character to the centre of the village.[83]

Most of the new building at the end of the 19th and beginning of the 20th centuries took place to the east of the village along Day's Lane, Vicar's Close, Main Road and New Road (now Biddenham Turn). In 1900 H J Peacock had a house built on New Road on his retirement from farming at Grove Farm.[84] This house was Three Gables and then Barringer, now number 17 Biddenham Turn. The well-known architect C E Mallows was H J Peacock's son-in-law. The house he designed and built for his father-in-law was the first house in New Road (Biddenham Turn). The house reflected the Arts and Crafts movement of the time, where the garden was designed to be integrated with the house. Mallows went on to live in the house later with his wife, Sybil, H J Peacock's daughter, whom he had married in 1899. In 1904 St. Aubyns, number 21 Biddenham Turn, was built, followed in 1906 by Beechwood, number 22, and in 1908 One Ash/Ashstead, number 23.[85]

Mr Sanders, a dental surgeon, moved on to Biddenham Turn, and sent his children to the Harpur Trust schools, as did Colonel Guays, a planter, who lived at The White House. Mayfield Lodge, number 1 Main Road, became the home of Mr Ednie, an accountant, and his family, who also attended the Harpur Trust schools.

The new houses were substantial houses of their time, well set in their own grounds. C E Mallows designed two other interesting houses. One was White Cottage on Day's Lane, and the other was King's Corner, number 9 Main Road. This was built in 1899 for John White, the son of J P White, who in 1896 had moved to Pyghtle works near the railway station to set up a larger joinery, metalwork and stonework business than he had been able to operate in Hassett Street. Between 1896 and 1914 White was producing quantities of carefully crafted furniture for house and garden, so his son would have demanded high standards for his house, which contained fine woodwork and many mullion windows on all floors. However, John White did not live there for long, as Kelly's Directory listed Mrs Charles Howard (probably the widow of Charles Howard of the Manor House) as living there in 1903.[86]

There are two houses in Biddenham that were designed by Mackay Hugh Baillie Scott, who was one of Britain's most important architects from 1890 to 1914. Scott had lived on the Isle of Man as a young man. In his architectural business he had developed his own style of building based on the precepts of William Morris and the Arts and Crafts movement: respect for tradition, a rational use of materials, no unnecessary ornament and fitness for purpose. Scott moved to 4 Windsor Place, St Cuthbert's Street in Bedford in 1901, and started an office there. It is thought that he was attracted to Bedford because he had been in contact with J P White, Bedford was conveniently situated, and he could educate his children at the Harpur Trust schools. While he lived in Bedford, until 1913, he worked with White to produce carefully crafted furniture for home and garden. The furniture was simple in outline and concentrated on fine woods and inlays for its effects. Scott also received commissions to design two houses in Biddenham. These houses reflected his belief that he should design the whole house from the roof line to door latches, and even the textiles that hung on the walls. One of the houses was King's Close, number 11 Main Road. The house was built in 1907 for a Mr Salmon, who had purchased the land from the Biddenham Estate.

The other Baillie Scott house in Biddenham is 17 Church End, The White Cottage, which was built in 1909 for £450 (only half the price of a Mercedes in 1909, but still expensive for a 'cottage'). The White Cottage is also listed Grade II, and is in a simplified Tudor style with white roughcast being largely used for the walls. The house has two storeys with gables, brick chimneys and a tiled roof. There is a two storey gabled porch to give the porch dignity. Baillie Scott liked the idea of the front porch for taking off coats and boots, as that would leave the hall, rather than being a corridor in which to take off one's coat, as the central room of the house, a place for eating and living as in the Middle Ages. At The White Cottage Baillie Scott had two doors leading off the porch, giving separate access to both 'parlour' and 'living room', the two main reception spaces, which were also connected by a wide double doorway.

Baillie Scott also liked inglenooks and window seats. He believed in keeping warm! He equipped The White Cottage with a large inglenook seat next to the fire in the parlour. He placed two long built-in window seats in the garden room at the back of the house, and in the living room at the front. Scott gave precise details in the building specifications about what materials were to be used in the construction of the house. Grey elm weatherboarding was used; the oak beams were 'adzed' in the traditional way rather than machine cut; sharp sand was used in the plaster mix, and the plaster was to be finished with a trowel rather than a float. One of the few concessions to modernity that Scott made was to insist on rippled glass for the window of the downstairs cloakroom.[87]

By 1914 Biddenham had a mix of grand, new houses and traditional cottages. The population was growing, and not all the residents worked in the village or in traditional occupations. However, much of the traditional way of life still remained. The farms had survived agricultural depression by diversification and making use of good communications and mechanisation.

The village was still largely self-contained, as there was no bus service, and cars were rare and belonged to the well-to-do. Most of the residents had to walk or cycle to get to Bedford. Their horizons were understandably limited. The outbreak of World War I in 1914 was to change the perspective that many of the villagers had of the wider world. The young men were to see service outside the Bedford area in the armed forces, especially after the introduction of conscription in 1916. Biddenham would no longer be a world of its own.

References:
1   Survey of Biddenham carried out for conservation section 1977, p 9.
2   1851 census.
3   Dorothy Richards, *Biddenham. A Parish History and Guide* (New Moon, 1991), p 34.
4   Survey of Biddenham carried out for conservation section 1977, p 10.
5   Dorothy Richards, op. cit., p 33.
6   Article in *The Bedford Bee*, 23 July 1879.
7   Report on the Ram Sale in *The Bedford Bee*, 30 July 1879.

8 Ibid.

9 Article in *The Bedford Bee*, 23 July 1879.

10 Ibid.

11 WI scrapbook, 1956, p 19, at BLARS.

12 Ibid, p 24 census figures for Biddenham.

13 R W Rideout, *Bromham in Bedfordshire: a History* (R W Rideout, 2002), p 42.

14 Survey of Biddenham carried out for conservation section 1977, p 10.

15 Dorothy Richards, op. cit., p 34.

16 Albert Church, *Recollections of my life in Biddenham,* p 30-32.

17 Ted Pile, Memoirs, 1988, p 5.

18 Ibid, p 5.

19 Ibid, p 5.

20 Ibid, p 6.

21 Ibid, p 6.

22 Ibid, p 6.

23 Ibid, p 7.

24 Ibid, p 5.

25 Ibid, p 5.

26 Ibid, p 7.

27 WI scrapbook, 1956, p 19, at BLARS.

28 Ted Pile, op. cit., 1987, p 7.

29 R W Rideout, op. cit., p 3.

30 WI scrapbook, 1956, p 31, at BLARS.

31 Ibid, p 31.

32 Information supplied to Bedford and District Tourism Association by the Aragon Lace makers.

33 WI scrapbook, 1956, p 32, at BLARS.

34 Dorothy Richards, op. cit., p 22-23.

35 Ibid, p 22-23.

36 WI scrapbook, 1956, p 24, at BLARS.

37 Dorothy Richards, op. cit., p 62.

38 WI scrapbook, 1956, p 42, at BLARS.

39 Ibid, p 6.

40 Dorothy Richards, op. cit., p 51.

41 Ted Pile, op. cit., p 6.

42 Ibid, p 6.

43 Dorothy Richards, op. cit., p 63.

44 Ibid, p 4.

45 WI scrapbook, 1956, p 17, at BLARS.

46   Ibid, p 18.

47   Ibid, p 18.

48   Ibid, p 18.

49   Ibid, p 18.

50   BLARS-SD Biddenham 1/1 School Logbook 1873-1910.

51   BLARS-SD Biddenham 2 School Logbook 1910-1936.

52   Ibid.

53   Ibid, p 19.

54   R W Rideout, op.cit., p 55.

55   WI scrapbook, 1956, p 39, at BLARS.

56   Ibid, p 43.

57   Ibid, p 48.

58   Dorothy Richards, op. cit., p 46.

59   Ted Pile, op. cit., p 10.

60   Ibid, p 14.

61   Ibid, p 14.

62   Dorothy Richards, op. cit., p 26.

63   Ibid, p 45.

64   Ted Pile, op. cit., p 13.

65   Dorothy Richards, op. cit., p 45.

66   Ibid, p 44.

67   Ibid, p 59.

68   WI scrapbook, 1956, p 43, at BLARS.

69   Ibid, p 43.

70   Dorothy Richards, op. cit., p 56.

71   Ibid, p 7.

72   Ibid, p 60.

73   Ibid, p 61.

74   *Stevington. The Village History* (Stevington Historical Trust, 2001), p 186.

75   Dorothy Richards, op. cit., p 61.

76   Ted Pile, op. cit., 1987, p 4.

77   Ibid, p 10.

78   Ibid, p 4.

79   Obituary of Claude Graham-White in *Bedfordshire Times,* August 1959.

80   WI scrapbook, 1956, p 29. at BLARS.

81   R W Rideout, op. cit., p 155.

82   Ordnance Survey map, 1887.

83   Dorothy Richards, op. cit., p 95.

84   Ibid, p 8.

85   Information from Bryan Norris about interesting older houses in
      New Road/Biddenham Turn/Main Road.
86   Dorothy Richards, *A Walk around Biddenham Village,* p.3.
87   Ibid, p 12, and an article by Matthew Sturgis in *The Daily
      Telegraph,* 2009: the century makers: 100 years of houses.

CHAPTER 8

BIDDENHAM 1914 TO 1939 - THE IMPACT OF WORLD WAR I

In the summer of 1914 most of the residents of Biddenham were preoccupied with the annual rhythm of the seasons and the need to get in the harvest. Those who had the time, money and education to buy and read the newspapers were aware that the storm clouds were gathering over Europe. On 28 June 1914 in the faraway Bosnian town of Sarajevo, the heir to the Austro-Hungarian Empire, the Archduke Franz Ferdinand, and his wife, Sophie, were assassinated by a member of the 'Black Hand', a Serbian group that aimed to unite all the Slav people of the Balkans into a single country which would be called Yugoslavia. Terrorism was the means by which they would achieve their aim. This act of terrorism activated the system of alliances that had developed in Europe during the 19th and early 20th centuries. The German Kaiser (Emperor) failed to reply to the British telegram ordering him to call back his army that was invading Belgium, so at midnight on Tuesday 4 August 1914 Britain found herself at war with Germany.

When the news of the outbreak of war reached the general public, there was an air of excitement. The young men thought that the war would be over by Christmas. It would give them a chance to do something different, and travel away from their village at government expense. When they returned home, they hoped that they would be treated like heroes, as had happened to Fred Simmons, the brother of the Misses Bertha and Edith Simmons of Church End, who, when he returned from the Boer War, was presented with a silver watch and chain at a harvest home supper by the grateful Biddenham parishioners.[1] They expected the war to be one of movement fought in traditional style. They did not know about the discomforts of trenches, the power of concentrated machinegun fire or high-velocity shells.

They would have been shocked if they had been told that gas warfare, mechanised warfare - the tank - and aerial warfare involving civilians would soon be used extensively.

With the knowledge and expectation available at the time, the young men obeyed the exhortation of General Kitchener in the famous recruiting poster 'Your Country Needs You' and rushed to volunteer to swell the ranks of the forces. There was no conscription until 1916. 83 men from Biddenham, out of a total village population of 451 in 1911,[2] served in the forces between 1914 and 1918, either as career soldiers or as volunteers in the army, navy and Royal Flying Corps after the outbreak of war, or as a result of conscription. Their names are inscribed on a Roll of Honour which hangs in the parvis in St James's church, Biddenham. There is no record of any women in the forces on the Roll of Honour.

Ten of the men who served died, and their names are inscribed on the war memorial. This can be compared with Stevington, where 109 villagers, including one woman, enlisted. Of these there were 12 who died and 20 who were severely wounded.[3] The casualty rate in World War I was high. Of the 10 men commemorated on the Biddenham war memorial, one, **Thomas William Riddy**, a mason's labourer, died at home on 24 June 1915, aged 33. He lived at Avenue Cottage, Biddenham, but had been born in Stagsden in 1882. He had served as a lance-corporal with the 486th Field Company of the Royal Engineers. The fact that he died at home and is buried in the churchyard of St. Leonard's, Stagsden, indicates that he may have been repatriated, and then died of his injuries. He left a widow who became a teacher at the village school, and three daughters - Celia, Monica and Nancy.[4]

Six of the Biddenham men who died in World War I were killed in the heavy fighting at the Somme in 1916 and at Vimy Ridge, Ypres and Passchendaele in 1917.

The Battle of the Somme began on 1 July 1916 when General Haig sent 13 divisions, 200,000 men, over the top. 20,000 British soldiers were killed and 35,000 wounded on that day alone, but the attacks continued through the summer and into the autumn. On 20 August 1916 **James Plain**, a private in the 1st battalion of the Northamptonshire Regiment, died at the Somme aged 29. James's father, George Plain, worked as a shepherd for Mr Whitworth, and James lived with his family in a cottage at Honey Hill as a boy. He enlisted in Northampton, and lived with his wife, Mary Plain, at Brixworth in Northamptonshire. He is commemorated in Biddenham, where he lived as a boy, and at Bazentin-le-petit cemetery, Somme, France.

In April 1917 heavy fighting was concentrated on Vimy Ridge, near Arras. The Germans had captured the ridge at the beginning of the war. The French had unsuccessfully tried to recapture the ridge twice, and had sustained heavy losses both times. The British and Canadians were at first more successful, as they made use of tunnelling, but then the Germans brought up reserve troops. There were 250,000 casualties in the battle that followed. Amongst them were two Biddenham men who are commemorated on the Biddenham war memorial and Bay 5 of the Arras Memorial in France. **Giles Havergal Shaw**, a lieutenant with the 5th battalion (Territorial) of the Bedfordshire Regiment, died on 10 April 1917. He was the third son of the Rev W H and Mrs Shaw of Biddenham Turn, Bedford. 'He was, we regret to hear, killed on 10 April by a sniper after capturing a valuable position which enabled the advance to be continued'[5] Private **Alfred Dudley**, whose parents Mr and Mrs William Dudley and brothers lived in the cottage next to the Three Tuns, was killed in action at Vimy Ridge on 23 April 1917. He was 31 when he died, and had worked on the Bedford golf links for 12 years before he volunteered and enlisted in the Bedfords in August 1914. He was sent to France in 1915 to complete his training with the 6th battalion of the First Bedfordshire Regiment. He took part in the Battles of Festubert, Loos and Arras and other engagements, and was wounded twice, including at the Somme in 1916, before being transferred to a line battalion of the Bedfords. After his death, Second-lieutenant E I F Nailer, his officer and an old Bedford School boy, wrote to his parents expressing deepest sympathy, and adding 'It will be some consolation to you to know that his death was without suffering. He was a very popular boy and did his work unflinchingly, and his NCOs loved him as a thorough, honest worker'. He was entitled to the 1914-1915 Star and the General Service and Victory medals.[6]

The offensives of 1917 claimed the lives of three more Biddenham men. On 25 July 1917 Rifleman **Wilfred Herring** died of wounds, aged 24. He was born in Walthamstow, Essex, the son of William Charles and Henrietta Maria Herring of Fairmead, New Road. He had been serving as a rifleman with the 15th battalion of the Royal Irish Rifles. He is buried at the Etaples military cemetery, Pas de Calais, France. Etaples, as Vera Brittain recounts in her autobiography, *Testament of Youth,* contained an 'area of camps, in which, at one time or another, practically every soldier in the British Army was dumped to await further orders for a still less agreeable destination'. It also contained a large general hospital where Vera Brittain worked as a VAD nurse after August 1917, nursing the wounded who had been brought in from the front line. She describes the big cemetery below the pinewoods at the top of the hill with its weather-beaten crosses, with their bright gardens of pansies and stocks and marigolds. Wilfred Herring's grave was marked by one of them.[7]

In August 1917 there was once again heavy fighting around Ypres. As the *Bedfordshire Times* reported on 17 August 1917:

Sir Douglas Haig has undoubtedly been hampered by the rain but he has pushed on with his plans in spite of it. There have been two important local attacks during the last week, both of them highly successful; and as we go to press, news comes of a third, apparently the biggest and most important of all, on a wide front east and north of Ypres.

Algernon Cyril Armstrong, who was born in Biddenham and lived at Ford End, Bedford, a private in 8th battalion of the East Kent Regiment, the Buffs, was killed in action at the start of these offensives on 10 August 1917. He is commemorated on Panel 12 and 14 at the Menin Gate Memorial at Ypres in Belgium.

As the summer of 1917 turned into autumn, the wet weather continued: it was the wettest period for many years. The shells churned the soaking ground around Ypres into a sea of liquid mud. The soldiers who fought the Third Battle of Ypres (Passchendaele) endured the most horrible conditions of the war. Soldiers sank into the mud up to their waists, and if they put down duckboards to help them to cross the mud, they frequently slipped off if they were tired, and they drowned in shell-holes. On 30 October 1917 **Richard Wright** was killed in action at Passchendaele, aged 19. He was born in Kempston, but by 1917 his parents, Frederick and Eliza Wright, lived in Duck End Lane, Biddenham. Richard enlisted in Bedford in February 1917, and was a private in the 4th battalion of the Bedfordshire Regiment. He was drafted to France later in 1917 after undergoing a course of training. In this theatre of war, he took part in important engagements in various sectors of the front, and was wounded. He was reported missing after the Battle of Passchendaele in October 1917, and was later presumed killed in action. He was entitled to the General Service and Victory medals, and is commemorated in Biddenham and also at the Tyne Cot Memorial, just outside Ypres in Belgium.[8]

More bad news was to come to Biddenham before the war ended on 11 November 1918. On 8 June 1918 **John Davison**, the son of the village blacksmith, died of wounds. He had enlisted in

Bedford and was a lance-corporal in the 6th battalion of the Machine Gun Corps (infantry). He is buried in Esquelbecq military cemetery, France.

Greville Shaw, a Canadian national whose father, the Rev William Shaw, was living in Bedford at the time of his officer declaration in 1915, died on 3 November 1918, aged 28. He was a major in the 12th battalion, the Royal Canadian Engineers. According to the battalion diary for 3 November 1918, preserved in the Canadian National Archives, 'Major Shaw went forward on a motorcycle about 14.00 hours to make a reconnaissance of the forward roads in St Saulve and beyond if possible. As he had not returned by 23.00 hours, he was reported to 4th brigade, Canadian Engineers as missing'. He left a wife, Annie C Shaw (née Strong), who was at the military hospital, Quebec. He is commemorated at Biddenham, and is buried at Valenciennes (St Roch) Communal Cemetery, France.

One Biddenham man who was wounded at the end of the war did not make it back to England. **Walter Clifford Rowney** was born in Stevington in 1891 to Thomas and Kate Rowney. He died on 31 January 1919, aged 28, more than two months after the end of the war. He left a wife, Emily Rowney who lived in Church End, Biddenham. Walter was a private in the 101st company of the Labour Corps. He is buried in Belgrade Cemetery, Namur, Belgium, next to the medical clearing station taking casualties from the Namur final assault.

Some soldiers managed to return home, but suffered the pain or incapacity consequent on their wounds for the rest of their lives. On 30 November 1917, under Biddenham news, the *Bedfordshire Times* reported that:

Mrs. Gray heard on Sunday that Captain Harry P T Gray had been received into Rouen Hospital suffering from gunshot wounds in the leg and side, received near Cambrai whilst leading the Seaforth Highlanders. He has since been brought over to the first Southern General Hospital at Birmingham University and is going on satisfactorily.

Captain Gray returned to the front, but on 14 April 1918 the *Bedfordshire Times* reported under Biddenham news that 'Captain Gray and Lieutenant Norman are reported wounded in the last Somme battle'.

Captain Gray was lucky to survive. Private Willie Dowler and Major Denys Firth were so seriously wounded that they had to be invalided home. Willie Dowler, who had grown up in Biddenham and attended the village school, volunteered in 1914, and in 1915 was drafted to Salonika. At the capture of Monastir he was badly wounded, losing his right arm and his right eye, and was consequently invalided home. He was finally discharged in December 1916, after being awarded the 1914-15 Star, the General Service and Victory medals.[9]

On 1 March 1929 the *Bedfordshire Times and Independent* reported on the death and funeral at Biddenham church of Major Denys Firth of Vicar's Close, aged 46. Major Firth 'had been for long a sufferer from a leg wound received in the Great War and it was this that ultimately resulted in his death'. At Oxford University in 1903:

….. He obtained a University Commission in the Duke of Wellington's Regiment. With this regiment, he served at home and in India, and when the Great War broke out he had risen to the rank of captain. In the early days of the war he fought in France, until in 1915 he was wounded in the leg in action near Ypres. He was invalided home and because of his wound, he had to retire from the Army in 1919, by which time he had become a major ….. With his wife and family, Major Firth took up his residence at Albany Road, Bedford, and about two and a half years ago moved to Biddenham ……

Despite his suffering, Major Firth had many interests and got through a prodigious amount of work:

His work included his job – an Assistant Commissioner to the National Savings Committee, his work with the Boy Scout Organisation (he was Assistant District Commissioner for several years), his chairmanship of the Bedford Branch of Toc H and membership of the local committee that supported the League of Nations. Only his family and intimate friends have any idea of the suffering he has borne since the war with such unbroken patience.

At least two Biddenham men became prisoners of war. On 3 May 1918 the *Bedfordshire Times,* under Biddenham news, reported that 'Mr and Mrs Jackson have received news that their son, Private Fred Jackson, is wounded and a prisoner of

50 – Biddenham men who served in World War I, 1919. Included are Brockett-Johnson, W Dowler, G King, F Jackson, T Trueman-Burley, Alfonso Johnson, Pearmain, Brookes, Faulkner, Simmons, A Sturgess, Cartwright, A Roberts, T Baden, Smith, Bransom, B Gudgin, A Burton, Major Grey, S Johnson, Trueman, W Stringer, W Peacock

war in Germany'. On 14 July 1918 the *Bedfordshire Times* wrote about the appeal that had been launched in Biddenham to raise £3 a month to try to get adequate food to Private Jackson. By 26 July 1918 it was revealed that Private Ernest Smith, who had been reported wounded and missing on 24 April, was a prisoner of war with a bullet wound in the foot and ankle, in hospital in Darmstadt, Germany. There was consequently another appeal for subscriptions for prisoners of war in the *Bedfordshire Times* on 9 August 1918.

The men who returned to the village after war service alive and seemingly unwounded had none the less seen and experienced terrible sights and conditions. The Women's Institute scrapbook for 1956 included a photograph of a group of Biddenham men who served in the 1914-1918 war, taken on Peace Day 1919. Amongst them on the third row was Arthur Burton, born in 1889, who was a sapper with the East Anglian Royal Engineers in France.[10] Three months after volunteering in September 1914, he was drafted to the Western Front, where he was engaged on road-making, pontoon bridge building and other important duties. He served in various sectors, and took part in the Battles of Ypres, Festubert, Loos, the Somme, Arras and Cambrai before being demobilised in November 1919. He held the 1914-1915 Star, the General Service and Victory medals.[11]

After the war, Arthur worked at Messrs J P White and Son, the Pyghtle Works, and became a highly respected cabinetmaker and joiner. He made the panelling for the Northern Ireland Parliament building, the Royal Naval College, Greenwich, the Stratford-upon-Avon Memorial Theatre and Worthing Town Hall. He made the altar and lectern for the Battle of Britain Memorial Chapel in Westminster Abbey, and was interviewed by Richard Dimbleby as the local craftsman for an edition of *Down Your Way*. As well as his work, he found time to be a parish councillor, a special constable and a member of

Biddenham village cricket team. His friends remembered him for his good sense, good humour, good nature and courage in adversity.

Next to Arthur Burton on the 1919 Peace Day photograph was Bertie Gudgin, who had also served (on the Western Front)[12] as a sapper in the Royal Engineers from May 1915. Further along on the third row was Arthur Roberts, who had served on the Western Front as a driver of motor transport and ambulances from June 1916 until the end of the war, in the Somme, Arras, Vimy Ridge, Passchendaele, Cambrai and Marne sectors.[13]

Missing from the photograph was 'Bert' Green, who had been born in Biddenham, where his father was landlord of the Three Tuns. He attended the village school, but left aged 11 to be a farm worker. He then became a regular soldier in the Royal Artillery. In the 1914-1918 war he fought in France and Salonika, and only returned to Biddenham in 1931 to succeed his father as landlord of the Three Tuns. Together they held the tenancy for 50 years.[14]

Several Biddenham men as well as Bert Green saw service in sectors of fighting other than the Western Front. Robert Shaw, the son of a retired farmer, had moved to Bedfordshire from Cartmel in Cumbria in the 1890s. He had worked as a groomsman and coachman at Cranfield Court, before transferring to Biddenham Manor. He married Alice, a lace maker from Wootton, in 1906, and they lived in Dawn Cottage overlooking Biddenham village green, and part of the Wingfield Estate. Although he was 40 when war broke out in 1914, and the father of three children, Robert felt that it was his duty to answer the call to serve his country. He volunteered in September 1914, and became a sergeant in the Royal Veterinary Corps. He served throughout the Gallipoli campaign in 1915. After the evacuation of the peninsula he was drafted to Egypt, and was in action during the operations at Magdhaba.

Later he was sent to Palestine, and played a prominent part in engagements at Gaza, Jerusalem and Damascus, and in General Allenby's offensive in 1918.[15]

E Branson of Church End, Biddenham, a driver in the RASC, saw service in Salonika and Egypt. He spent some time in hospital suffering from fever, and was invalided home in 1918.[16] Edward Brooks, a driver in the Royal Engineers, and Willie Dowler, who was badly wounded, both served in Salonika.[17]

Not all Biddenham men saw service in the army. Ernest Dowler, Willie's brother, joined the Royal Navy in August 1917. For two years he was engaged on patrol duties in the North Sea on board HMS *Torch*.[18] Willie Sargent joined the Royal Flying Corps in June 1916 and (after training) was sent to Egypt as a mechanic. For the rest of the war he was attached to service flying squadrons, chiefly at Cairo.[19] Frank Green joined the RAF in September 1918, and until his demobilisation in June 1919 he was stationed on Salisbury Plain 'where he was employed on highly technical work in the aeroplane sheds'[20]

As previously stated, there is no record of any woman who saw active service in the forces on the Roll of Honour for 1914-1918 in Biddenham church. Locally, women were encouraged to join the Women's Land Army (a civilian organisation) or to be VAD nurses.[21] Dorothy Richards described a strong nursing tradition in the village.[22] In 1911 the Biddenham-Kempston number 10 detachment of the British Red Cross Society was formed. It met in the thatched building in the garden of the Three Tuns with Mrs Carpenter as commandant. Dorothy Richards includes a photograph of the founder members on duty at the Biddenham Show in 1911. The ladies in the photograph show a wide span of ages. Unfortunately only the surnames of the members are given, but Chibnall was the name of the farmer at Grove Farm, and we know that a Hilda

Chibnall was awarded the Royal Red Cross for her work on a hospital ship off Gallipoli during the war.[23]

Certainly the members of the British Red Cross Society worked hard even if they stayed in England. They did first-aid and ambulance work, nursing and cooking. The Biddenham members regularly held jumble sales to raise funds, and in 1915 helped at the Goldington Road measles hospital.[24]

Even though they were not serving abroad, the women of Biddenham were aware of and fully involved in the war. Several had the worry and anxiety of knowing that their husbands and sons were at the front. They dreaded the arrival of the telegraph boy with a telegram bearing bad news, and as we have seen, some Biddenham families such as the Herrings, the Davisons, the Dudleys, the Armstrongs, the Wrights and the Rowneys received this news. Other families could not put the war to the back of their minds as people in some villages could, because soldiers were all around them. First a Scottish and later a Welsh regiment were billeted in Biddenham.

51- Welsh soldiers with Mrs Pile and two neighbours, 1914

144

Although he was only nine in 1914 (he was born in 1905), Albert Church retained vivid memories of the soldiers in his *Recollections of My Life in Biddenham,* which he wrote when he was an old man. Albert remembered that a lot of the Scottish soldiers, about 200, were billeted in Biddenham. Every cottage had to have two or three soldiers, and the farmers had

52 – Scottish Highlanders, with School House in the background

the officers.[25] Each soldier was in charge of a horse, mule or pack pony, and some were in charge of two animals. Every farmer in the village and his workmen had to clear out all cart hovels of wagons, trolleys and carts to make way for stabling of horses and mules. All used horseshoes were commandeered from the blacksmith and driven into the stone walls of cart hovels, and horses and mules were tethered to them.[26] Fortunately for the Biddenham residents, none of the soldiers had meals at their billet. Each farm had its own cookhouse for the soldiers, one of whom went into Bedford each day to fetch bread and provisions.[27] In addition, the Red Cross ladies were instrumental in getting the straw barn belonging to Clay Farm converted into a canteen for the troops, so that they could get together in the evenings and their spare time. A counter was built at the east end, so that the Red Cross ladies, on a rota system, could serve tea, chocolate, cake and cigarettes. Tables, chairs, cards, dominoes and draughts were bought for the soldiers, but there was a strict rule that no alcohol was to be consumed on the premises.[28] The soldiers used Ford End fields for training.

However, the highlight of the early part of the war for Albert Church was on 22 October 1914, when King George V came to inspect the Black Watch Regiment in Gallows Field and the golf course before they marched to the old Bedford Midland Road station at the corner of Ashburnham Road to go to France. A pupil at Bedford High School, Joyce Marsh, caught the atmosphere of the day in a poem that she wrote called '1914':

Trudge, Tramp, Tramp, Trudge,
The kilted battalions go filing by,
By the Bromham Road, and over the bridge
Rain or sunshine, damp or dry.

Over the bridge and round to the right,
The lengthy column wends its way,
Straight through a gate (you know it by sight),
On to a field once devoted to play.'[29]

Albert Church recalled:
There were thousands of troops, Gallows Field was overflowing with them, as well as three parts of the golf course. Each battalion was headed by a brass band or bagpipes. The King mounted his horse in front of the golf course. He wore the uniform of the Scots Guards and his bearskin. I had a wonderful view of him. That was the only time I remember playing truant from school. Would you believe it, on this great historic occasion for Biddenham, we were not granted a half holiday or even a couple of hours from school. I can't remember what our punishment was, probably two strokes of the cane or to stop in

after school and write 50 or 100 times with a slate pencil on a slate – I must obey the school rules.[30]

Albert's recollection is vivid, but Mr Richard Galley, who has researched the Highlanders in Bedford, has pointed out that the King wore khaki uniform and a peaked cap, not a Scots Guard bearskin. The High School girls, along with the Boys' Grammar and Modern Schools, had a holiday to watch the review, and did not have to play truant like Albert Church. As one of the girls wrote:

About 11.30 am we heard a sound of cheering, and the King drove up in an open motor car. He wore a khaki uniform, as did the officers accompanying him; following him came members of his suite and staff officers. The car stopped at the gate leading to the golf links and the King first inspected the troops there, passing on to those in the nearer field. In a few minutes he took up a position near the gate and then the march past began. The Highlanders came in a continuous stream through the gate and along the road to the town – their bayonets gleaming in a broad line as far as we could see across the field. It took about an hour and a quarter for all the regiments to pass; at intervals there came bands of pipers, but we heard no brass band music. The long columns came to an end at last, the rear being brought up by the Scottish Horse.[31]

The soldiers fulfilled a useful purpose in the village in March 1916 when in a terrific gale about 20 trees were blown down, including two across Gold Lane and two across the road at Buttercups. The children were sent home from school, as one of the two elm trees next to the school was blown down, just missing the school playground. Albert Church recalls that it was lucky that there was a shop and baker in the village, as nothing could get in or out of the village by road, and the farmers had to go through the fields with their pony and float to get milk to Bedford. The soldiers in the village provided manpower and horses, as the fallen trees had to be cut up by crosscut saws and axes, which took days. The trunks and large branches had to be shifted by horses.[32]

The war did not just impact on the villagers through the anxiety they felt for their loved ones at the front and the presence of the billeted Scottish and Welsh regiments. There was a need for the nation to respond to war conditions, though not on the scale that World War II was to require. Zeppelin raids affected London from 1915, and necessitated fire brigade practice in London institutions[33] but not in villages like Biddenham outside London. The Biddenham residents did their best to support the soldiers. The *Bedfordshire Times* reported regularly on the meetings of the Biddenham miniature rifle club. At the meeting reported on 22 February 1918, the chairman congratulated the club on the good percentage of members who were now serving in His Majesty's forces having learnt the art of handling and using the rifle at the club.

Albert Church mentions knitting for the soldiers in the early part of the war. 'Some of my school mates were very good at it, but I made a very poor job of it.'[34] He also went into Bedford with a friend to collect wooden boxes that had been used to pack chocolates. 'Our job was to knock the slats off, take out the nails and sandpaper the wood, and the ladies of the Biddenham Red Cross would use them to make splints.'[35] As has been mentioned already, the *Bedfordshire Times* reported in July 1918 on an appeal for funds for food for prisoners of war. The renewal of the U-boat war in 1917, along with the bad harvest of 1916, helped to cause shortages of many basic foodstuffs, such as margarine, meat, potatoes, sugar and tea, and the doubling of prices. In August 1917 a food control committee was appointed for Bedford Rural District, and information was printed in the *Bedfordshire Times* about preserving fruit without sugar, though rationing was not introduced until February 1918, initially for butter and margarine[36]. Government posters urged people to eat less bread in order to make wheat supplies last longer. To increase food supplies and make up for the loss of men's labour on the land once conscription was introduced in 1916, boys aged 12 could leave school if they wished to do so, provided that they went to work on the land. Albert Church and several other boys availed themselves of this opportunity in 1917.[37]

Albert went to work for Mr Anthony Chibnall at Grove Farm, where his father worked. He remembers that he was paid 4s 6d:

This was for a 60-hour week, six o'clock in the evening and the same for Saturday. In the winter, which I think was four months, it was seven o'clock until five-thirty. In the summer you had an hour for breakfast and dinner. In the winter you had only half an hour for breakfast. Now, if you were working in the field with the horses you had to have your breakfast packed up and a nosebag for the horses. If it was very cold you could collect rotten wood from the hedges and make a fire.[38]

Albert emphasised that 'things on the farm were tough in those days. If it was wet or snowy and frosty and you could not get on to the land to do anything, and all the jobs in the barns had been done, you would be sent home. There was no unemployment pay.'[39] Despite the privations, Albert did enjoy fetching and carrying the beer for the men from the Three Tuns at hay time and harvest:

I have been at the Three Tuns knocking up the landlord, or the barmaid. They had one living in in those days, as early as six-thirty ….. when I arrived from the Tuns with the first lot they drank it quickly and handed back the jars and money for me to fetch some more for them to have with their breakfast at eight.[40]

Another job Albert liked doing on the farm:

….. Was going to Bedford with a horse and cart. It was a thrill to go through the streets being watched by the townspeople. One journey took us a good way through the town. It was to the brewery of Newland and Nash, and also Charles Wells brewery in Horne Lane. Mr Chibnall, the farmer for whom I worked, had the contract to clear away horse manure and spent hops.[41]

Albert and the non-conscripted men and boys left working on the farm did their bit to keep food production as high as possible during the war. However, their work was impeded by the terrible influenza epidemic of 1918. Albert remembers that 'hundreds of people died in the Bedford area and many of them were Scottish soldiers who were billeted here.'[42] Mr Chibnall, Albert's employer, supplied his workers with bottles of quinine, as he had been told that 'if people drank plenty of quinine they would escape influenza.'[43] So serious was the 'flu epidemic that in November 1918 Bedford's elementary schools were closed.[44] At the time of the armistice in November 1918, therefore, the people of Biddenham were trying to cope with the influenza outbreak. They then had to wait for those serving in the armed forces to be demobilised. This was a staggered process; for instance, Arthur Dudley was demobilised in February 1919, Edward Brooks in May 1919, Robert Shaw in July 1919 and Harry Burton in November 1919. William Church was not demobilised until February 1920, as he served with the army of occupation in Germany.[45] Alfred Sargent and William Williams were also with the army of occupation at Cologne, and were not demobilised until March 1920.[46]

By 1920 the pattern of rural life was being resumed, but the war had had a lasting impact on the village. The relatives of those who had died, such as the Davisons, received a plaque and scroll from the King in commemoration of their loved one. The citation read:

He whom this scroll commemorates was numbered among those who at the call of King and country, left all that was dear to them, endured hardness, faced danger and finally passed out of the sight of men by the path of duty and self-sacrifice, giving up their own lives that others might live in freedom. Let those who come after see to it that his name be not forgotten.

53 – Unveiling of the war memorial, 1922

In 1922 a war memorial was erected to commemorate publicly the 10 Biddenham men who had died on active service or as a result of wounds sustained during the war. The memorial is on the green in the centre of the village on the north side of the Main Road. It was designed by Frederick Landseer Griggs (1876-1938) in the form of a small Celtic cross on a plinth, with a three-stepped base. The names of the men commemorated are inscribed around the base of the cross, along with the words 'to the greater glory of God in proud memory of Algernon Armstrong, John Davison, Alfred Dudley, Wilfred Herring, James Plain, Thomas Riddy, Walter Rowney, Giles Shaw, Greville Shaw, Richard Wright men of Biddenham who died for the honour of their country

1914-1919.'[47] The memorial was unveiled on 18 May 1922 by Lady Wingfield.

In the immediate postwar period the Wingfields were still the largest landowners in Biddenham and Bromham. The farmers were their tenants, apart from William Manning at Green Farm.[48] The other farms - Church Farm, Manor Farm, Honeyhill, Grove Farm and Clay Farm - were therefore part of the Wingfield Estate in Biddenham, and remained so until 1954, when much of the estate was sold off. When Lady Wingfield died, she left the Biddenham estate to one nephew, and the Bromham estate to another. The new owner of Bromham was not interested in running an estate, and in 1925 he sold out. The Biddenham estate was considered to be the more valuable because of valuable building land near to the town.[49]

54 – Harry King, agent, at the gate of Rose Cottage

The Wingfields still had extensive property in Bedfordshire, including Ampthill House, so in the 1920s they left the management of the Biddenham estate to their foreman,

Mr Harry King, who lived at Rose Cottage in the centre of the village.

Albert Church left Grove Farm when he was nearly twenty and went to work for the Wingfield Estate. In his memoirs he wrote that he was a general labourer and his wage was £1.8s per week:

I stayed with the Biddenham Estate for over thirty years and very happy years they were. The money was poor but the work was varied and interesting and I had a nice bunch of men to work with. Through working with them I gained a fair knowledge of bricklaying, thatching, carpentry, stonewalling and my duties also included hedge laying, repair, and maintenance of gates, fences and water pipes. I was also involved in water meter reading and rent collecting. ….. Roofs on all buildings were kept in good repair and this included thatching and tiling. In some cases thatch on farm buildings which was in bad repair was stripped off, rafters and lathes replaced and tiled instead of thatch.[50]

Albert was a loyal employee of the Wingfields. He had some interesting comments to make about the rents the Wingfields charged, and the services that they supplied:

Rents of some of the cottages were very cheap. Rents to older tenants were never raised. Some who had been tenants before the First World War were still paying the same rent at the time the Estate was sold in 1954. The rent of one such cottage was 10 old pence per week and several others only paid one shilling and sixpence or two shillings. Stone built and tiled cottages were two shillings and sixpence and more modern ones paid four shillings.

If a tenant died or left a cottage the Estate would do it up a bit inside, probably put in new grates, paper and paint the rooms and possibly a sink and water laid on. If the rent had previously been four shillings it would go up to six shillings.

There were always some cottages that went with the farms. These were tied cottages and the tenants were usually stockmen, cowmen or horse keepers. Rent for these cottages was stopped out of the men's wages and the farmer paid the Wingfield Estate with his farm rent. ..... Cottage rents were due on 25 March and 29 September but the Estate owners always gave them two months' grace, which meant it was paid in May and November. The rent was paid at Rose Cottage, the home of Mr Harry King. Each tenant, on paying his rent on the day due, was given back two shillings.[51]

Albert also pointed out that if a man died, the widow and family were never turned out, but sometimes they were offered alternative accommodation if the cottage was tied to a job.[52] In what were economically hard times (Mr Chibnall at Grove Farm went bankrupt in 1929),[53] the Estate provided useful services for its tenants. Cottages were repaired and painted every three years, and in this way, the row of thatched cottages on Main Road, Day's Lane side that had been condemned by the RDC in 1920 had a reprieve.[54] Allotments were provided for any tenant who wished to have one. The allotments were either at the lower end of Day's Lane between number nine and Deep Spinney Farm, or along the causeway path between the 'kissing gate' and the church. The tenants could grow vegetables and keep hens. They paid one shilling a year rent to Harry King. There was no sewer through the village in the 1920s, so the Estate supplied lavatory buckets, disinfectant for lavatories and drains, dustbins, coppers for washing, and gravel for paths was free to cottagers if they fetched it from the pits.[55]

As well as the cottages that were tied to the tenant farmers of the Wingfields, there were six cottages for the gardeners and grooms that were tied to the large houses in the village: the Manor, Lavender Lodge, Biddenham House and Biddenham Close. As the 1956 WI scrapbook shows, despite lacking modern facilities, some of the cottages looked very picturesque. The photograph of the old cottages at Church End and the plough team returning from work, with Arthur Burton sitting on the first horse, is redolent of many people's cherished image of Old England. However, cottage life had its dangers and privations. In 1929 some cottages in Church End were gutted as a result of a spark from a passing steam engine starting a fire at about 12 noon one Saturday. Neighbours rallied round and formed a bucket chain until the fire brigade arrived. Water had then to be pumped from a nearby pond until the fire was put under control. Although the contents of the cottages were saved, they had to be demolished, and the Johnson and Trueman families lost their homes.[56]

Even if your cottage survived, cottage life was very cramped. The 1956 WI scrapbook reveals that in the middle cottage of the row of 17th century cottages in the main street opposite the village hall, Mr and Mrs Sargent raised nine children. Mrs Wynne Stringer, Albert Church's sister, in an article in the *Biddenham Bulletin*, August 1990, remembered that the cottage where she was born, and where she moved back to as an old lady, was 'two up and two down'. There was a large barn at the back, housing a copper for hot water, and an earth closet at the far end. She recalled that conditions were cramped when she was a child, as she was one of five children. They were also cramped for the Dowlers next door.

By the 1920s and 1930s not all the residents of Biddenham lived in either large old houses or cottages. Houses for middle-class professional people were being built. Albert Church recalled that 'several houses had been built in Day's Lane early in the 20th century but the plots really began to sell in or about 1930. At that time the price was £400 an acre'.[57] However, later when a five-inch water main was put in by the Biddenham Estate, who owned the water supply in Biddenham, and the cost of a sewer was shared with the purchaser, the price of building plots reached £600 an acre in New Road (now Biddenham Turn) and £500 in Day's Lane.[58] Piped water, sewerage and electricity were new luxuries that some of the villagers had by 1934. In his memories in the *Biddenham Bulletin* in July 2003, Alan Evans wrote that:

Biddenham Turn in the late thirties and during the war was vastly different from now. There were very few houses on the right side towards Bedford and no schools. However, the left-hand side was full of houses to the right hand turn to Bedford. Amongst the residents were Mr Swift, a Westminster Bank manager, and the Honourable Romola Russell, the Duke of Bedford's aunt.

The 1939-1945 war stopped new building, but just before the war Alan remembered that as a boy after he came to Biddenham

55 – Spring drilling in the Baulk field, 1922. Leading – Len Wiliams age 14); at the drill Albert Church (16), at the rear Ted Brooks

in 1937, Thorpe House and lodge were built for a Bedford doctor. 'It was a lovely new large house with a ballroom. It also had a green baize door like the other large houses in Biddenham, which of course led to the servants' quarters. Many Christmas parties were held there which I went to!'

Biddenham in the 1920s and 1930s was a hard-working community. The men laboured on the land, (Ted Pile, in his memories in the *Biddenham Bulletin* in July 1987, said that the farms employed about 30 men as well as the tenant farmers), in the gravel pits on Day's Lane and at the forge. Some commuted to Bedford, or to London, as Mr Stanton, who lived at Abbotsbury near the war memorial, did by 1935. The farm and gravel pit workers laboured outdoors in all weathers, and as we have already learnt from Albert Church's memoirs, they were glad to get the work. M L Simpson, in her Regional Survey of Biddenham in 1938, pointed out that although the climate of Biddenham is temperate, 'the land surrounding the parish of Biddenham is very flat, thus allowing the bleak cold winds in winter to sweep over the village. There is consequently a great deal of frost during the winter months.'[59]

56 – Church Farm House, 1922

In addition, there could be heavy rain to contend with - 'in the February of 1937, the Ouse was in flood,'[60] or drought - 'in 1938 there was a spring drought, causing great loss and anxiety for the farmers. The rain which occurred at the end of May saved the farmers' crops.'[61]

The men working at the gravel pits braved all the elements, their hard work by hand with pick and shovel being alleviated only by beer. Albert Church remembers that 'it would be one man's job every two hours to fetch beer from the Tuns in a jug.'[62] The pits, at the top of Day's Lane, were worked by Jarvis of Midland Road, and most of the carting of sand and gravel was done by Hull of Queen's Park, using horses. The horses had to work hard to take the gravel to the tip on the Bromham Road on the Bedford side of Day's Lane. A massive black shire horse had to pull the trams full of gravel up to the tip: at the steepest point, the horse could only manage two trams. The Biddenham Estate collected the royalties from the gravel workings.[63] By about 1930 the Day's Lane pits had been worked out. The pits were closed, and all topsoil was put back on the bottom, and banks sloped so that they could be cultivated or sown down for pasture. M L Simpson wrote that Mr Rawlins used the land as chicken run[64]. Two other places were tried where there was known to be gravel – on the Baulk on the right-hand side, and by the river to the left of Honeyhill Farm - but in both places there was not enough depth of gravel to make working it a worthwhile proposition.[65]

The gravel pits provided work for the village smithy, sharpening the picks. A man would bring half a dozen each night, and collect them in the morning.[66] The forge was also a vital part of village life, and an important employer in an age when horses were still widely used, and tools needed to be repaired quickly and locally. William Davison, whose son was killed in World War I, was the village blacksmith from 1884 until 1929, when Leonard Herbert took over. Mr Davison had been apprenticed at Lavendon, and he in his turn took a number of pupils, including his cousin, William Branson of Queen's Park. William Davison did not just shoe horses and repair machinery; he also crafted scrollwork for St James's Church, and made bicycles, which were inscribed with his name and proprietary 'Cable' brand.

57 – The smithy, 1921.
Left to right: Donald Dowler, apprentice to blacksmith; Joe Davison, brother of Bill Davison; Len Herbert, succeeded Bill, and was the last blacksmith in Biddenham. He died in 1966.

Bicycles provided a useful means of transport out of the village for school and work in the inter-war years. Alan Evans, in an article in the *Biddenham Bulletin* in April 2004, remembered that after his family moved to Biddenham in 1937, his brother cycled to the station each day to catch the train to London to go to work. The London Midland and Scottish trains ran through Bedford from Midland Road station, and the London North Eastern ran from St. John's.[67]

Alan Evans's brother was not the only man to use these trains.

Albert Church and Alan Evans both mention in their memories that Maurice Stanton, who had joined the Bank of England after leaving Bedford Modern School, cycled from Abbotsbury, the house that he built on Main Road, Biddenham, in 1935, to the station to catch the train to London. Alan Evans remembers that he had 'a very upright bicycle and wore a homburg hat and city suit. If it was wet he always cycled with his big black umbrella up.'

Many of the Biddenham residents who worked, or went to school, in Bedford used the bus service. There were about 15 buses a day, run by the Eastern National Company, linking Bedford, Biddenham and Bromham.[68] Alan Evans used the bus to travel to Bedford to attend Bedford Modern School after September 1939. He caught the bus from the village green.[69] Very few people had their own cars. Mr Percy Shurety, the sexton and son of the church caretaker, had two cars which he had available for private hire.[70] By 1938 M L Simpson commented that the village was more of a dormitory for Bedford.[71] The gravel pits were worked out, therefore apart from the farms and businesses like the forge, the men had to look further afield and rely upon improved transport to get employment.

Some women also worked outside the village. At Easter 1920 Emmeline Tanner became headmistress of Bedford High School. During the summer holiday in 1920 she found her home for the four years that she was to spend at Bedford High before moving on to be Headmistress of Roedean in 1924. The home was Murree Cottage (now Buttercups) in Biddenham. She remembered the glory of the thatched cottage, and particularly its garden: sweet-scented in the spring with purple violets, and later heavy with fruit - greengages, plums, apples, raspberries and strawberries. Emmeline, or more often her gardener, Mortimer, grew vegetables too, to lavish seasonally on her friends and relations. From the cottage she cycled daily to the school behind a large basket crammed with books and papers, even when evening events were in prospect, decked in the full evening dress which was de rigueur on many occasions.[72]

Alan Evans mentioned that his sister, Rita, known as Peg, first worked in E P Rose's shop (now Debenhams) after leaving school. She then went on to work in a drawing office in Elstow Road, before nursing at Bromham hospital at the start of World War II.[73] Other women either moved to the village as a consequence of their employment, or found jobs in the village. Edith Church, Albert's wife, came to Biddenham as a nanny in 1927, when her employers, the owners of the Bridge Hotel, moved into a new house on Biddenham Turn.[74] M L Simpson pointed out that by 1938 lacemaking was a declining industry in the county. In Biddenham there were two very old ladies who were still making lace to give away as presents or to sell to a small circle of people. They were Mrs Sharpe, who lived at Church End, and Mrs Tysoe, who lived at the end of the village street just near Gold Lane. It was a contrast to earlier days remembered by Mrs Davis, the Postmistress, who said that when she was seven, she had to make so much lace a day before she was allowed out to play.[75]

The post office was a steady source of employment for men and women. By the beginning of the 20th century the post office had moved from the school house to the post office row of cottages. Mr and Miss Ingram were postmaster and postmistress for many years. In 1934 the post office moved to Penny Black Cottage, and Mrs Davis, a widow, became postmistress and ran a general store as well as the post office.[76] Mrs Davis was a formidable woman who, perhaps unknown to her customers, had two truncheons hanging behind the door. It was possible to buy a wide variety of items, and not just stamps. Telegrams could be sent, and there was a public telephone box. There was a postbox outside, and also one near

Manor Farm, Church End. There were two collections and two deliveries each day.[77] George, the postman, delivered letters and collected and repaired shoes. Alan Evans remembers that:

Houses had no numbers then, only names, and he walked up the long driveways to each house and he always read any postcards before he put them through the door. On Boxing Day he used to call for his yearly Christmas box; each year he had a small notebook where he recorded each payment, and used it to check back on previous years' amounts.[78]

Miss D D Steel (sister of Miss Evelyn Steel) became a legend in the croquet world. Before World War I she was already considered the finest exponent of the game in the world. She went on to win the open croquet championship (for men and women) four times between 1925 and 1931, and won the women's championship 15 times. According to a press report at the time '... Vigorous, small, sturdy, with red country cheeks and Irish blue eyes, she hunts in winter and croquets in summer'.

The school employed a schoolmistress, Mrs Cork, who had lived next door to the school. She used to have two helpers when the school was much larger, but by 1938 there were only 16 pupils. They only stayed at the Biddenham school until they were 10, when they were collected by bus each day and taken to school in Kempston.[79] M L Simpson commented that by 1938 some of the older boys and girls who lived in the village attended either Bedford High School or Bedford School, or one of the Modern Schools (boys or girls).[80]

The village policeman did not live in Biddenham: he lived in a police house in Bromham, and had to look after Bromham, Stagsden and Biddenham. Alan Evans remembers he patrolled the village on his bicycle, and could be seen most times of day and night somewhere in the village. He knew everybody by name, and used your name when he met you. He was a nice person, and was liked by all the villagers. House doors and cars were never locked: crime hardly existed. In 1938 the young van drivers from the Bedford shops were racing each other through the village to be first in and then on to Bromham. PC Wells stood at the Green and stopped each vehicle, so the racing stopped. There was the occasional £2 fine for the odd cycle without lights, and you had to be out of the Tuns when 'time' was called![81]

By the mid-1930s the level of public services depended upon where you lived in the village. This was because in 1934 the eastern part of the parish of Biddenham was transferred to the Borough of Bedford.[82] As a result, street lighting stopped at St Mary's House on Main Road and there was a distinct line in Biddenham Turn coming into the village, where the tarmac on the road finished and gravel started.[83]

In 1938 the parish council managed the western part of the parish of Biddenham, except for Day's Lane, which was managed by Tristram Eve as part of Colonel Wingfield's estate. [84] The council met every quarter. In 1938 there were a clerk and six councillors, all men. The chairman was Mr Henman, and the other councillors were Messrs Pile, Herbert, Holland, Burton and Church. The topic for discussion in the summer of 1938 was air-raid precautions, and further orders were awaited.[85]

The straw barn at Clay Farm, which had been converted into a canteen for the soldiers billeted in the village during World War I, had become a village hall, used as a centre for plays, whist drives, dances and meetings by the late 1930s. Alan Evans recalls in his memoirs in the *Biddenham Bulletin* in 2004 and 2007 that the hall was a large barn with a stage at one end and a counter for refreshments at the other. The ladies' cloakroom was next to the stage, but the men put their coats in the hallway at the entrance. The hall was heated by a coke stove which was against the wall on one side, to the right of the door. Apparently if you were near the stove you roasted, but if you were opposite to it you froze. The area outside the hall was still used as a farm 'with cattle in enclosures on the right as you came to the entrance. You arrived at the hall dressed for a dance, with cows and bullocks watching your every move.'[86] The *Bedfordshire Times* reported on 7 January 1938 that a New Year's Eve social had been held in the village hall, with games and dancing arranged by the village hall committee.

Although many people worked or went to school in Bedford, there was a thriving social life in Biddenham in the 1920s and 1930s, much of it using the village hall as a base for meetings. For men and boys, there was the boys' club, which met in the village hall every week, the Three Tuns darts club and the cricket club. Alan Evans remembers playing other clubs from Bedford and the surrounding villages on a field that was 'far from flat, had many weeds and where the players had to watch out for cowpats.'[87]

Boys and girls could go to the youth club started by Muriel Cork, the daughter of the schoolteacher, which had outings to places such as St Alban's Cathedral. The 1956 WI scrapbook records that by the 1930s there was a flourishing branch of the Girls' Friendly Society under Miss Haffenden, and in addition to Sunday school, Mrs Dobbs had started a handwork class for boys with the Reverend William Norman's approval. About 12 boys met one evening a week in the schoolroom during the winter months. They made useful things such as calendars, jigsaws, wool mats and rush seated stools, which were sold at the annual social in the village hall. The boys had an annual trip to London, and by the time the Reverend Douglas Carey came to the village, they could join the men's fellowship, which he organised for when the boys were older.[88]

The Biddenham branch of the Women's Institute, which was

formed in 1922, was an important activity for the women in the village. There was a close link with the church, as the first president was Mrs W B Norman, the wife of the vicar, and the secretary was Mrs Manning, the wife of the churchwarden.[89] In 1938 Mrs Carey, the new vicar's wife, was president.[90] Meetings were held every second Wednesday in the month. There was a variety of activities, though one of the most popular was the annual tea and social evening for the older village inhabitants. At the earlier teas, the vicar said grace, and after the tea there were plays, games, competitions, community singing (Mr W West gave an old-fashioned song in rollicking style when he was 86), and gifts for the old people.[91] The *Bedford Record* of 31 May 1938 had a photograph of 40 old people from the village attending the annual tea provided by the WI.

The WI also had activities for its own members. There was an annual supper and social, when prizes were presented for the year's competitions. The drama group put on plays to entertain other WIs. In 1922 a folk-dancing team was formed, which performed at the popular annual garden meetings of the WI. The team only dispersed in 1939, due to the outbreak of World War II. The WI also revived the flower show, which it ran until the outbreak of World War II. 1931 was an exciting year for the Biddenham WI, as the members took part in the pageant presented by the county federation. The home-made costumes look beautiful in the photographs preserved in the 1956 scrapbook. Finally, for women, many of whom might not have travelled very far, there was the annual outing to a place of interest. In the 1930s Windsor Castle, Chatsworth, the Royal Worcester China factory and the Huntley and Palmer's biscuit factory at Reading were all visited.[92]

Music, especially choral singing, brought men and women together in the village. In 1927 the Glee singers, which had started as a men's choir in 1925, became a mixed choir with

39 members. The choir disbanded at the end of the 1920s, but it was re-formed and conducted by Mrs Paul, and then Mrs Slaughter, until it lapsed in 1939 with the outbreak of war and other demands on men's and women's time.[93] The *Bedfordshire Times* of 8 April 1938 reported a very successful concert by the village choral society in its heyday at the village hall.

A more unusual activity was reported by the *Bedford Record* of 31 May 1938. This was a meeting of the Walter Hines Page chapter of the Daughters of the American Revolution at the home of Mrs F Carpenter-Holland-Griffith, The Close, Biddenham. Alan Evans remembers her as an 'American living on her own in a very large house with a large garden. The house was more or less a club for American officers during the war at her invitation.'[94]

In the interwar years not many people were able to afford holidays, as Ted Pile remembered in the *Biddenham Bulletin* in July, 1987, so the main excitements for Biddenham residents were the annual outings like those organised by the WI. Albert Church in his memoirs described an outing that the Biddenham farm-hands had to the Wembley Exhibition in 1921.[95] Mr Whitworth of Church Farm paid for his workmen to go on the new double-decker bus as a treat after harvest. Albert Church and his friends filled up the spare spaces. However, their boss, Mr Chibnall of Grove Farm, let them have the day off, but they had to pay their own fare and lose a day's pay.

Albert remembers:

My mother made an extra large clanger on Friday so that it would be cold for Saturday morning for my father and me to share. We also took the bottom of a cottage loaf and one or two raw onions - in fact the same routine as if we were having our dinner in the fields at Biddenham. I believe it was put into my father's old rush basket. A nine-gallon barrel of beer was put on the back of the bus, under the stairs on a proper wooden trestle and tapped.

Plenty of beer was drunk on the way, but dinner was eaten on the steps of Wembley Stadium:

We younger ones were sent back to collect the baskets and everyone got seated on the steps. What a sight this must have been for onlookers to see about forty men from the country sitting with their baver baskets complete with strap or cord and opening a lovely white cloth to reveal the pork and onion clanger together with the cottage loaves and onion to go with it.

The older men had more to drink at the workingmen's club at Potters Bar on the way home: a man called Joe 'to use his own words was "full of beer right up to his collar stud" ..... what a day to remember.

Early aviation had already provided excitement in 1911 when Claude Graham-White, who attended Bedford School from 1892 to 1906, and was a friend of Bill Davison, the village blacksmith, had landed a plane on the field below the church. This event had attracted the crowds, and after World War I people were prepared to pay two shillings to be taken up in a biplane from the fields east of Biddenham Turn. Such was the novelty of flying. These rides were stopped when one of the biplanes crashed, killing a man, whose body was taken to the village morgue behind the Three Tuns.[96]

Tragedy struck again in 1930. At 7 pm on 4 October the giant airship R101, which had been built at Cardington, circled Bedford and came over Biddenham, before setting off for India. On the Sunday morning, 5 October, it crashed at Beauvais in France, and 48 men aboard were burned to death.[97]

Royal occasions also provided a reason for celebration for everyone in the village. In 1935 King George V's Silver Jubilee was marked by a procession led by the drum and fife band of All Saints' Church Lads' Brigade. Fancy dress was worn for the procession. Mr H Peacock was particularly splendid in Tudor costume. The procession went to the sports field, where there were games, races and competitions. Mrs A Dowler won the ankle competition for the ladies! In the late afternoon, the villagers sat down to a meat tea in the village hall. There were so many wanting to attend that the partition in the hall was taken down, and two other barns had to be used to accommodate all the people. Dancing in the evening rounded off the day. [98]

The coronation of King George VI and Queen Elizabeth on 12 May 1937 was celebrated with a peal of the church bells, a well-attended church service and a civic procession from the far end of the Green to the field opposite Day's Lane, where sports were held. For the procession a mayor and corporation were elected for the day only. Mr Herbert Green, the landlord of the Three Tuns, was the mayor, and Mr H Peacock invested him with the chain of office. The mayor promised to:

Guard the rights and privileges of his fellow men, cause to be kept open and maintained all pathways and roads, taste all beer and see that it is of good quality, encourage young people in healthy games, see that lovers are not disturbed in their pleasant walks, punish all rogues and vagabonds, succour the aged and infirm and act as father and counsellor in all cases of difficulty and domestic quarrels. He then presented new coins to the old age pensioners and a good day was had by all.[99]

The new reign saw the village in celebratory mood. Although more people were leaving each day to work in Bedford, they returned at night and took part in the village activities. The church and the Wingfield Estate still played an important part in village life. John Rawlins, the son of Fred Rawlins who farmed at Church Farm, Manor Farm, Honeyhill Farm and Grove Farm by 1937, recalled in an interview with Mary McKeown in December 2010 that he met Mr Wingfield once in the village and asked him who he was. He replied 'I'm the landlord'. John said, 'He was GOD!!'

Nevertheless, events in Europe were once again about to impact upon Biddenham and affect the social order. In September 1938, the British Prime Minister, Neville Chamberlain, arrived back from meeting Hitler at the Munich conference waving the 'scrap of paper' whereby Britain and Germany renounced warlike intentions against each other. Chamberlain remarked 'I believe it is peace for our time'.

It was not to be.

References.

1   WI scrapbook, 1956, p 33, at BLARS.
2   R.W.Rideout, *Bromham in Bedfordshire: a History*, (2002), p 155.
3   *Stevington: The Village History* (Stevington Historical Trust, 2001) p 269.
4   We are grateful to Martin Edwards and his website www.roll-of-honour.com for helping to provide information about the men commemorated on the Biddenham war memorial.
5   Report in the *Bedfordshire Times*, 27 April 1917.
6   Information obtained from a report in the *Bedfordshire Times*, 27 April 1917, and the *National Roll of the Great War*, 1914-18 Section XII Bedford and Northampton, p 74.
7   Vera Brittain, *Testament of Youth* (Virago, 1978), p 371.
8   Information obtained from the *National Roll of the Great War*, 1914-18 Section XII Bedford and Northampton. His family commented 'His memory is cherished with pride'.
9   *National Roll of the Great War, 1914-18* Section XII Bedford and Northampton, p 74.
10   WI scrapbook, 1956, p32, at BLARS.
11   *National Roll of the Great War, 1914-1918* Section XII Bedford and Northampton, p 39.
12   Ibid. p 101.

13   Ibid.

14   WI scrapbook, 1956, p 26, at BLARS.

15   *National Roll of the Great War 1914-1918* Section XII, Bedford and Northampton, p 200, and information supplied by his grandson, Richard Church in *Biddenham Bulletin* February 2009.

16   Ibid, p 28.

17   Ibid, pp 30 and 74.

18   Ibid. p 74.

19   Ibid.

20   Ibid p 100.

21   *Bedfordshire Times*, 11 January 1918 and 31 May 1918.

22   Dorothy Richards, *Biddenham. A Parish History and Guide* (New Moon, 1991), p 40.

23   Edited J Godber and I Hutchins, *A Century of Challenge. Bedford High School 1882-1982*, Charles Elphick, Bedfordshire, p 480.

24   Dorothy Richards, op. cit., p 40.

25   Albert Church, *Recollections of My Life in Biddenham*. p 10.

26   Ibid. p 10.

27   Ibid. p 10.

28   Ibid. p 43.

29   *Aquila*, November 1914, at BGS.

30   Albert Church, op. cit., p 10.

31   *Aquila*, November 1914, at BGS.

32   Albert Church, op. cit , p 13.

33   *Aquila*, November 1915. Letter from the Bedford College, London, correspondent, at BGS.

34   Albert Church, op. cit , p 10.

35   Ibid. p 10.

36   *Bedfordshire Times and Independent* 17 August 1917.

37   Albert Church, op. cit., p 21.

38   Ibid. p 21.

39   Ibid. p 24.

40   Ibid. p 22.

41   Ibid. p 23.

42   Ibid. p 26.

43   Ibid. p.26.

44   *Bedfordshire Times and Independent* 1 November 1918.

45   *National Roll of the Great War, 1914-1918* Section XII Bedford and Northampton, p 48.

46   Ibid.

47   Dorothy Richards, op. cit., p 21.

48 Ibid. p 34.
49 Albert Church, op. cit., p 29.
50 Ibid. p 30.
51 Ibid. pp 30 and 31.
52 Ibid. p 31.
53 Ibid. p 29.
54 Ibid. p 35.
55 Ibid. p 32.
56 WI scrapbook, 1956, p 21, at BLARS.
57 Albert Church, op. cit., p 33.
58 Ibid. p 34.
59 M L Simpson, *Regional Survey of Biddenham,* 1938, p 14.
60 Ibid. p 14.
61 Ibid. p 14.
62 Albert Church, op. cit, p 32.
63 Ibid. p 32.
64 M L Simpson, op. cit, p 90.
65 Ibid. p 33.
66 Ibid. p 32.
67 M L Simpson, op. cit., p 12.
68 Ibid. p 12.
69 Alan Evans in *Biddenham Bulletin*, April 2004.
70 M L Simpson, op. cit., p 12.
71 Ibid. p 89.
72 Susan Major, *Doors of Possibility – The Life of Emmeline Tanner 1876-1955* (Lutterworth Press, Cambridge, 1995), p 181.
73 Alan Evans in *Biddenham Bulletin,* April 2004.
74 Profile of Edith Church by Diana Toyn in *Biddenham Bulletin*, March 1994.
75 M L Simpson, op. cit., p 85.
76 WI Scrapbook, 1956, p 22, at BLARS.
77 M L Simpson, op. cit., p 13.
78 Alan Evans in *Biddenham Bulletin*, November 2003.
79 M L Simpson, op. cit., p 117.
80 Ibid. p 118.
81 Alan Evans in *Biddenham Bulletin*, November, 2007.
82 Dorothy Richards, op. cit, p 10.
83 Alan Evans in *Biddenham Bulletin*, February 2004.
84 M L Simpson, op. cit., p 119.
85 Ibid. p 119.
86 Alan Evans, op. cit.

87   Alan Evans, op. cit.

88   WI scrapbook 1956, p 43, at BLARS.

89   Ibid. p 37.

90   M L Simpson, op. cit, p 120.

91   WI scrapbook, 1956, p 37, at BLARS.

92   Ibid. p 37-41.

93   Ibid. p 42.

94   Alan Evans in *Biddenham Bulletin*, November, 2003.

95   Albert Church, op. cit., p 27-28.

96   Dorothy Richards, op. cit., p 10.

97   Ibid. p.10.

98   WI scrapbook, 1956, p 35, at BLARS.

99   Ibid. p 35.

CHAPTER 9

EDUCATION - PART 1
THE VILLAGE SCHOOL 1832 TO 1944

58 – St James' school

St James's Infants' School opened in 1832, in Main Road opposite the Three Tuns. Later the name was changed to St James Church of England Voluntary Aided Lower School, and it is now known as St James' Church of England (VA) Lower School. The school is maintained by the state, being part of Bedford borough council's provision for state education. However, the Church of England owns the school buildings, and is responsible for their repair and upkeep.

The earliest reference to education in Biddenham was in 1706, when a Bishop's Visitation reported that there was no school in Biddenham[1]. However, by 1818 (when the population of the village was 310), the vicar, the Rev Shuttleworth Grimshawe, stated in his reply to a circular letter from the Select Committee on Education of the Poor that there were no endowments for education in the village, although there was by this time a day school, with numbers varying from 10 to 30, supported by parental contributions. There was also a Sunday school, which would also have taught children to read the Bible, maintained by Mr Grimshawe, with 70 to 80 pupils. Mr Grimshawe observed that 'the poorer classes are desirous of having the means of education'.[2]

The 1833 Factory Act introduced a compulsory two hours of schooling each day for children, and in the same year the education returns now refer to three daily schools, principally for lacemaking, with 30 pupils (presumably all girls). There was also an evening school for 'about 15 males'. These schools were supported by parental payments. In addition there were now two Sunday schools – one for 35 males, supported by the minister, and the other for 40 females, supported by the parish. Books for both these schools were provided by Mr Grimshawe.[3]

The demand for education was growing, and the first purpose-built school opened in 1832, with accommodation for 90 pupils. Financed by private subscription and the church, it consisted of one classroom, which was attached to the schoolteacher's house, built the same year. St James's church, through the Vestry, subscribed £6 a year, [4] and the vicar, Mr Grimshawe, gave £5 per annum.[5]

From the 1841 census returns for Biddenham, we find that the population was 345, living in 61 inhabited houses. Of these, 69 were children between the ages of four and 12. The census does not record how many of these children were attending the village school.

However, by 1843 the school had 41 pupils and a school return says 'In reading 31 not advanced beyond monosyllables, but two boys and one girl able to read with ease … five boys wrote on slates, and one boy and one girl on paper. None seem to have attempted arithmetic. … The children are clean and orderly'. The mistress at this time 'was trained in the Home and Colonial establishment'.[6] The school house had a small yard, and the size of the schoolroom was 32 x 18 x 10 ft.[7] (There were no wells, no pumps and consequently no water. There were only outside earth closets for the pupils, which were emptied once a week).

Minutes of the Committee of Council on Education in 1845 state that the school was now aided by grants from the Lords of the Treasury, and Mr Grimshawe was the sole trustee of the school. 'The children are in good order, cheerful and well behaved. Ten read the New Testament; four write their names; spelling good; arithmetic decent; very good and intelligent answers on religious subjects. Mistress intelligent and successful in teaching'.[8] Mrs Grimshawe, the vicar's wife, also took a keen interest in the school.[9]

The following year a Church School Inquiry reported that the infant school, consisting of 23 boys and 27 girls, was 'united to the National Society'.[10] This was as a result of the nonconformist churches having inaugurated the 'British Schools' in order to make similar provision for nonconformist schools in 1814.[11] The National Society, and hence the church, owned the Biddenham school building, and was responsible for its repair and upkeep.

An assistant mistress had been added to the staff. The mistress was paid £40 per annum, and the school was funded by 'endowment, local subscriptions and school pence from the children'.[12] The school house was attached to the school, the site having been donated by the Rice Trevor family of Bromham.[13]

Craven's Directory, 1853, notes that Mary Nichols is the infant schoolmistress and also the postmistress. 35 boys and 25 girls attended the school then. Since the 1851 census notes that there are 37 infants and 52 'scholars' in the village, it seems that most of the children in the village were now attending school. A second classroom, the infants' room, was added in 1860. This room originally had a gallery backing on to the north wall (it was removed in 1918).

The state did not take responsibility for education until the 1870 Education Act (commonly known as the 'Forster Act'), which made provision for the elementary education of all children aged five to 13. These elementary schools were for the working class. They provided a restricted curriculum, with the emphasis almost exclusively on the '3Rs' (reading, writing and 'rithmetic), and they pursued other, less clearly defined, aims including social-disciplinary objectives (acceptance of the teacher's authority, the need for punctuality, obedience and conformity). The schools operated the 'monitorial' system, whereby a teacher supervised a large class with assistance from a team of monitors (usually older pupils).[14]

Six years later, 'Sandon's Act' placed a duty on parents to ensure that their children attended school. In 1880 a further Act made attendance compulsory for children between the ages of five and 10. Schooling was also compulsory up to the age of 14, unless an exemption certificate was granted. For this, the child had to have attended school 250 times per year for 10-12-year-olds, and 150 times for those over the age of 12. An exemption certificate could also be granted if the child had obtained a labour certificate, which was proof that the child had reached the educational standard required by local by-laws, and/or had a paid job to go to.

We have no record of admissions in the 19th century, as St James school admissions register doesn't begin until 26 March 1900. At the front of the book the pupils are listed alphabetically, and each is given a number, starting at 1. In the second part of the register the pupils' details are given –

date of birth, parent's name, date of admission, date of leaving, reason for leaving, and, at the far right-hand side, columns for recording whether the child has had measles, whooping cough, chickenpox, diphtheria, scarlet fever or mumps. The reasons for leaving, in the early years of the 20th century, were 'left the village', '14 years old', 'gone to work', 'labour certificate' or 'certificate of exemption'. However, one in 1907 had 'gone to Modern School', and in 1909 and 1910 two children had 'gone to private school'. Ages on admission were surprisingly young in some cases – occasionally a child only three years old was admitted, and several aged four.

Not until 1877 do the school logbooks (which began in 1873) record the number of pupils attending the school. In that year the average attendance was about 40, and by 1885 the average had risen to nearly 60. However, during the next 15 years the numbers fluctuated between the 30s and the 50s. In 1882 there is a comment 'many of the boys are absent on account of the haymaking'. There is little mention of bad behaviour or punishments during this time, except that in May 1873 a boy was expelled because of 'his mother's interference', and he wasn't reinstated until early in September.

Teachers' pay in those days was 'by result', and Miss Nichols, headmistress from 1847 to 1875, was not, by the last year of her tenure, doing very well. In October 1875, after the diocesan inspector's annual visit, the grant for the school was reduced by one-tenth because of the pupils' 'poor performance in arithmetic'. Miss Nichols was replaced later that year by Miss H Felts, and immediately the Rev Henry Wood, the vicar, in addition to his regular visits to the school, usually three times a week, for religious instruction, and 'lessons on singing from notes', began teaching arithmetic. However, the following year's report from the diocesan inspector praised Miss Felts for having 'improved the school considerably. The sewing, writing and spelling more especially are good'. But this time the report criticised the instruction of the infants, and there was a threat that the school's grant might again be reduced.

Several times during this period the school was closed for up to two weeks because of an outbreak of measles, whooping cough, mumps or chickenpox. Often children did not come to school if the weather was bad – presumably because they lacked suitable clothing or footwear.

The vicar's wife visited the school about once a month, and from 1876 regular needlework lessons for the girls were arranged, Miss Golding coming to the school for this purpose. In 1881 she was joined by Miss Wood (presumably the vicar's daughter), who came to 'assist with knitting'.

Over the years the logbooks gradually became more detailed. From 1877 mention is made of the annual examination of the pupils for bible knowledge and the catechism. In the 1880s prizes were being given to the girls for sewing. In 1895, when Miss E M Goodwin was appointed headmistress, there were the first recorded instances of punishments, including for disobedience, idleness, inattention, untruthfulness and for 'being dirty' - although we are not told what form the punishment took.

Diocesan inspection reports improved greatly over the rest of the 19th century. From the early 1880s the school attendance officer was visiting the school about once a month – this was the time when the head teacher's salary was linked to school attendance figures. During the 1890s the leaving age was raised twice – first to 11 in 1893, and then to 12 in 1899.

At the beginning of the 20th century the staff consisted of Miss Goodwin (a 'certified teacher'), C West, pupil teacher (4th year) and G Smith, probationer. By now there was an average of 40 pupils in the school, and the vicar was giving religious instruction three times a week. Object-lessons became popular: subjects covered in 1901 and 1902 included 'hive bees', 'coffee', 'the care of lamps' and 'the Post Office Savings Bank'.

Ted Pile started at the village school in 1906, when he was five years old. He recalls:

The headmistress was Miss Goodwin, who lived in Bedford, and the infants' teacher, Miss Hebbes, lived in Biddenham.

In the big classroom the desks were in three lines, parallel to the wall behind us, and we sat facing the other wall, on which were hung large pictures which reflected what was going by on the road behind us. When the horses and hounds went by, and the huntsmen in their red coats, we knew they were fox hunting somewhere in the village. This was a signal for us boys to follow the hounds and not go home for our dinners, nor back to school in the afternoon. Once after fox hunting all day, we ended up along the Turvey Road about five miles from home, and, being hungry, we went into a farmer's field and pulled some white turnips, which went down jolly well, and then we had to walk all the way home. The next morning we had to go before the Head Governess [the headmistress] and explain why we played truant, away from school all day. After we had the cane, we were made to stand in the porch, and when it was all over we went back to our desks. We had a good day fox hunting, and it was well worth a good hiding.

I stayed at Biddenham school until I was 11 years old, when father thought I should go to Bromham school where there was a headmaster named Mr Grundy, who was very strict. I was just under 13 years old when I left.[15]

From 1907 all schoolchildren had to receive a medical inspection. In the same year there is the first record of prizes being given by the county council for perfect attendance, good conduct and progress. Children could still obtain a labour certificate, enabling them to leave school a year early, at the age of 13, if it could be demonstrated that their school work was of a reasonable standard.

59 - Labour Certificate, Mary Mason, 1908

The school was still receiving 'excellent' reports at the annual diocesan inspection. The 1908 diocesan report commented on the pupils' *viva voce* examination that 'in each of the three divisions of the school all the subjects have been well taught, the children answered remarkably well, and showed much intelligence'. At the beginning of 1910 there were 32 pupils. Albert Church, who started at the school in about 1910, did not remember his school days with Miss Goodwin as his happiest:

Although this lady was the headmistress of the school, she was referred to as the Governess, and her assistant was the infant teacher. The Governess always wore black, and during school hours a black apron. This was kept at school in her desk, with the cane and the pointer. The pointer was always in the Governess's hand. It was used just as much to give you a rap on the knuckles as to point out something on the blackboard. More often than not our fingernails were dirty, and if you were writing [at your] desk and the Governess came behind you and your nails were noticed, down would come the pointer on your fingers, and you would be told to clean them before you came to school again. You could not clean them at school, as there was no water, not even a well or a pump. There was an old tub standing against the coal barn, which caught a little rainwater off the roof, but the tub was so cracked with age, and the bottom full of rotten leaves, that the water was filthy. Of course our hands were dirty, because we did things we should not have done after our parents had us ready for school.[16]

In Albert's time at the school, the pupils were taken on a 'class walk', usually to the Baulk, by the infant teacher. On Ascension Day they marched down to the church with the vicar for a short service, after which the rest of the day was a holiday (a practice that continued for many years).

In January 1913 there were 46 pupils, and Bedford education committee awarded prizes for merit as well as the usual attendance prizes. This year two boys were sent home with 'verminous heads'.

The 1914-1918 war affected village life – on 23 April 1915 a pupil was excluded by the schools medical officer until 10 May 'as a soldier billeted in the house has measles'. A month later 'a lecture on hygiene and temperance was given'.

Miss Goodwin resigned in February 1916, and Miss Chitham was appointed later in the year. Towards the end of March 1916 there was such a heavy fall of snow and rain that only 21 pupils attended. 'Two girls … arrived at school in such a wet condition that they had to be sent home again' – by which time they must have been really wretched.

During the War the children were frequently taken for a nature ramble for about an hour in the afternoon, and also we first find mention of exams (other than in religious subjects) – the 3Rs in the upper classes, and 'an examination' in the infants' room. In 1917 a lesson was given on 'inadvertent disclosures of military information', as requested by the Education Committee. On 8 June 1916 'the children were taken this morning to see the inspection of the Welsh Division of the troops stationed in Bedford by Lord French. The inspection took place in the village'. An inkling of some of the problems of daily life at the school is gained from the following entry for 1 February 1917 – 'Miss Hebbes left school at 10 o'clock to get the cheque cashed at Bedford. Owing to a puncture, she had to walk, arriving back at 11.30'. It is interesting that this event was considered worthy of record. On 22 March there is a note that 'The upper girls have been allowed to view an aeroplane in an adjoining field'. Maybe the upper boys weren't considered well behaved enough to go too, but it would certainly have appealed to them. On 27 June 1918 'The school is closed this afternoon owing to the visit of the King and Queen to Bedford'.

Very little was mentioned in the logbook during the 1914-1918 War about its impact on the village. There was a similar reticence in the logbook for Felmersham village school.[17] However, Biddenham school did close on the afternoon of 11 November 1918 'For the signing of peace'.

In October and November 1918 – the year the school leaving age was raised to 14 - the school was closed for two long periods because of an outbreak of influenza. This was no doubt due to the pandemic which swept through Europe between June 1918 and December 1920. In 1918 and 1919 there must have been some concern about food shortages, as the children were given three afternoons of holiday in the blackberrying season in both these years. Kenneth Shrimpton quotes Felmersham village school logbook recording that the children 'continue their work of National Importance viz Blackberry picking'. He comments 'No mention is made of why it was so important, but they picked over 4 cwt each week and received 1¾d per pound towards school books'.[18] A programme of weighing schoolchildren began at this time too, and the children were weighed four times in 1919.

In 1919 five girls were sent home 'with dirty heads' – presumably head lice. About this time nature walks were started.

From the turn of the century until 1925 the average attendance was between 30 and 40. 1918 was the first year that the observation of Empire Day was recorded for the school – on 24 May 'The Education Committee programme was observed this morning'. Thereafter Empire Day was observed every May until 1958.

60 – St James' school Empire Day celebration, May 1908

On the first anniversary of the end of the War, it is noted that 'The request of the King concerning fallen soldiers and sailors was observed this morning', and on 11 November 1921 the Two Minutes' Silence was observed by the school.

A new sign of the government's concern over the health of the country's children is the visit early in 1920 of the school dentist and nurse, which thereafter became a regular feature of school life. Also in 1920 there are the first references to regular examinations in the school, taking place in December, and then the following March.

61 – St James' school group, 1920.
Left to right: Back row: Mrs Riddy (teacher), Flora Sergeant, Irene Jackson, Charlie Bransom, ? Burley, Eva West.
Middle row: Marjorie Burton, Dorothy West, Phyllis Wiles, Mary Faulkener, Lily Stringer, Queenie Cartwright, Eunice Frossell.
Front row: G Davis, E Church, R Tebbutt, E Johnson, C Shaw, S Dudley, G Cambers.

In 1921 Miss Chitham noted on 7 November 'On my arrival at school this morning 2 fires were out and the rooms registered only 40°'. She resigned in 1923, and was followed by a series of temporary headmistresses. The school was reorganised so that it now catered for children only up to the age of 11, when they moved on to Bromham school, or occasionally to Queen's Park or Kempston. Miss H M Haffenden was appointed headmistress in 1925. The Rev William Norman was taking religious instruction three times per week. [For a photograph of Miss Haffenden and the Rev William Norman with the scholars, see Chapter 4, Figure 38].

Three years later Miss Haffenden was replaced by a temporary headmistress, Miss B E Hill, and the number of pupils had fallen to about 20. Miss Hill was followed by a series of temporary headmistresses until 1934, and the average number of pupils dropped until in 1934 there were only 10 pupils. The diocesan inspection in 1932 was non-committal, commenting that the school was 'Conducted with great kindness, the children are kept well occupied and are evidently happy'.

By 1933, however, the diocesan report was more encouraging:

It is evident that the work in this school is being undertaken earnestly and capably. The children were questioned quite closely over a fair range of the work taken, and the answers given, although almost entirely confined to the older children, showed a very good grasp of the work. It is quite clear that the children normally take an active share in the instruction given, and in their response they were lively and intelligent. There is a singularly happy tone in the school, which reflects a friendly relationship between those who teach and those who learn.

At last in May 1934 a new headmistress was appointed – Mrs Ruth Cork. Mrs Cork had a very difficult start, due to the long period during which the school was run by temporary head teachers, and also because an outbreak of illness brought the attendance figures down to a very low level.

By May 1936 the number attending the school had dropped to eight, and the school attendance officer was making frequent visits. The vicar, Mr Douglas Carey, was visiting twice a week for scripture lessons.

The outbreak of World War II caused a significant upheaval in the school, with the arrival of the teachers and 40 pupils of Mora Road School, Cricklewood, London. In addition to about 14 children who were evacuated privately to families in the village during the course of the War, the village school now had to absorb the Mora Road infants, while the older evacuees were accommodated in the village hall. (See Chapter 10).

References:
Unless otherwise stated, sources are the St James' school logbooks and register at the Bedfordshire and Luton Archives and Records Service (BLARS), reference nos. SD Biddenham 1/1, 1/2, 1/3 and 1/4 (logbooks), and SD Biddenham 2/1 (admission register), and the two later school logbooks which are held by the headteacher at the school. These logbooks cover the period from 1873 to 1992, when they were discontinued.

1   BHRS Vol. 81, p 11.
2   Ibid.
3   Ibid.
4   BLARS P74/5/1.
5   BLARS Z614.
6   An Anglican institution founded in 1836 'for the Improvement and Extension of the   Infant School System at Home and Abroad, and for the Education of Teachers'.
7   BLARS CRT130BID/4.
8   BLARS CRT130BID/4.
9   *Kelly's Directory*, 1847.
10 The National Society for Promoting the Education of the Poor, founded in 1811 in order to educate poor children in Church of England schools.
11 BLARS CRT130BID/4.
12 Ibid.
13 Ibid.
14 D Gillard, *Education in England; a brief history* (2007).
15 Ted Pile, unpublished memoir, 1988, in the possession of his son Michael.
16 Albert Church, *Recollections of My Life in Biddenham,* p 2/3.
17 Kenneth Shrimpton, *Felmersham, the History of a Riverside Parish,* Impress Print (Corby), 2003, p 116.
18 Op. cit., p 117.

CHAPTER 10

BIDDENHAM DURING WORLD WAR II, 1939 TO 1945

At 11 o'clock in the morning on Sunday 3 September 1939 the Prime Minister, Neville Chamberlain, announced on the wireless that Britain was at war with Germany. Appeasement had failed, and for the second time since the outbreak of the World War I in 1914 the residents of Biddenham were to be involved in a conflict that was to take on a global proportion. This time, though, both men and women would be conscripted, and civilians were well aware that they were not safe from attack: the Zeppelin raids of World War I had developed into the blitzkrieg (lightning bombing) tactics of the Luftwaffe that had already been demonstrated in the Spanish Civil War (1936 to 1939).

There was no sense of exultation at the outbreak of war, or any feeling that it would be over by Christmas.[1] The preparations for war that started long before 1939 in Bedford and the villages were stepped up. The *Bedfordshire Times* noted that in Bedford 'men in khaki were everywhere. Wooden barricades were being erected in front of the plate glass windows in the High Street. On St Peter's Green the sandbags were being piled high to form a shelter against bomb splinters.'

The war had an immediate impact on the young men of Biddenham, who soon joined 'the men in khaki.' In September 1939 the government announced that all men aged between 18 and 40 would be conscripted for military service. Starting with 20- 23-year-olds, they had to register in turn for service in the army, navy, or air force. Many volunteered before their turn came up, and by the end of 1939 over one-and-a half million men and 43,000 women (at this stage all women were volunteers) had joined the armed forces. Not everyone was conscripted. Certain essential jobs such as skilled industrial workers, firemen and doctors were reserved.[2] In an interview in the *Biddenham Bulletin* in December 1987, Edith Church remembered a Christmas greeting in 1939 that was sent to those from Biddenham who were away serving their country:

Best of luck and a safe return
Is Biddenham's wish to you,
Duck End folk, and Biddenham Turn,
Day's Lane and Main Street too,
Each Bromham Road and Ford End friend,
Norman's and Vicar's Close, Church End,
Hearty and grateful greetings send,
And trust that shortly all will here
Meet again in Victory Year.

Not all the Biddenham men who were in the forces did meet again in victory year: three died on active service, and their names are now on the war memorial in the village.

Terence Hugh Creed, the son of Edward Cecil and Olive Agnes Creed of Biddenham, served as a pilot officer with 608 squadron of the Royal Air Force. Terence died on Sunday 1 September 1940, aged 27, and he is commemorated on the Biddenham war memorial and on Panel 7 of the Runnymede memorial near Windsor.[3]   As a pilot officer, he was a junior officer, and his squadron, an Auxiliary Air Force squadron, was based at Thornaby in North Yorkshire. From June 1940 the squadron had been equipped with Blackburn Bothas which had superseded the AVRO Ansons.

The Bothas were used for North Sea patrols until November 1940. However, they were seriously underpowered, and they gave poor visibility for downward and lateral observations. They were not issued to other squadrons as planned, and were subsequently confined to operational training duties. On

1 September 1940 Pilot Officer Creed took off in one of these training flights, but was unable to land because of the presence of intruders. The Botha was presumed to have ditched into the North Sea.[4]

Douglas Harold Everett, the son of Bennett Henry and Lily Ethel Everett and the husband of Lilian Francis Everett of Biddenham, was a lieutenant commander in the Royal Naval reserve. He died on 7 November 1944, aged 30. He had been a pupil of Bedford Modern School, and he was mentioned in despatches. He was commander of a tank landing ship, HMS LST 420 (LST 420), formerly USS LST 420, from 20 July 1944 until 7 November 1944, when it was mined and sunk in the English Channel.[5] Douglas Everett is commemorated by Biddenham, Bedford Modern School and on Panel 92, Column 2 of the Plymouth naval memorial.[6]

John Norman Campling, MBE was a lieutenant in the Royal Navy whose father, Percy George Campling, an electrical engineer, lived in Vicar's Close, Biddenham.[7] His sisters, Peggy and Monica, were old girls of Bedford High School, and they reported to their old school in March 1944 that John had been awarded the MBE for enterprise and skill in repair work after his ship had been bombed.[8] A year later, in March 1945, the news was not so good. John Campling was missing and presumed killed on active service.[9] He had been serving on HMS *Aldenham*, an Escort Destroyer, Hunt type III. The *Aldenham* had been commissioned for service in January 1942, and had been deployed in convoy service in the Eastern Mediterranean, including support of the assault on Tobruk in September 1942.[10] In 1943 the *Aldenham* was still in the eastern Mediterranean, deployed for anti-submarine and convoy interception patrols before in September leading the convoy of tank landing- craft from Malta to the beachhead during the landings in Sicily. After the Italian surrender, the *Aldenham* returned to Alexandria for the support of military operations in the Aegean to prevent the Germans replacing Italian garrisons. In January 1944, though, the *Aldenham* was transferred to 22nd Destroyer Flotilla and took passage to Algiers, where she was deployed on escort of military convoys in the central Mediterranean. By May she was deployed for support of operations in the Adriatic, and in July she was deployed as part of the escort for convoys to Naples, Syracuse and ports in Southern Italy as preparation for Operation Dragoon (the allied landings in the South of France under US command).

At the end of the first phase of Dragoon, the *Aldenham* returned to Royal Navy control and resumed deployment in the Adriatic with the flotilla from September to December 1944, with a break for a refit in Malta in October. On 13 December, along with HMS *Atherstone*, the *Aldenham* was deployed for support of partisans. On Thursday 14 December the *Aldenham* landed partisans at Pag Town as part of operation Exterminate. During the return passage to Karlobag the *Aldenham* detonated a mine in position W.30N 14.50E in the NE Adriatic off Velebit in Croatia 45 miles SE of Pula. The ship sank quickly, with many casualties. Out of a complement of 189, only 67 survived. 65 were rescued by HMS *Atherstone*, and one each by HM Landing Craft (Gun) 12 and HM Motor Launch 1162. HMS *Aldenham* was the last Royal Navy destroyer to be sunk in World War II[11] and Lieutenant Campling was amongst the five officers and 111 ratings who were missing. He is commemorated on the Plymouth naval memorial, Devon, panel 85, Column 1,[12] as well as on the Biddenham war memorial.

Other men who lived in Biddenham in 1939-1945, or came to live in Biddenham later in their lives, saw active service and survived. Jack Matthews (1920-2009), who was born in Great Staughton but who lived in Biddenham from 1960 until his death in 2009, used his journal to write his war memories for the *Biddenham Bulletin* in 2005. In May 1939 Jack joined the Territorial Army, Royal Engineers when he was 18 years old. By the end of 1940 he had qualified as a fitter first class in the Royal Engineers, and was sent to London to blow down dangerous bombed buildings and repair damaged sewers.[13]

He was later sent to North Africa, and in his memoirs he wrote:

It was whilst we were at El Alamein about 6 weeks before the main battle on October 23rd 1942, that another sapper and myself were sent on detachment to the Durham Light Infantry for patrol duty. They sent patrols out nearly every night to No Man's Land, the area between the two armies' forward minefields. The sapper carried no arms except a bayonet, which he used to prod for mines. Sometimes we went out and up to the enemy minefield, when the sapper had to take and disarm one of the enemy mines to find out what mines were on that part of the front. Sometimes we had to try and take an enemy prisoner to see who was on that part of the front, German or Italian, and what regiment. Sometimes we just went out looking for trouble, which we often found, as there were enemy patrols in No Man's Land as well. We had several narrow escapes ..... Each soldier who survived the Battle of Alamein was allowed to send one telegram which he had to pay for, to his next of kin. A telegram stamped 17 November 1942 was received by my mother in Willow Road, Bedford. It read 'Please don't worry, all well and safe. Writing.' There were nearly 14,000 British and Commonwealth soldiers killed in this battle.[14]

Later in 1942 Jack was at Misratah, near Leptis Magna in Libya. He developed septic scabies, and had a spell in the base hospital where he was treated and kept until his scabies healed. He wrote:

Conditions in the desert were really terrible. It was bad enough to be shelled, bombed, strafed and shot at, and if you were not careful, blown up on a mine, but we had never enough to eat or drink and water was very scarce. Petrol was more plentiful than water. We never had any bread, always biscuits, corned beef, tinned cheese, hard margarine, dried potatoes and rice with a handful of sultanas thrown in. Nearly everybody had desert sores. They just used to break out anywhere and then the flies, of which there were millions, settled on what food we had. In addition to all this, we were all infested with lice. You never washed your clothes because you just could not. You wore your shirt until the back rotted out and then got another one. We all had to shave every morning. We used the same water over and over again for this by filtering it through the corner of our blanket. We slept two to a bivouac, dug in where possible with a blanket, a groundsheet and a greatcoat with your pack or haversack for a pillow.[15]

Jack went on to fight in Italy, and was the only survivor from his platoon in the assault on Monte Cassino. By 8 May1945, VE Day, he was with the 56th Field Company, Royal Engineers, in camp near Gorizia near the frontier with Yugoslavia. He wrote that 'it was whilst we were here that the war in Europe officially finished.'[16] He did not return to England until April 1946. 'I was officially discharged on 26 July 1946, and I had served seven years all but 36 days. Of this time, five years were served abroad. Eight months in France in 1939-1940 and four years four months in the 8th Army in North Africa, Sicily and Italy. I now had to start again from scratch, so to speak, at the age of 26.'[17] In her address at Jack's funeral at St James's church, Biddenham, printed in the *Biddenham Bulletin* in February 2010, the Rev Jane Nash said that Jack felt that his survival in a war when so many had perished had laid on him the responsibility to use his life well, and he did, doing his very best for his family and his community.

Ian Robertson had a long post-war connection with Biddenham, as he moved to the village in 1957. As a young man in the 1930s he was determined to learn to fly.[18] In 1938 he was serving a premium five-year apprenticeship with a Luton company, and he joined the RAF Volunteer Reserve. When war broke out, he was called up and sent for training to Hastings, where he had plenty of PE and some very good mathematics teaching. By September 1939, as a sergeant, he was posted to Marshall's Flying School at Cambridge to learn to fly Tiger Moth aircraft. In the summer of 1940 he was posted to Little Rissington in Gloucestershire to fly Anson aircraft. He was commissioned as a pilot officer, sent to the school of navigation for a month, and then sent to RAF Cottesmore for operational training on Hampdens. In April 1941 he married Pat in Luton, and they managed to have a honeymoon in Scotland as, being an officer, Ian was given a rail pass.

62 – Ian Alexander Robertson, DFC

After the honeymoon, Ian joined 83 squadron at Scampton, and flew his first nine operational tours as a pilot/navigator. Ian then did 200 hours operational flying, and was awarded the DFC for flying a Hampden at low level to take out the enemy searchlights along the Belgian coast. His plane was hit by shrapnel during this operation. In October 1941 Ian was posted to Upper Heyford as an instructor. Pat went with him, and gallantly put up with the problems of living in the old cottage which constituted married quarters. The main event while Ian was at Upper Heyford was the first 1,000-bomber raid on Cologne in May 1942. Ian has written about this for the BBC World War Two People's War archive:[19]

I well remember 30 May 1942 the date of the first 1,000-bomber raid on Cologne. To muster 1046 bombers, aircraft from training units had to be used to supplement the operational squadron of the RAF. These aircraft were mostly old Wellington bombers relegated to training duties, obsolete for operational use. We took off from Upper Heyford in Oxfordshire in one of these Wellingtons with a full load of fuel and incendiaries. At full throttle the aircraft was very slow to climb, and by the Dutch coast we had only reached 9,000 feet. Shortly after crossing the coast, the starboard engine failed and as the aircraft could not maintain height on one engine, the bomb load was jettisoned. Even after this, the aircraft was losing height, and some fuel was jettisoned. We hoped to be able to reach an emergency landing ground at Woodbridge, near Orfordness. On reaching the coast of England at Orfordness, at 800 feet, it was obvious that we could not make the airfield, and it was decided that rather than crashland on land, we would try to land on the beach, as near to the sea as possible. In the dark at least the seashore could be seen. The landing was successfully achieved, no-one was injured and there was no fire. We were rescued by coastguards from Orfordness lighthouse, who had heard and seen us land, and taken by rowing boat to Orfordness and then to Woodbridge. The following day, with another pilot from Upper Heyford, our crews borrowed an aircraft and flew back to Heyford.

Ian later learnt that they had landed on the only stretch of beach for some miles around that was not mined, as it was a pebble beach and pebbles would have detonated mines.

Later in 1942 Ian was posted to RAF Hixon in Staffordshire as a flying instructor. When reminiscing in 2010, he described the station as a sea of mud, but he and Pat found lodgings in a pub, which was noisy, but they eventually had a lovely time. In his memories for the BBC People's War archive, Ian told an interesting story about his time at Hixon and what the airmen could get up to:[20]

Hixon was a wartime-built station which opened in 1942. The airfield was one side of the railway line to Stafford and the buildings and messes the other side. The buildings were built round the farmyard where land had been taken over for the airfield but the farmer still cultivated a small area remaining. The ploughing was done by a white horse, and the sheep herded by a white dog. There was a certain tension between the farmer and the airmen, as his eggs seemed to be disappearing, and also now and then the odd chicken vanished. Eventually the farmer complained to the station commander, and the airmen were all confined to camp for a period. The next day the farmer's white horse appeared with red, white and blue RAF roundels on each side and one round its tail. The white dog experienced the same treatment. The matter was then closed, but the roundels remained for a long time.

In 1943 Ian was posted to RAF Manby, near Louth, on a nine-month Armament Officers course, and was retained as officer commanding flying wing at what was to become the Empire Air General Training School. He left Manby in December 1944 to become commanding officer of the Twin Armament Testing Flight at Boscombe Down. He was in charge of rocket and bombsite testing and looking after the bombing ranges. Ian's career in aviation did not end with the cessation of hostilities in 1945. He worked in civil aviation at Hunting Air Travel at Luton, became chief test pilot at Cranfield for 21 years, and ended his working life as HMI for professional pilot training and sundry other aeronautical-related subjects, from which he retired in 1980 to enjoy life in Biddenham.

As well as his peacetime achievements, Ian had a very distinguished career in the RAF in the war. He knew he was lucky to survive. Out of seven RAF officers who attended his wedding in 1941, Ian was the only one who was still alive at the end of the war.[21]

At first, war service for women was voluntary. However, it soon became clear that to supply the armed services and support for them, all able-bodied people of both sexes would be obliged to take on some form of 'national service.' Very reluctantly the government announced in 1941 that unmarried women aged between 20 and 30 would be called up for war work. In 1942 19-year-olds were also conscripted. They were offered a choice between the auxiliary services and jobs in industry. Married women were not called up, but they could volunteer, and were encouraged to do so by government propaganda.[22]

Both sisters of John Campling, who is commemorated on the war memorial, undertook war service. Monica, who left Bedford High School in 1941, was mentioned by the Headmistress, Kate Westaway in her book *Old Girls in New Times*:

W H Allen Sons & Co Ltd, the largest engineering firm in Bedford of very conservative views on the question of sex, opened its doors during this war just a crack wider than before, and Monica Campling became their first woman apprentice. She was solemnly bound for a certain period of time on certain conditions which was a great advance on the comparatively casual labour which the firm gladly accepted in this war as in the last.[23]

Her sister Margaret (Peggy) left school in 1938 and started a degree course at Royal Holloway College, London. After the declaration of war, she volunteered at Bedford County Hospital, then entered training and became an SRN. On 3 April 1943 she married at St James's church, Biddenham. Her husband, Nathan Tilley, was a sergeant in the US army.[24] It was the start of a very happy marriage and, eventually after the war, life in America.

Penelope Ronn and her sister, Phoebe, had both been very active in the Girl Guide movement before the outbreak of war. Penelope had represented England in August 1938 at an international Ranger conference in Switzerland. Phoebe had been one of the Bedfordshire representatives at the Guide service at St George's Chapel, Windsor in June 1938. In 1939 Penelope had left school and was teaching at Rushmoor School, where she was in sole charge of the Rushmoor Cub pack and was starting a Biddenham Guide company.[25] With the advent of conscription, both girls joined the WAAF (Women's Auxiliary Air Force). Before her marriage at St James's church, Biddenham on 2 October 1944 to Lieutenant Carson of the Intelligence Corps,[26] Penelope had an interesting time in the WAAF. In 1942 she was in balloon command, helping to run a balloon flight of barrage balloons somewhere in Birmingham. She wrote an account of her war so far to her school magazine:[27]

If three years ago, on leaving school, I had been told today I would be in uniform, I would not have believed it. Yet it is a fact, and there must be many hundreds of girls in the same position. For war-time, it is well worth while and a grand life, with plenty of scope in your own line, whatever it may be, with a chance of seeing the world (I have been to eight different places in that number of months since I joined up) and of meeting people and making good friends.

This is a job that demands a love of the open air – or rather an ability to stand up to the English climate – also proficiency on a bicycle ..... The sites are naturally scattered about the city, and with the universal petrol shortage, the bicycle has come into its own ..... A balloon operator's life is by no means easy. Some people think it is a simple life, merely entailing putting up a balloon and then sitting out in the sunshine until it is time to bring it down again. They wouldn't think that if they saw girls turning out at all hours of the night to stand on guard, or turn the balloon every time the wind veers; or to carry out a difficult operation in the rain and wind with the balloon 'hitting the deck' on either side. Unless you have done it, you can hardly realise how cold it can be out on a balloon-bed in mid-winter, when ropes and wires get frozen or buried in snow.

You will say I am painting a black picture, but I want to prove that despite the difficulties, the hardships and the exposure, 'balloonatics' as we are called, enjoy life tremendously ..... My particular job is to look after the girls on sites: to see that their billets and food are all right, to keep an eye out for illness, to clear up the hundred-and-one problems that arise, and to arrange games and entertainments for them. Those entertainments can be the greatest fun, especially when there are born comediennes, as on our Flight. You can imagine the fun we have with impromptu concerts in the huts on bleak winter nights.

Penelope was heard on the wireless in 1942 in the show 'Ack Ack Beer Beer.' This was an entertainment programme for anti-aircraft and barrage balloon workers, featuring the comedian,

63 – Milton Ernest hostel 'land girls' having a break from summer work
in the fields at Rawlins' farm, Biddenham, 1945.
N Wallace, courtesy of Stuart Antrobus

Kenneth Horne, that ran for over 700 episodes. Kate Westaway described it as 'a quite formidable entertainment.'[28]

Women could also join the other auxiliary forces: the women's branch of the army, the ATS (Auxiliary Territorial Service), the WAAF (Women's Auxiliary Air Force) and the WRNS (Women's Royal Navy Service). Leonie Quarry, whose parents lived at the Manor House, Biddenham, joined the WRNS.[29] Others joined the Women's Land Army, which had operated on a smaller scale in World War I and was re-formed in June 1939. At first the 'land girls' were volunteers, but later recruits were brought in by conscription.[30]

There was a great need of 'land girls' in Biddenham, which was still a largely agricultural community, where the farmers had to be helped to increase vital food supplies. The largest farm was Church Farm, which now included the Manor Farm, Honeyhill and Grove Farm.[31] The tenant was Fred Rawlins, who used modern methods in his farming. He had five tractors,[32] lorries to take the vegetables, mainly potatoes, to London, and he used artificial manure. He kept horses (to pull carts), cattle at Church Farm, doves and 138 pigs at Grove Farm. He grew corn, barley, potatoes, Brussels sprouts and oats. He had two hayfields with two tents to keep the rain off the haystacks. Fred Rawlins had help from at least eight 'land girls', who lived at a hostel at Milton Ernest. They went out in gangs to do seasonal work on local farms, in the summer harvesting corn, and in the winter threshing.[33] The photograph of the Milton Ernest hostel girls having a break from summer work in the fields at Rawlins' farm, Biddenham in 1945 is from Stuart Antrobus's book on the Women's Land Army in Bedfordshire.[34]

Ann Brodrick, who had worked at Rawlins' farm as a hostel girl, and was treated as one of the family, asked to move there in 1945.[35] When interviewed by Stuart Antrobus, she told him that she had her own Allis Chalmers tractor. She was a dogsbody, but loved it. She could drive lorry-loads of potatoes into Bedford, and fetch the vet. She was well fed on the farm, as opposed to having very limited hostel food. Marjorie Rawlins gave Ann's food coupon book to Ann's mother, who was living on her own by this time in Luton. At the time of VE Day she was given time off to attend the victory celebrations in London. She even met her husband-to-be 'Tich' on the Rawlins' farm. Looking back on her years as a 'land girl', Ann remembered that some of the farmers 'just reacted to you as though you were not there.' Some, like the ones on her final farm, were delightful.

64 – Fred Rawlins (4th from left), with C W (Bill) Rawlins (behind dog) and Phil Rawlins (right foreground). Others have not been identified.

Fred Rawlins could also be forgiving. Mary Pakes told Stuart Antrobus that the only time that she and her gang from the Milton Ernest hostel got into trouble was at Fred Rawlins's farm. It was very hot, and they had been hoeing all day. 'One girl said "I can't do any more." She flopped down, threw away her hoe and they all did the same. They had only been down for a few minutes when the farmer came along, saw them and reported them. But he was very nice afterwards.'[36]

In some respects the pattern of village life continued during World War II. The farms and businesses were operated by those who were too old for conscription, or were in reserved occupations, with extra help such as that from the 'land girls'. As well as Church Farm, there was Green Farm where the bungalows are now in Gold Lane.[37] Mr Favell farmed there, and ploughed the fields himself. He had eight ploughs pulled by horses, and sometimes by a tractor which he hired. He had eight cows and a dairy and he delivered milk round the village and to Biddenham Dairies, a shop on Bromham Road, Bedford. At the back of the farm he had a few haystacks, and two others in another of his fields.

There were two smallholdings in the village. Ouse Valley Farm was a dairy farm farmed by Mr Treerise. He had eight cows, two horses and four pigs during World War II.[38] He sold milk to people in Biddenham, using bikes to transport it round the village. The other smallholding was Frossell's Farm, opposite the church.[39] Theed Frossell kept five cows, two horses and

65 – The village blacksmith, Len Herbert, 1962

chickens. He took milk into Bedford on a milk-float. He did the work himself, despite being in his 60s, and used a plough pulled by horses. He had two hayfields at the Baulk. He and Mr Treerise were tenant farmers, as the village was owned by Lord Dynevor of Bromham, and then the Wingfield Estate until 1954, when much of it was sold off.[40]

Other services in the village were provided by the older men and women. Len Herbert was the blacksmith at the smithy on Main Road. He had machines to sharpen instruments, and mended many things, from ploughs to bicycles. This saved people a trip into Bedford.[41]   Mr Greetham had a shoe repair shop opposite the village green. Nearly all the people in Biddenham took their shoes there for repair.[42]

66 – The smithy, 1962

The Three Tuns not only sold beer, but also mineral waters, biscuits, cigarettes and matches.[43]   Mrs Davis, who ran the post office in Penny Black Cottage in Main Road, sold writing paper, sweets and cigarettes as well as stamps.[44] Carpentry work was carried out by Arthur Burton, who had been apprenticed to J P White of the Pyghtle Works, Bedford, and by Albert Church, who was also a thatcher. Albert Church, who died in 1979, left an interesting set of memoirs of his life in Biddenham, including comments on his working life and his wartime experiences. Of his working life, he says that he 'gained a fair knowledge of bricklaying, thatching, carpentry, stonewalling and my duties also included hedge laying, repairs and maintenance of gates, fences and water pipes. I was also involved in water meter reading and rent collecting.'[45] However, there was no baker in Biddenham at that time, so bought bread and cakes had to come from Bedford.[46]

In the early days of the war the village was still expanding. The population had risen from 460 in 1921 to 568 in 1931, and a few new houses were being built: two in Vicar's Close and two in Day's Lane.[47] However, the population of the village expanded in 1939 because as the danger of war grew greater, Bedford and the surrounding villages had been assessed for potential as an evacuation area. During the first weekend of September 1939 evacuation was well under way. Bedford was the reception area for those coming from London. School children arrived, loaded with bags and parcels, including the compulsory gas mask. They were accompanied by their teachers. There were also expectant mothers and mothers with children under school age. In the BBC Project *The People's War*, Joy Loffman, who was evacuated from Cricklewood to Biddenham, recalled being taken to the Market Square in Bedford, where trestle tables were laid out with lemonade and biscuits. Each table was earmarked for a different village.

Biddenham families took in evacuees for the whole of the war period. Albert Church helped with the billeting when the evacuees first arrived. He commented 'Some took them with open arms and love for them: others had to be forced to take them, and a few with larger houses, were sorting them out and looking for girls from 12 to 14 years old with a view to helping with the housework.'[48]

The whole of Mora Road Primary School, Cricklewood, London, numbering about 40 children, came to Biddenham.[49] They arrived by coach on 3 September 1939, and with them were their headmaster, Mr Rattenbury, his wife and daughter, and two women teachers. At first the Rattenburys were billeted with Miss Huntingdon, a music teacher, in Church End, before moving to a home of their own. The younger children went to the village school and the older ones attended school in the village hall, which had been commandeered by the Education Authority.[50]

At first the village children were hostile to the newcomers from London. However, in the Christmas holidays, 1939, it snowed a lot, and they all took part in a great snowball fight between the villagers and the evacuees in the pig field in Church End. After half an hour, there was no sign of a winner, but all the children became friends.[51]

During their stay in Biddenham the evacuees gave a concert in November 1939, and a performance of extracts from *Julius Caesar* in the village hall.[52]

We have further details about the stay of the Cricklewood evacuees in the village because the headmaster, Mr Rattenbury, kept diaries from 1939 to 1942, and Mr James Roffey of the Evacuees Reunion Association, who wrote about the teachers' role in the evacuation of British children during the Second World War, has given us permission to quote from them. The children of school age were evacuated with their schools, so that they could be with their friends and be taught by teachers they knew. This all placed a huge responsibility on the teachers, and especially the head teacher. With his wife and daughter, Rose, as helpers, plus the other teachers, he found himself responsible for 93 evacuated children in Biddenham. The responsibility was not just for the term time, but also for the holidays. Mr Rattenbury's diary reveals that in 1939 the schools closed on 22 December for the Christmas holiday. However, on that day Mr Rattenbury, helped by other adults, took 64 children to the Picturedrome in Bedford to see *Treasure Island*. The next day he was preparing for the Christmas party in the village hall. At 11 am on Christmas Day the children gathered in the hall to exchange cards and letters. In the afternoon there was a party between 3.30 pm and 7.30 pm. On Boxing Day there was also a party from 2 pm to 6 pm, and there was a dance for the 13-year-olds in the evening. The diary records that there were games in the village hall for the children throughout the holidays, along with visits to the cinema and the pantomime. As we have seen, the snow provided another distraction. By the time term started again on 8 January 1940, Mr Rattenbury and his fellow teachers had done their best to organise plenty for the children to do, and to make their holiday as happy as possible.

The following Christmas he had to repeat his attempts to make the festival as enjoyable as possible for the children, but it was much harder. On 24 December 1940 he wrote about trying to buy presents for his evacuees in Bedford. 'Well, a peculiar kind of Christmas Eve, shops very poorly stocked, many lines unobtainable.' He did organise a Boxing Day party, but he wrote 'I think all the children enjoyed themselves. Got home feeling tired and needing a respite. Still, it was all worthwhile I think. Hope it will be the last Christmas at Biddenham.' Being on duty every day of the week for over a year, teaching, coping with air raids and occupying the children in fund-raising and war effort schemes such as the collection of scrap metal and waste paper, and 'Dig for Victory' were exhausting.

Further problems gradually emerged. Many local people had lost enthusiasm for taking in evacuees, and some wanted to be rid of them. When a new billet had to be found for an evacuee, it became increasingly difficult. As children reached the school leaving age (14 for those attending elementary schools), they returned home. The foster parents could no longer draw an allowance for the young person's keep, and the government considered that the evacuee was now an adult and no longer its concern. By May 1942 there were only three evacuees on the school roll at Biddenham out of the original 93. Mr Rattenbury was ordered to parcel up any remaining school stock and return it and himself to London in June 1942. The diary has no more entries in it.

There is no record of any official thanks to Mr Rattenbury, but a former evacuee pupil of his did write after his death in 1982 'he was always a very reassuring figure for me, a lonely ten-year-old, to have around ….. he really cared about all the children in his care. He was a real father figure for me and I valued that.'

Peter Carey agreed about being an evacuee in Biddenham. He wrote in the *Biddenham Bulletin* for September 2005 that he lived with the Creeds at Arleen in Day's Lane. 'In all honesty, I cannot recall how long I was under the Creeds' roof, but I remember the time as being one of the most enjoyable and happiest times of my evacuee experience.' (The Creeds lost a son during the war; his name is on the village war memorial).

Mr Creed had a car, but no petrol, so the vehicle was on blocks in his garage. Mrs Creed was most caring, and treated me extremely well. Like me, they were Catholic and I used to walk into town each day to attend the Priory Road school and church on Sunday. Although I was about 12 years old at the time, I was well-built and must have looked older, because I had a Saturday job, as delivery-cum-errand-boy for Wallenger's the greengrocer near to Union Street and the then 'TOC H' Club nearby. Another pocket money earning exercise was to act as caddy at the nearby golf club on Bromham Road to the many American servicemen who played there.

Some Biddenham families took in elderly people, some took in mothers with young children, and some gave a home to friends and relatives from the danger zones for intensive bombing.[53] Musicians from the BBC lodged in Biddenham, including Paul Beard, the leader of the BBC orchestra, before he moved to Stagsden Road.[54] Maurice Leczycki, a Jewish Polish refugee who lived with Mrs Faulkner in Church End, wrote a 24-page book about Biddenham, in which he concluded 'Biddenham itself is one of the thousands of villages in England and it is very pleasant and healthy to live there.'

67 – Maurice Leczycki, 1946

As well as taking in evacuees, the residents of Biddenham who were not conscripted for active service were also expected to play their part in civil defence, notably air-raid precautions, the fire service, the invasion committee, first-aid, the Home Guard, the Royal Observer Corps and keeping the village and the troops supplied with food ('Dig for Victory', the Fruit Preservation Centre and food parcels) and warm clothes (knitting parties). This was in addition to holding down a full-time paid job or running a home and looking after children. Everyone was fully occupied.

As early as 1935, the fear of a future conflict led to civil defence measures being introduced into Bedfordshire under the name of air-raid precautions. The civil population had never been mobilised before, and there was no real understanding of the complexity of the arrangements that would be required to deal with an air attack - in particular an effective warning system and the handling of casualties.[55] By 1938 a full-time County ARP officer had been appointed, though, and an ARP structure of six areas was in place. This was followed by the recruitment of volunteers, and training in the Shire Hall.[56]

In 1937 the government had chosen Bedford for experiments in the control of street lighting, and the painting of white lines on the road and on the side of the lampposts and telegraph poles, to assist drivers moving with very reduced or no headlights. The RAF flew over Bedford to test the first 'blackout' in 1937, and by July 1939 the first blackout exercise for real took place, preceded by the civil police sounding the warning alarm system. On the night of 1 September 1939 all windows had been blacked out, and all the adult population and babies had received their gas masks.[57]

In Biddenham, according to Albert Church, there were several meetings in the village hall in the build-up to the start of the war in 1939, at which volunteers were asked to join the ARP, but there was no response. When war finally came, and ARP staff had been recruited,[58] it was left to Albert Church, who, as he was crippled in his right leg and foot, had problems[59] getting on the Wellington boots which were part of a warden's equipment, and Mr Gunnell, who was about 70 years of age, to make a start with ARP.[60] Albert did get one or two more men to join, and briefly took on the leadership when Mr Gunnell wished to withdraw on account of his age and poor health. He then persuaded the Town Clerk, Mr Darlow, who lived in the village, to take on the leadership.[61]

Recruitment for the ARP, or CD (civil defence) as it became known, speeded up when the government announced that everyone at all capable must do something for the war effort.[62] Mr Darlow held the post of chief warden, and he was assisted by Albert Church, H Groot, F Salmons, W Eyre, A H Dowler, D Dowler, P Shaw and L A Williams (until he was called into HM forces).[63] Whereas the two ARP Wardens in Stevington slept in the church room store and ran a nightly roster system with other members of their team,[64] Mr New lent the lounge of the Old Vicarage in Biddenham and the use of his telephone until the wardens' post could be transferred to a more spacious outbuilding of Biddenham House, lent by the owner, Mr Campbell. The building offered was the groom's quarters over the stables, as W Eyre, who was a warden, was groom/chauffeur to Mr Campbell. A telephone had to be installed for the sole use of the wardens by government orders, and a double tier bed was sent out to every post for the wardens to sleep on. They also had an iron bed provided by Mr Campbell.[65]

In his memoirs Albert Church told a couple of stories illustrating the lighter side of civil defence duties in 1939. The first involved himself and his fellow Warden, Nobby, dozing off one Friday evening and then waking up and thinking they saw a black lizard-shaped creature with large eyes:

I went to the fireplace and picked up an old army bayonet which Mr New used as a poker, and clouted the creature about the head until I thought it was dead, then I picked up a coal shovel out of the grate and ….. pulled the creature into the shovel with the bayonet. We both looked at it and wondered what it could be. I said. 'Let's throw it outside and look at it in the morning when it is daylight' ….. When morning came ….. we spent a long time looking for it, but found nothing ….. As it was never found, we had our legs pulled about it, especially as it was a Friday night when, unless the air-raid warning had gone, we would nearly all meet at the Tuns with some of our friends who were in the special police.[66]

The second story involved a morning warning. 'One morning early in the war the warning went about 6.30 am, and did not clear until 9 am. Nobby and I were on duty, and quite a few men were on their way to work between 7.30 and 8 am. We told them the warning had gone and that they should take shelter.' Timmy Trueman was with his horse and cart going to help the roadmen repair Bromham Road near the bridge:

When the siren went, Tim shut his horse out of the cart and tied it to the wheel. Yes, those were his instructions. Then Tim went and got into one of the arches under the bridge and there he stayed until it was all clear. This happened several mornings that week and still Tim did the same. The road foreman got rather annoyed with Tim, as, of course, some of the roadmen went with him. He commented that if the warning went when Tim was on his way home he never heard it.[67]

The St James' school logbooks record:
16.5.1940   'Air raid' practice and 'air raid dispersal.'
24.6.1940   School closed one week so that protective measures against air raids may be provided. [The school was then closed for 2 more weeks, and ended up closed for four weeks].
4.9.1940   One-hour air raid – 'therefore the composition lesson was omitted.'
11.9.1940   Another air raid 11 to 11.30 am. Also two air raids the next week.
Two air raids on 24.9.40 and another two on 26.9.40.
Two more air raids 'so children were in the Refuge Room.'
3.10.1940. Children in Refuge Room most of the day.
More air raids on 9 to 31 October 1940, and in November and December.
1941 – More air raids in January.

In 1941 the logbooks record the arrival of supplies such as blackout curtains, mattresses, respirators, kettle, teapot, mugs, biscuits in tins, tinned milk, sugar, tea and blankets.

However, although people in Bedfordshire were kept on their toes with nightly air-raid warnings as enemy aircraft flew over to targets in the industrial Midlands, the attacks became more irregular until the last bombing attack in August 1942, and the last rocket attack in December 1944. [68] In that time, over 1,000 high explosive bombs and over 8,000 incendiary devices were dropped in Bedfordshire.[69] Fortunately Biddenham only had three bombs dropped in the parish, and all were dropped by the same plane. One fell in the garden of Mr Dillingham (on Bromham Road opposite Windmill Hill) within four yards of the main road. The bomb fell in soft ground, penetrating to a considerable depth before exploding. All the blast went upwards, luckily causing no structural damage to the houses in the immediate vicinity. The other two bombs fell to the north side of Bromham Road in fields.[70]

The civil defence did not relax their efforts, and manned their post every night from 10 pm until 7 am during the whole of the war period. The wardens took their duty in pairs on a rota system, and patrolled the village during every 'alert.' Mr Darlow also operated a canteen, which enabled extra equipment to be bought for the warden's service from the profits made. At the end of the war, the surplus profit (£54) was handed over to the village hall committee.[71] The school also retained its vigilance. The logbook records that on 12 November 1943 'Policeman visited to talk to children to warn them about picking up dangerous objects.'

In 1940, after the fall of France, Mr L E H Roberts, a director of Meltis Ltd, who lived on Day's Lane, was requested to form a fire service for Biddenham, as it was felt that Bedford borough fire brigade could take no responsibility for Biddenham in the event of an aerial attack. Mr Roberts held a meeting in the village hall, and young men who were in reserved occupations, such as working in the munitions factories, enrolled in the fire service.[72]   Dorothy Richards reproduced a photograph of the men in the fire service in 1942 with their hoses.[73]   There was no equipment for the fire service at first, and the £68 profit from an entertainment that was held had to be used to buy

68 – Biddenham Fire Service, 1942.
Back row: G Rose, R Chapman, R West, K Green, E Green,
A Smith, E Church, S Hillyard, R Hall.
Front row: J Shaw, J Hillyard, L E Roberts, R Watts, F Wright.

simple stocks of hoses. The Rural District Council had also to be persuaded to extend the water main from where it ended at the Old Vicarage to near Biddenham church.[74]   Drills were held twice weekly at Biddenham House, where those two men on duty each night could sleep in the stables on the two camp beds provided. So well run was the service that at the end of the war, Mr Roberts could hand over £168 to Harry Peacock to be used for village activities.[75]

In the approach to war, there was an awareness that aerial warfare could produce numerous casualties and prompt first-aid would be essential. In late September 1938 15 first-aid posts were set up in North Bedfordshire with 45 additional mobile first-aid posts complete with supporting vehicles, stretchers and medical supplies. These were supplied by the Red Cross and St John's Ambulance. In Stevington the first-aid point was in the village shop, and was covered by trained and readily available villagers.[76]   In Biddenham, in 1939 a number of village residents were approached to form a first-aid team, and they opened a post. The County Council supplied them with poor and inadequate equipment, so they successfully made a house-to-house collection. They were able to meet once a week in the grounds of Biddenham House, thanks to Mr Campbell. The leader of the team was Mrs Demery, who lectured on first-aid and home nursing. She was helped by Mrs Burdett, Mrs A Church, Mrs G Church, Miss D Gammons, Miss A Haines, Miss M Haines, Miss E Steel and Miss E White.

Visiting officials praised the team for their bandaging, splinting and general knowledge.[77] Fortunately the team's skills were not to be tested out in a large-scale local bombing raid, but in anticipation of such an event they worked enthusiastically and conscientiously. They took part in Home Guard exercises and treated mock casualties. They also attended courses on gas warfare and resuscitation at the village hall, and took and passed the exams at the end of the course.[78]

In an interview with Mary McKeown John Rawlins, who was born in 1934 and whose parents farmed at Church Farm, remembered taking part as a 'casualty' in a civil defence exercise in the village when he was six or seven years old. He turned up at the village hall pretending that his arm had been blown off, thinking that it would be rather dramatic, but he was immediately put in a wheelbarrow as a corpse and wheeled to the 'mortuary' in the skittle alley. He also recalled that the wealthy American Mrs Carpenter-Holland-Griffith, who lived on her own in a very large house up the lane beside Parsonage Cottage, offered a commode and a truss towards the first-aid equipment.

In 1940, after the fall of France and the evacuation of our troops from the beaches of Dunkirk, the national situation was very serious. It seemed likely that an invasion of Britain would take place. In June 1940 the government sent instructions to all parishes, requiring the establishment of a parish invasion committee which would act as a focal point for implementing instructions from the central government and coordinating the civil defence work. As in other parishes, such as Stevington,[79] a Biddenham invasion committee was formed from the heads of different organisations serving Biddenham. The residents rallied round, but it was yet another draw on their time, along with the civil defence, fire and first-aid duties. Nevertheless, preparations were made so the village could be run as a self-contained unit in the event of invasion and Biddenham being isolated.[80]

The other major organisation which took up the time of the non-conscripted male residents of Biddenham was the Local Defence Volunteers, or Home Guard, as they were known after 31 July 1940. Bedfordshire was divided into zones, with commanders and a devolved structure down to sections and platoons at parish and village level. In November 1940 army ranks were introduced, and in time, civilian dress with an LDV armband was exchanged for a uniform. The Home Guard had three specific roles:
(1)To patrol and guard the local area and any key facilities.
(2)To support the civil defence organizations.
(3)To create the nucleus of and support for auxiliary units in the coastal areas (embryonic resistance units).[81]

Brian (Dick) Crisp, whose parents had the Globe public house in Ford End Road, and who now lives in Biddenham, has written down his memories of the family connection with Biddenham platoon, 8th battalion, Bedford Home Guard.[82] His father, a World War I veteran, was among the first to report to the police station and to volunteer when the local LDV was formed in May 1940. It was a part-time, unpaid force for men aged 17 to 65. Dick's father was 'a godsend', as in the appeal for weapons 'he had a 1900 model .303 rifle with ten rounds of ammunition.'[83] Dick remembers that his father and the other early members of the LDV had to parade at Biddenham golf course, as it had been identified as a possible landing ground for parachutists if the Germans invaded. 'Every time an air-raid warning was sounded the volunteers would turn out and assemble at the golf course armed with an assortment of weapons ranging from shotguns, air guns, sporting rifles, bows and arrows, harpoons - in fact any sort of weapon that could be used to repel the German hordes.'[84]

69 – Biddenham platoon, Home Guard, in the yard of the Globe, Queen's Park, about 1942. Back row, left to right: Private Les Crisp, Corporal Ted King, Lance-corporal Peter Crisp. Front row, left to right: Private Brian (Dick) Crisp, Private Jock Paterson.

The weapons and equipment gradually improved. Instead of the early uniform which consisted of 'thin denim battledresses, which were intended to be used as overalls for the regular soldiers', standard army battledress and overcoats were issued. With winter coming on, the members had asked for a set of the early uniform 'three sizes larger than required so that they could put plenty of their own clothing underneath.'[85] By the end of summer 1940 batches of 0.300 Springfield rifles from the USA, together with Ross rifles from Canada, arrived for the Home Guard. They also acquired medium machine guns, light machine guns, sten guns, revolvers, grenades, a 2016 HE Spigot Mortar and a Northover projector.[86]

Dick's brother, who was two years older than him, joined the Home Guard after his father 'so, not to be left out, in 1942 I put my age on by two years and joined Biddenham Platoon, 8th Battalion, Bedford Home Guard. At my very first parade, a lecture on anti-gas training, who should be sitting in front of me but Captain F T Johns, MC, my old headmaster. I give him credit for not giving me away, apart from saying that the years fly by quicker these days.'[87]

Dick stayed in the Home Guard until May 1944, when he left and went into the army. His platoon commander was Captain Fred Rawlins, of Church Farm, who employed the 'land girls'. He was in charge of the command post in a field opposite the Manor.[88] The other command posts were a trench dug just inside the hedge surrounding the Spinney, a trench dug into a ditch at the side of the footpath running from the farm road to Vicar's Close, and at the barn to the south of Honey Hill Farm. In addition, an anti-tank barrier could be erected into preset metal boxes set into the carriageway on the Bromham Road just north-west of Gallows Corner, but this only happened once, and it took a lot of physical effort. There was also a brick-built pillbox at the east side of the Bromham Road opposite the end of Biddenham Turn, but Dick Crisp does not think this was ever used. The platoon paraded on Wednesday evenings and Sunday mornings. The place of the parade varied from the golf course, Queen's Park School playground, Honey Hills adjacent to the Allen Park allotments, Manor Farm and occasionally Church Farm.[89]

The training on these occasions consisted of rifle or light machinegun training, bayonet fighting and grenade throwing while the specialists concentrated on signals, using flags; first-aid; medium machinegun and anti-tank weapons. Later two of the younger and fitter members were sent on an unarmed combat course. On their return as fully-trained instructors, Captain Rawlins started a 'commando squad'; the things we were going to do to any German invaders. If the training took place in Biddenham, the dismissal always took place outside the Three Tuns. When in the Queen's Park area most of the members made their way to my father's pub, the Globe. (Well, we did put a lot of hard work into our training, and replacement of lost fluid was essential).'[90]

Dick recounts another incident, the culmination of which was photographed for the *Bedfordshire Times*:

Several 24-hour or 36-hour exercises were carried out, sometimes against other Home Guard units and occasionally against the army. One in particular against the army we should have had rations issued. With typical army efficiency, the rations were not issued and cash in lieu was eventually paid. Rather than distribute the money between those who took part in the exercise, it was decided that we would have a grand dinner to be held in Biddenham village hall.[91]

A photograph was taken for the *Bedfordshire Times* at the start of the evening.

Dick remembers that as well as training:

….. While the invasion scare was on, we had to man defence positions around the Biddenham area. We had to man these positions one hour before dawn for two hours, then two hours before dusk. My position was Honey Hill Farm. We had converted one of the barns on the south-west corner into a strongpoint by building sandbag walls within the external timber walls, and forming removable portions of the timber cladding to provide firing positions covering the river and across to the fields to the Dutch barn ..... my father and I made the most of these occasions and went out with our shotguns looking for additional food for the pot. Mind you, we still kept a good lookout for enemy parachute landings.[92]

As time wore on and the invasion scare diminished, the Home Guard no longer had to turn out whenever an air-raid warning sounded.[93] Instead, the intelligence system would notify Home Guard headquarters, and the church bells would be rung to warn of impending invasion. Dick remembers that there were practices without the church bells being rung, but they were not very successful. 'We would have had to rely on the bells. Thank goodness the bells were never rung.'[94]

Dick records that gradually the administration of the Home Guard was improved:

At first there was no administrative back-up. However, on 24 June an army council instruction was issued making the County Territorial Army Association responsible for all the administration of the Home Guard. Also, they were to be responsible for all the records. A paid administrative assistant was allocated to each Home Guard Battalion. On 14 February 1942 compulsory enrolment into the Home Guard came into force. Many were hostile to this idea, and much trouble was caused. Records were kept of the number of parades that each soldier attended. If his attendance was not up to standard, the administrative assistant would send a letter to the individual drawing this to his attention. If the person concerned did not improve his attendance, he could be prosecuted and, if found guilty, fined. There were several cases of this happening in Bedford. A very different attitude to the volunteers of May 1940![95]

The members of the Home Guard had to do all of this in addition to a hard day's work. They also had to start developing an attack role as well as a defence role once the threat of invasion reduced. There must have been some relief when, on 1 November 1944, with the allied forces well established in Europe, the order was given to the Home Guard units to stand down, and on 3 December 1944 the Bedfordshire Home Guard units held their final parade in Russell Park.[96] By then, Dick Crisp was in the army. He writes that he has been asked 'was the Home Guard anything like the antics shown in the popular series *Dad's Army*? Yes, in many ways, but to be honest the films exaggerated to a very large extent.'[97] Fortunately the six rows of brick-lined sockets set in concrete on Bromham Bridge never had to be used to anchor a blockade so that the road would be impassable. The Home Guard could have delayed the Germans, but never have defeated them. It had been a very good civilian morale-builder; as one member of the Middlesborough Home Guard said: 'It made us feel we could do something useful.'[98]

In 1943 an interesting voluntary organisation affiliated to the RAF moved to Day's Lane, Biddenham, from its original headquarters in Bedford Telephone Exchange. This was the Royal Observer Corps.[99] Kate Westaway wrote of that 'queer, long low building just outside Bedford ..... from which some of us, mostly the younger ones, watched the skies.'[100] The above-ground buildings were support offices, and the original operations room was used in tracking aircraft. The British subjects aged 16 to 55 who applied to be 'observers' were male and female, and they were subject to the Official Secrets Act. They had to have a sense of service, dedication and commitment, and if they passed the highest standards, they could wear the Spitfire badge, the hallmark of an expert observer. They were trained to take immediate action if any enemy launched an aerial attack on Britain.[101] They had played an important role in the Battle of Britain, as radar could not tell the types or number of aircraft coming over, nor their precise height. The Observer Corps had to supply this information, and in 1941 as a tribute to this work, was granted the prefix 'Royal.' This vital work in aircraft recognition reporting to Fighter Command Group HQ was continued at Biddenham. Amongst those who worked in the Royal Observer Corps was Eric Green. His son, Dennis Green, emailed Mary McKeown from New Zealand, where he now lives, to say that 'Dad was an engineer (at Allen's in Queen's Park) a reserved occupation which kept him out of the forces. Dad had been an air cadet, and was keen to be a navigator, but had to be content with the Observer Corps. He was also in the village fire brigade.' The Royal Observer Corps branch in Day's Lane continued after the war until 1992, when a parade marked its disbandment.

70 – ROC parade for the closure of the Day's Lane branch in 1992.

War service for the non-conscripted was not just restricted to civil defence, the fire service, first-aid, the Home Guard and the Royal Observer Corps. The Ministry of Food had appealed to the nation to grow as much food as possible. A 'Dig for Victory' campaign started all over the country, and took up any spare time that might have been left for the non-conscripted. Doreen Locke entered a 'Dig for Victory' writing competition in her Junior School Magazine, the *Eaglet*, in 1940. She wrote:

The gentleman next door said he had a plot of ground in Day's Lane and if Daddy would like a piece of this ground, Daddy could have it, so Daddy said he would like it. This year we have planted 14 rows of potatoes, 2 onion beds, 3 rows of beet, 3 rows of carrots, 2 rows of peas, 2 rows of beans and about 6 rows of lettuce. Our lettuce have some lovely crisp hearts. We are able to have lovely lettuce straight from our garden instead of paying 8d in the shops. I help to weed the garden but I do not like to see the large worms which sometimes come up with the weeds. This is our small part in the big Dig for Victory campaign.

Much of the fruit produced in the Biddenham orchards was turned into jam. Mrs Mooring ran a fruit preservation centre and 341 pounds of jam were produced.[102] By 1945 706 pounds of jam had been produced from fruit grown in Biddenham gardens and sugar provided by the government. Some was sent to Bedford shops, and some went to the forces.[103]

Enough vegetables were produced for the Flower Show to continue under Mr H Green at the Three Tuns, and for the proceeds to contribute to the Red Cross Fund.[104] Albert Church's wife and his sister-in-law, Alice Church, went round the village every month with a wheelbarrow and collected vegetables from the residents to fill a hamper to send to one of the minesweepers:

They took the produce to Miss Steel's house in King's Close where hampers were filled and Miss Steel would take them in her car to Bedford to put them on their journey to the coast. When there was a surplus of marrows, Albert's wife and Alice had to wheel a barrow laden from Bromham Road to Miss Steel's and then go back perhaps twice before starting on the rest of the village. They must have walked and pushed that barrow many miles.[105]

Rationing was a major feature of wartime life, and even after the war, until it was ended in 1954. The residents of Biddenham were not daunted by this. The members of the Women's Institute spared food from their rations to provide afternoon teas for evacuees and troops.[106] On 13 November 1943 the WI held a 21st birthday party in the village hall. There was even a splendid birthday cake made from pooled ingredients given by the members.[107] Later on, the WI entertained a party of men from a nearby RAF camp in the village hall to an evening's dancing and musical games, and they were able to provide refreshments.[108] Gifts of vegetables, fruit and flowers were donated for the harvest festival at the church in October 1944. The produce was auctioned, and the proceeds divided between the Royal Agricultural Benevolent Institution and the Bedford County Hospital.[109]

So short was food at times that Derek Frossell remembered with pride when writing in the *Biddenham Bulletin* in 2003 that he could give his box of harvest rations to his mother. This was when he was working on Rawlins' Farm, Church Farm, during the summer holidays from 1940 to 1947 whilst attending Bedford Modern School. The rations, which were only issued to the farm workers who were actually engaged on harvest work, consisted of extra cheese, butter, jam and tins of meat and fish: all very useful to the family.

The comfort of the troops was a major consideration. The president of the WI, Mrs Lilley, organised a knitting party so that 200 pairs of socks, scarves and helmets and 80 pairs of gloves and mittens could be sent to the forces.[110] Albert Church recounts that 'My wife was also an excellent knitter and knitted dozens of pairs of socks for the army. Mrs Lilley would bring wool to Mrs Church on a Friday evening and say 'I need one more pair to make so many dozen. Can you get them done for me by Monday?' and on Monday morning they would be ready for collection.[111]

Christmas parcels were also sent to the men serving in the forces, and money was raised for the prisoners of war.[112] Biddenham residents would have been reminded of POWs if they saw the Italian POWs, captured in North Africa, working in the fields, straightening the brook in Bromham and digging spectacular deep ditches round Bowles Wood. They were very friendly, and made aluminium rings set with celluloid stones as gifts for the Bromham villagers.[113] The German POWs were kept in a camp near Clapham. They were not seen until the surrender of Germany in 1945, but then they too were allowed to go out of the camp until they were repatriated.[114]

Anthony Laing, who lived in Biddenham for more than 45 years and built up a large and successful architectural practice, was one of the 600 allied POWs who marched out of camp PG49 at Fontanellato near Parma, Italy, after the Italian armistice on 8 September 1943. In 1997 he contributed his experiences to a collection of POWs' stories made by Ian English to raise money for the Monte San Martino Trust, which provided bursaries for children and grandchildren of Italians who helped British POWs on the run from the Germans in Italy in 1943 and 1944. The bursaries were to say 'thank you' to those who had risked their lives, and to enable the recipients to come to Britain for a period of study.

Lieutenant A R Laing, RE, MC, walked west into the hills on leaving Fontanellato. He was recaptured when near the Allied lines, but he managed to jump down from a train that was taking recaptured prisoners to Germany, near Orte, on 3 December 1943. He made his way to a Franciscan monastery where he and Jack Clarke, another escapee, were looked after by monks. Fed, restored, re-clothed and given money by the monks, they took a train to the outskirts of Florence. In Florence, they stayed with the Valvona-Buti family, who had risked their lives looking after Allied escapees:

The family were delightful and treated us as a family and we passed a memorable and very happy and comfortable Christmas 1943 with them. They did not want us to leave, but Jack Clarke, Teddy Mumford and I thought that they had done more than their share and that for their own safety they should have a rest. Having tried the Lines and Yugoslavia we then thought it prudent to make for Switzerland. We left them on 21 February.[115]

Anthony Laing's adventures were not over, though. A train journey to Venice and Padua and back to Florence was followed by a final attempt on the Swiss border:

The following morning we left at dawn and, like all good Italian businessmen, in gents' natty city suits and shoes and carrying briefcases, we slipped and slithered our way up to a col, which we were assured was the Swiss frontier, and where we said goodbye to our guides. We descended similarly on the other side and, having just reached the tree line, were happily and carelessly talking when a voice behind us called 'Alt.' Turning, I saw a German soldier in the usual field grey uniform. My heart sank; had we failed again? But no, he was a Swiss soldier.'[116]

Anthony Laing commented movingly on the relationship between the allied ex-prisoners and the Italians:

There must be very few of the 50,000 Allied POWs who

enjoyed freedom, for however short a period, in Italy in 1943/4 who do not freely acknowledge a great debt of gratitude to the Italians who helped us in so many ways to find and maintain our liberty ..... We can only hope that they escaped punishment and did not suffer for helping us.[117]

Another Biddenham resident, Major Alan Martin, spoke to the May meeting of the wives' fellowship in 1991. His talk was reported in the June 1991 edition of the *Biddenham Bulletin*. Major Martin had joined the Territorial Army just before the outbreak of World War II. He was taken prisoner by the Japanese when they captured Singapore. He endured terrible privations in a Japanese prisoner of war camp: the food was mainly rice, with the occasional piece of pork. When he returned to Biddenham after the war, his weight was half what it was when he had set out for the Far East. Mrs Martin heard little from her husband when he was a prisoner. She occasionally received a small card giving brief details of her husband's health, and a little other news. She kept these cards and showed them to the wives' fellowship. She was grateful for their support during these difficult years and for the young mothers' discussion group which Mrs Carey, the vicar's wife, had started in June 1942.

Grace Harral, who was to become one of the vice-presidents of Biddenham's Women's Institute and was instrumental in designing the Jubilee Collage in 1965, had an eventful war in the Far East.[118]   Grace was a trained nurse who had been maternity ward sister at Bury St Edmunds Hospital before going to live in Malaya (now Malaysia), where she was married to the head of the geological department in Batu Gajah. As the Japanese advanced through Malaya, Grace's husband 'saw her on to one of the last boats that left Singapore, but had himself to stay behind and he became a prisoner in Japanese hands. The boat was bombed and fired at most of the way to Australia.'[119]   Once she reached Australia, Grace did some interesting pioneer work when she took charge of the 'Baby Train' in South Australia. This was a railway coach beautifully equipped as an Infant Welfare Centre, and it was hitched on to a passenger train or freight train and taken to remote country districts that were too poor to have a centre of their own. Each village was visited about once in eight weeks, and when the train arrived, all the mothers and babies would come down to it from miles around to get help or advice from Grace and her assistant. She comments 'It must have been a blessing which we town dwellers can hardly imagine.'[120]

Grace herself described the Baby Train in an article that she sent home:

The coach is all white enamelled inside, with little green curtains at the windows, and is fitted up with everything that can be desired - electric light, wireless, kerosene refrigerator, kerosene stove, sinks, taps, water. I do wish you could see it. There is one bed and a divan, which has the added glamour of having been in the vice-regal coach, recently dismantled, and therefore has probably been sat on by most of the British royal family and all the governors since 1900.[121]

Grace did eventually hear that her husband was safe, and she was able to rejoin him in Malaya in 1946. She reported home that:

The voyage out was very crowded indeed, but conditions in Malaya are not so bad as she had expected. She and her husband are sharing a large house with another family, but furniture is very expensive and her own heavy baggage has not yet arrived, but she has got a lovely piece of coco-matting! Prices are very high, and the natives are feeling the rice shortage, but the Government is buying rice and selling it cheaply at a loss in an effort to stop inflation and the black market.'[122]

Back in England, the D-Day landings and invasion of occupied France, as Churchill said, marked 'the beginning of the end.' The St. James' School, Biddenham logbook records that on 21.7.1944 there were '17 scholars on roll and one evacuee.' It was now safer to return home, although there was the threat of flying bombs and rockets. However, the government asked parents of evacuated children to contribute to the financial cost of fostering their children. Most simply could not afford to do so, and children had begun to drift back to their homes in increasing numbers, which was why there was just one evacuee left on the school roll in July 1944. On 17 September 1944 the total blackout was modified to 'dim-out', followed by a relaxation of full civil defence duties. On 22 April 1945 all restrictions on light were removed. By 2 May 1945 all civil defence services were stood down, and on 10 July 1945 the North Bedfordshire area held a farewell supper at Kempston.[123]   In December 1944 the vicar of Biddenham was able to comment that 'The sound of the bells is cheering after so long a silence which the exigencies of war imposed on us.'[124] The end of the war came in 1945, and the St. James School logbook recorded that

11.5.1945 School closed Tuesday and Wednesday for VE holiday and Thursday for Ascension Day.

The paraphernalia of war was duly collected up. The logbook stated:

14.2.1946. The earthenware, beds, blankets etc. stored in school were collected by Mr Farmer, Shire Hall on 26.6.45.
19.9.1946. The gas masks were collected today.
10.12.1947. A man from Shire Hall has just been to collect 2 camp beds stored in the classroom.

The village tried to return to normality, but rationing continued. There were also the gaps, and the memories in particular, three residents who would never return and whose names were inscribed on the war memorial. For those who did return, there were not the support services that are available today. As Jack Matthews recalled:

I was officially discharged on 26 July 1946 ..... I now had to start again from scratch, so to speak, at the age of 26. I would add that after nearly seven years of stress and life-threatening situations, none of us received or had even heard of counselling or any particular syndrome. Had these facilities been available at the time, some of us may have benefited from them.'[125]

Although government-sponsored counselling was not available for the men returning home after World War II, the vicar of Biddenham, the Rev Douglas F Carey, was aware of the need for the church to offer help and support. In the Biddenham Church Leaflet of December, 1944 he wrote:

The Parochial Church Council has appointed a small committee to consider the Church's responsibility and opportunity in connection with the men and women who will in due course be returning home from their service with the Forces.

It is a known fact that very many, while on service in time of war, are brought into closer touch with religion, and a considerable number pass through quite definite spiritual experiences, which have - or should have - a lasting influence on their lives.

The end of the last war, which came more suddenly than was expected, found the Church unprepared. There was much loss to the cause of Christianity because the Church failed to establish contact with those returning, on their return.

We do not want that to happen again ..... We have talked matters over and are sending a letter which we hope may reach all who are at present serving. If you have any of your family who is with the Forces will you very kindly when they return to civil life in Biddenham, let one of us know of their return? That would be a great help and would enable us to extend them a welcome and invite their much-needed co-operation in facing the problems which lie ahead of us all.

In July 1945 Mr Carey used the occasion of the patronal festival of St James on 25 July to urge the residents of Biddenham to treat the return of the men and women from their service with the forces as 'a reason for heartfelt thanksgiving ..... it would contribute greatly to the joy of the Festival if we had that uppermost in our celebration.'[126]

Another important source of support for ex-servicemen and women was the Royal British Legion. In 2008 Biddenham resident, Mrs Joy Bean, was presented with a unique medal in recognition of 75 years' fund-raising work for the Legion. In an interview with the *Bedfordshire Times and Citizen* Mrs Bean said:

I started collecting for the Poppy Appeal with my mother when I was about 16 years old. I've always lived and collected around Bedford and Biddenham. I'm still a great supporter of the Poppy Appeal and the work the Royal British Legion does ..... What would we have done without the men who fought in the wars? ..... I had three family members in the war and lost my brother.

In 2010 Joy received special recognition at an 'evening of appreciation' hosted by the Royal British Legion at the Addison Centre, Kempston. As Joy had now sold poppies for 79 years, an extraordinary achievement, the Lord Lieutenant for Bedfordshire, Sir Samuel Whitbread, presented her with a special letter from the Queen which paid tribute to her commitment to and support for the Poppy Appeal. The Lord Lieutenant explained he had met Joy on numerous occasions, and 20 years ago he had presented her with the British Empire

Medal. Joy wore her Royal British Legion Medal with great pride at this latest presentation.[127]

The events of 1939 to 1945 have now passed into memory. Alan Evans, writing in the *Biddenham Bulletin* in March 2000, could recall the throb of the German bomber engines as they flew over Biddenham on the night of the Coventry raid and flew back again later. Derek Frossell, writing in the *Bulletin* in 2003, remembered leaning against a corn stook having his breakfast, looking up and seeing large formations of American B17 bombers going to bomb Germany, and at the same time British Lancaster bombers straggling back from night raids on Germany. Every year the residents of Biddenham still gather at the war memorial on the Sunday nearest to Armistice Day, 11 November, to remember those who gave their lives for the village and their country. It is always a poignant and moving occasion.

References:
1   Nigel Lutt , 'Bedfordshire and the "Phoney War"' 1929–40
    in *Bedfordshire Magazine*, vol 22, p 47.
2   Caroline Lang, *Keep Sailing Through. Women in the Second World War*
    (Cambridge University Press, 1989), p 8.
3   www.roll-of-honour.com/Bedfordshire/BiddenhamRollofHonour.html
4   Information supplied by Lauren Woodward,
    Assistant Curator, RAF Museum, London.
5   Allied Warships website Commands section, still being worked on.
6   www.roll-of-honour.com/Bedfordshire/BiddenhamRollofHonour.html
7   Parish marriage registers, microfiche BLARS.
    April 1943 marriage of John's sister, Margaret.
8   *Aquila*, March 1944 – News of Old Girls from Miss Westaway's
    Wartime Notebook. Brothers, at BGS.
9   Ibid, March 1945 - News of Old Girls from Miss Westaway's
    Wartime Notebook. Brothers.
10 www.naval-history.net/XGM-Chrono-10BE-Aldenham.htm
11 www.naval-history.net/xGM-Chrono-10DE-Aldenham.htm
12 www.roll-of-honour.com/Bedfordshire/BiddenhamRollofHonour.html
13 *Biddenham Bulletin*, June 2005, article by Rosemary Harris about the

end of the war and Jack Matthews.

14 *Biddenham Bulletin,* September 2005, Jack Matthews, War Memories from his journal July-October 1942.

15 *Biddenham Bulletin,* November 2005, Jack Matthews, War Memories from his journal - the end of 1942.

16 *Biddenham Bulletin*, June 2005.

17 Ibid.

18 The authors are grateful to Ian Robertson for supplying the information in this section during a conversation with Katherine Fricker on 21 September 2010.

19 www.bbc.co.uk/dna/ww2/A4120246

20 www.bbc.co.uk/dna/ww2/A4120381

21 Information supplied by Ian Robertson to Katherine Fricker in September 2010.

22 Caroline Lang, *Keep Smiling Through. Women in the Second World War* (Cambridge University Press, 1989), p 30.

23 K M Westaway, *Old Girls in New Times* (Bedford, 1945), p 54.

24 Biddenham Parish registers, marriages, Microfiche, BLARS.

25 *Aquila*, December 1939, at BGS.

26 Biddenham Parish Registers, marriages. Microfiche, BLARS.

27 *Aquila*, July 1942, at BGS.

28 K M Westaway, *Old Girls in New Times* (Bedford,1945), p 21.

29 Ibid, p 100.

30 Caroline Lang, *Keep Smiling Through. Women in the Second World War* (Cambridge University Press, 1989), p 32.

31 Dorothy Richards, *A Parish History and Guide* (New Moon, 1991), p 33.

32 Memoirs of Maurice Leczycki, p 13.

33 Stuart Antrobus, *We Wouldn't Have Missed It For The World: The Women's Land Army in Bedfordshire, 1939-1950* (Book Castle Publishing, 2008), p 156.

34 Ibid, p 206.

35 Ibid, p 86.

36 Ibid, p 157.

37 Dorothy Richards, op. cit., p 33.

38 Ibid, p 34.

39 Ibid, p 34.

40 Ibid, p 34.

41 Memoirs of Maurice Leczycki, p 21.

42 Ibid, p 21.

43 Ibid, p 22.

44 Ibid, p 20.
45 Albert Church, *Recollections of My Life in Biddenham,*. p 29.
(Albert Church read the proofs of his recollections, but sadly he died
before the printing was finished).
46 Memoirs of Maurice Leczycki, p 22.
47 Ibid, p 23.
48 Albert Church, op. cit., p 43.
49 WI scrapbook, 1956, p 46, at BLARS.
50 Ibid, p 46.
51 *Biddenham Bulletin* July/August 2007, article by Alan Evans.
52 WI scrapbook, 1956, p 46, at BLARS.
53 Ibid, p 46.
54 Dorothy Richards, op. cit., p 10.
55 *Stevington – the Village History*
(Stevington Historical Trust, 2001), p 283.
56 Ibid, p 283.
57 Ibid, p 283.
58 Ibid, p 283.
59 Albert Church, op. cit., p 1.
60 Ibid, p 40.
61 Ibid, p 40.
62 Ibid, p 40.
63 WI scrapbook, 1956, p 44, at BLARS.
64 *Stevington – the Village History*
(Stevington Historical Trust, 2001), p 284.
65 Albert Church, op. cit., p 42.
66 Ibid, pp 41 and 42.
67 Ibid, p 42.
68 *Stevington – the Village History* (Stevington Historical Trust, 2001),
p 284.
69 Ibid, p 284.
70 WI scrapbook, 1956, p 44, at BLARS.
71 Ibid, p 44.
72 Ibid, p 45.
73 Dorothy Richards, op. cit., p 11.
74 WI scrapbook, 1956, p 45, at BLARS.
75 Ibid, p 45.
76 *Stevington – the Village History* (Stevington Historical Trust, 2001),
p 283.
77 WI scrapbook, 1956, p 46., at BLARS.
78 Ibid, p 46.

79 *Stevington – the Village History* (Stevington Historical Trust, 2001), p 287.

80 WI scrapbook, 1956, p 45, at BLARS.

81 *Stevington – the Village History*, (Stevington Historical Trust, 2001), p 280.

82 Brian L (Dick) Crisp 'Some Memories of Biddenham Home Guard, May 1940 – May 1944,' in *Biddenham Bulletin,* October 2010.

83 Ibid.

84 Ibid.

85 Brian L (Dick) Crisp, op. cit., p 2.

86 Ibid.

87 Ibid.

88 Dorothy Richards, op. cit., p 10.

89 Brian L (Dick) Crisp, op. cit., p 2.

90 Ibid.

91 Ibid.

92 Ibid.

93 Ibid.

94 Ibid.

95 Ibid.

96 *Stevington – the Village History* (Stevington Historical Trust, 2001), p 282.

97 Brian L (Dick) Crisp, op. cit., p 3.

98 Patrick Bishop, *Battle of Britain: A Day-by-Day Chronicle* (Quercus, 2009).

99 Dorothy Richards, op. cit., p 36.

100 K M Westaway, *Old Girls in New Times*, (Bedford, 1945), p 91.

101 Dorothy Richards, op. cit., p 36.

102 WI scrapbook, 1956, p 40, at BLARS.

103 Dorothy Richards, op. cit., p 42.

104 WI scrapbook, 1956, p 41, at BLARS.

105 Albert Church, op. cit., p 43.

106 Dorothy Richards, op. cit., p 42.

107 WI scrapbook, 1956, p 38, at BLARS.

108 Ibid, p 40.

109 Biddenham Church leaflet, September 1944.

110 WI scrapbook, 1956, p 40, at BLARS.

111 Albert Church, op. cit., p 43.

112 WI scrapbook, 1956, p 40, at BLARS.

113 R.Rideout, *Bromham in Bedfordshire: A History*, (Roger Rideout, 2002), p 61.

114 Ibid, p 61.

115 *Home by Christmas*, ed. Ian English (privately published, 1997),
     p 46.

116 Ibid, pp 60, 61.

117 Ibid, p 50.

118 WI scrapbook, 1965, p 23, at BLARS.

119 K.M. Westaway *Old Girls in New Times*, (Bedford, 1945), p 29.

120 Ibid, p 13.

121 *Aquila,* July 1944, 'Our Nurses Overseas',
     Report from Mrs Harral, at BGS.

122 *Aquila*, December 1946, 'News from Abroad', at BGS.

123 *Stevington – the Village History* (Stevington Historical Trust, 2001),
     p 287.

124 Biddenham Church Leaflet, December 1944.

125 Jack Matthews in article by Rosemary Harris
     in *Biddenham Bulletin*, June 2005.

126 Biddenham Church Leaflet, July 1945.

127 Article by Michael Hurford in *Biddenham Bulletin*,
     December 2010 – 2011.

CHAPTER 11

MEMOIRS

1 - EDWARD WILLIAM ('TED') PILE 1901 – 1992 FROM A MEMOIR WRITTEN IN 1988

This is an extract from a long memoir in the possession of Ted's son, Michael, of which the authors have a copy. Ted, born on 14 September 1901 in Barnes, London, was the only child of Mr and Mrs E C Pile. The family came to Bedford in 1904, living in Pembroke Street before they moved to 11 Day's Lane, Biddenham. Ted's father worked at W H Allen's as a patternmaker - he was brought up from London by Allen's when they worked underneath the railway arches. Ted's years at the village school are recounted in Chapter 9. When he was almost 13 years old, Ted started to work on Mr Whitworth's farm at Church End, as a stable boy, helping with the nine or so shire horses. His pay was 8d per day.

71 – Three generations of the Pile family, 1905.
Left to right: Ted's grandfather, Ted, Ted's father

We had a new Saunderson tractor at the farm in about 1916, and I had been sent over to Saundersons' works for about four weeks to learn about the tractor, how to drive it and repair it, etc.

The first job was ploughing, and a Mr Brown came from Saunderson's to photograph the tractor at work. We also had a threshing drum wheel come to the farm (it was made by Fosters of Lincoln), and a Maynard chaff-cutter. The chaff-cutter had a blower attached, which was used to blow the chaff up into the chaff barn, instead of putting the chaff into bags and carrying it up to the loft. Other jobs for the tractor were sawing wood, grinding flour and the usual jobs on the farm. There was plenty of road work – carting bales of clover to the station and bringing goods back to the farm; there were 104 bales in a load, which made a truckload on rail. One day a load fell off at the bottom of Biddenham Turn just as everybody was going to work, and it held all the traffic up. There were bales everywhere.

72 – Pile family picnic, Bromham Bridge, 1911. Ted, front left, holding fish; Ted's father holding cup; Ted's mother holding jug.

Nearly all the boys in the village could swim, and we learnt in the river by pulling a small armful of rushes and laying them across our chest, and then striking out for the bank. As soon as one boy could swim a yard or two, there was keen competition among the rest to try and beat him. Bill Williams was a man who couldn't swim, but they taught him. They would tie a cart rope around his waist and let him jump into the main river, and when he went under, they hauled on the rope. He soon learned to swim.

We always kept a pig in a sty at the bottom of the garden for our own use, so we always had half a pig hanging up in the kitchen. When we killed a pig we used to live on pig meat for a fortnight. The butcher was a local man from Stagsden, who used to walk and push his wheelbarrow and scalding tub

73 – Pile & Co truck

and all his knives a distance of three miles to Biddenham. He would then kill the pig, clean all the insides out, and scald the pig in boiling water to remove all the hairs, and then it was hung up to cool till morning. The next day he would return and cut the pig up into ham, two sides and two fore hams. The head was cut into two halves to clean out the eyes and nostrils, so that it could be made into brawn. It was now ready for curing. The leads [huge lead-lined wooden troughs] were now brought out, and the sides laid in them. The hams were put into some more leads with the two fore hams, all ready for covering with salt. My mother made brawn with the pig's head and from the trotters. Pork pies and lard were made from the leaf [the visceral fat deposit surrounding the kidneys and inside the loin]. The chitterlings and lights were given away to men in the village.

Ted started looking for another job in the early 1930s, as the wages were very low on the farm, and he and Gladys were now married. Mr Gunnell, captain of the Church Lads' Brigade, offered to invest £400 in a road haulage business, and Ted's mother lent him £60. He started with a Morris one-ton lorry. Ted's haulage business flourished, and he won contracts with Allen's and Robertson's through his reputation for hard work, reliability and integrity. It was a sad day when in 1949 he lost the business when road haulage was nationalised. However, Ted was able to return to farming, having acquired 250 acres of land in the village. His record of service to the village includes 29 years on the Parish Council (17 of them as chairman), and Biddenham's elected representative on the old Bedford Rural District Council. He also served for 28 years as a special constable, retiring with the rank of inspector in 1968. (From the address given by Dudley Peacock at Ted's funeral on 21 December 1992).

2 - FROM A MEMOIR WRITTEN BY W R N ('TIM') BARNETT, IN SEPTEMBER 1973, after visiting his childhood home, Lavender Lodge.

The Barnett family lived in the village from 1907 to 1936. Lavender Lodge is a two-storey 17th or 18th century farmhouse, standing in 1.27 acres and built of limestone rubble with a slate roof. Like much of the village, it was owned by the

Wingfield family, Lords of the Manor of Biddenham. When the Barnetts moved in, the rent was £77 per annum. The valuer commented: 'House poorish, old and badly planned ... No electric light, water laid on ... Grounds also poor. No tennis court.' Another valuer took a rather different view: 'House nicely shut in, wants some money spent on it, done up worth £110 [per annum], would fetch £130.'[1]

74 – Lavender Lodge

I was born at Lavender Lodge, Biddenham, in June 1908, the youngest of four children. Very early I recollect a grey car in the ditch bordering Bromham Road on the north side near Gallows Corner. The accident gave me a peculiar feeling of foreboding, perhaps the fact that car deaths were to amount to more than those killed in two world wars.

In my very early days there was a field to the north-west side of Lavender Lodge always used for mowing grass (rotation did not seem to be practised much in those days), but in this hay field there was a wealth of dog daisies and quaking-grass, a few cowslips, and even orchids. This was the field in which the Biddenham flower show was once held.

There were three ponds where the children of Biddenham really enjoyed themselves in our early days. One large pond was behind what was then Chibnall's farm, about 100 yards to the east of Day's Lane, and another smaller pond in front of the farm house at the beginning of the path to Queen's Park. There was another pond – and still is – behind Biddenham Manor. The first two have been filled in.

We used to slide and skate on those ponds. An outstanding winter (I think it was 1916-1917) brought about six weeks of skating. It was around 9 January, and it had been raining with a south-west wind which veered north-west and then north-east. In the afternoon large flakes of snow began to fall, which came on more heavily, and then got thick and small as the temperature dropped. The snow continued until the next morning, the deepest and most beautiful fall of snow (one foot, without any drifting) I have seen as a child at Biddenham. Never after, in Switzerland or anywhere else, did I enjoy skating so much as on Chibnall's pond. The late Mrs Chibnall, out of the kindness of her heart, would lend chairs and ask her son Bernard's friends in to tea, to give us never-to-be-forgotten gingerbread and eggs, and tea with cream. The chairs were used for skating beginners. Mr Chibnall would brush the ice, and once Mrs Chibnall said to me 'she has fallen in'. 'Oh', I said, 'how terrible! Who is she?' It was a cow which had been drinking from one of the holes cut in the ice at the side of the pond, and 'she' was easily pulled out.

I remember sliding on the ponds with Ruth Shaw, Gladys Williams, Tommy Sargent, Jim Church, Jessie Keens (who lived in the cottage that 'went with' Lavender Lodge), Teddy Brooks, Bobby Cartwright and his little sister Queenie who tragically died through hanging on to the back of a cart and falling off. The ponds were full of life in those days, newts and frogs and a wealth of frogs' spawn in March. Frogs and toads seem very much reduced in numbers now. This is probably due to the use of insecticides and the burning of stubble, flame-throwers for killing weeds, and so on. It is a pity that we are killing all the good insects and frogs and toads while destroying the harmful insects like aphids, certain caterpillars and the wasp, which I doubt is harmful at all, except when one stings me. An eft or newt would sometimes crawl into the hall at Lavender Lodge; 'yellow bellies', Violet Stringer's grandfather used to call them. After a thunderstorm there would be as many as a dozen toads on the lawn at the west side of Lavender Lodge. Talking of thunderstorms, although the rain was not great in quantity on 9 July 1923, thunder and lightning started at about 10 pm, and continued until 5 o'clock the next morning, with vivid lightning and crashing thunder.

An unusual blizzard for so late in the year occurred on, I think, 28 March 1916. There was sunshine after a snowy night, then rain which changed to snow and howled down from the north-east, causing drifts. Elms crashed everywhere (there were far more in those days). I remember the Rev W E B Norman visiting his parishioners on this bitter afternoon barefoot. Perhaps he thought it would be useless to try to keep shoes and socks dry. Here come back joyous memories of tea at the old vicarage, with its magnificent and superb hornbeam and cedar (still standing), and the vicar throwing sweets for the children to scramble for.

Some of the happiest boyhood memories were bathing in the Ouse above the weir at Bromham; the fields were accessible in those days, but I can't get in now. The waterweeds could be treacherous, and I remember being pulled out of the river, gasping for breath, by my eldest brother Maurice, just in time. Although, as everyone knows, the Ouse is usually quiet, those lush meadows can be covered by a torrent in winter floods, and

I remember hearing of the tragedy of two girls flung out of a boat, and both drowned, when on the flooded river with a man friend, who survived.

Finally I must thank Mr and Mrs J L Knight for allowing me to see my old home after thirty-seven years. We lived at Lavender Lodge from 1907 until 1936. This visit meant a very great deal to me, and memories of every flower and of every tree came flooding back. The Wellingtonia still stands on the lawn, *Sequoiadendron giganteum*, the great redwood of California, and *Quercus ilex* which only grows in the south of England, and I believe will live for over 1,000 years. Mr Glass is proud of his Wellingtonia at the Three Tuns. I sometimes wonder if they were both planted by the late Billy West, as was the Wellingtonia at Lavender Lodge. For boys, climbing the branches was like climbing a ladder. The big may tree (*Crataegus*) has gone, and the *Robinia* or false acacia – but so much is left. It was one of the happiest afternoons of my life to have tea with Mr and Mrs Knight and their son Timothy in the well-kept garden. To see the house and garden looking so beautiful despite modern difficulties gave me infinite pleasure.

Reference:
1   Bedfordshire Borough Council Archives and Records Services website
    – community archives, Biddenham.

3 - DEREK FROSSELL AND ALAN SIMS - CHILDHOOD MEMORIES OF LIFE IN BIDDENHAM

Derek, who lives with his wife Sheila in Duck End Lane, was born in 1931, and grew up in Queen's Park. He is the grandson of Theed Frossell, nicknamed 'Old Nodder', who worked in the gravel pits in Day's Lane. Derek wrote an account[1] of his time on the farm:

I lived in Queen's Park with my parents and younger sister, but all my grandparents lived in Biddenham. I went to Bedford Modern School, where we had very long summer holidays, of eight or nine weeks, and with our local contacts, my father arranged for me to work on the farm. I worked there every summer holiday from 1940 to 1947.

Rawlins' farm was rented from the Wingfield estate. It was over 1,000 acres, and covered nearly all the Biddenham Loop, which is now Great Denham and the golf course. It was mainly arable, but the flood plain was used to graze cattle and horses. There were four farms, three of which were in the village. The buildings still exist today, having been converted into houses: Church Farm, near the church, where Mr Rawlins lived, consisted of the outbuildings housing the stables, cow byres, bull pen and various cart barns; Middle (Manor) Farm, near what is now Manor Hospital, having buildings for the farm workshop, farm machinery, carts and storage for corn, etc; Lower or Bottom (Grove) Farm on the corner of Day's Lane and Main Road, mainly pigsties; and Honey Hill Farm, now demolished, on the other side of the golf course near the river, which had a house and cow byre. Lastly there was a cow byre on the Main Road side of the village hall.

I never saw the farmer, Mr Fred Rawlins. His father farmed at Cardington, and he had a brother who farmed in north Bedfordshire. The farm workers I can remember were Don Dowler, the farm foreman; his brother Nobby who looked after the machinery and carts; Mr Shurety who looked after the horses and cattle; Mr Smith who lived at Honey Hill Farm, a general labourer and cattle man; and Mr Boon, a general labourer and thatcher. There were others, but I cannot remember their names. One was a very large man who drove the Crawler tractor. I remember him because there were very few large people at that time. He lived in a small cottage in Main Road, and had difficulty in getting through the front door.

In total there were about 10 full-time workers. To supplement these farm labourers, a piece-work gang would gather potatoes, pick Brussels sprouts, hand hoe, and do many other jobs that could be paid for by how much they did. These men only worked when jobs were available, and they had a ganger who organised them. Also a gang of Land Army girls from the hostel at Milton Ernest came and helped out during the busy times, as did the five or six Modern and Bedford School boys from Queen's Park.

I left home before half-past six, and cycled across the fields to Middle Farm, where most of the farm workers and casual labourers congregated to wait for Don Dowler to arrive from Church Farm with the orders for the day's work. If it was raining or there was no work, the casual workers were sent home. The start of the day was a time for a laugh and leg-pulling. I am sure that many of the lads received as much education here as they did at school, and it was here that I got my nickname of 'Young Nodder' when the farm workers realised who I was.

The motive power on the farm was a combination of tractors and about a dozen very large shire horses of various colours and dispositions. It was my job to be a horse-boy during harvest. I had to go to Church Farm each day of the corn harvest and fetch the horses in from the meadows along by the river if they had been turned out the previous evening. At the stable I helped to put on their harnesses and collars. This last job of putting the collar on a horse over six feet high by a young lad of four-and-a-half feet, without the horse's co-operation, was very difficult. The horses were also fed and groomed before I took them to their carts either at Middle Farm or out in the fields. To do this, I put a corn sack over one of the horses' backs, and with difficulty climbed aboard to ride side saddle leading two or three others down Church End.

At the start of the day there was usually a delay while we waited for the corn sheaves to dry out from dew or overnight rain. This was a time of relaxation; on many occasions I can remember leaning against a corn stook having my breakfast, looking up and seeing large formations of American B17 bombers going to bomb Germany, and at the same time British Lancaster bombers straggling back from night raids on Germany.

When the corn dried out we put the horses into the shafts of the carts. The carts that Mr Rawlins used were two-wheeled, with ladders extending over the horses' backs and the rear of the cart to increase the load that could be carried. The horse and carts were taken to the cornfield, where they were loaded by a team of people who pitched the sheaves up from the rows of stooks to a person who loaded the cart. The job of pitching required a good technique in the use of a pitchfork – also a great deal of strength to do this all day. I have seen Land Army girls do this job for hours on end. The loader had the job of keeping the cart balanced, loaded in a fashion that ensured the sheaves did not fall off, and getting a good sized load. As I became older and more experienced, this was one of my jobs. The horses walked from stook to stook on verbal commands, and when loaded, the horse-boys took them to the ricks, the red Dutch barn or the threshing drum to be unloaded.

The corn sheaves were either made into ricks to be threshed at a later date, or threshed in the field. The site of the threshing drum and ricks was usually adjacent to the hard farm track that goes from Middle Farm in Church End to Queen's Park, approximately in the middle of the cornfields, but allowing easy access.

If the sheaves were to be made into ricks, the work of unloading was easy until the sheaves had to be pitched up because of the height of the rick. Usually three men worked on the rick, the most important being the man working on the outside, who controlled its shape and stability. The man working behind the builder made certain that the outside sheaves were bound in. The third person had to take the sheaves from the man who was pitching them up from the cart. All the movement of the sheaves was achieved by passing them from one pitchfork to the next; it was very tiring work, and not without danger. I know of one person who was impaled through the thigh by the tine of a pitchfork, and I received a very black eye when I got too close to the man in front and the butt end of his fork poked me in the eye. The strongest man always worked in the pitch hole, taking the sheaves from the man on the cart. One harvest I can remember a Land Army girl doing this work; some of these girls were big and tough. The ricks were then thatched to keep them dry, until threshing took place later on in the year.

Harvest was always the busiest time of the year, and was far from being the rural idyll that many of the younger generation imagine. Some years the corn was taken straight from the fields to the threshing drum to be threshed. During harvest the drum was usually located on the middle track to Queen's Park near the corn ricks. The drum was a large piece of machinery that separated the corn from the husks and straw, doing the same job as the combines do today. Also, as a part of the rig there was the elevator that moved the straw to the straw stack from the drum. The power for the drum and elevator was provided by a stationary tractor via very long webbed belts which had a tendency to fly off, and even break at times.

The cartloads of corn sheaves were taken to the drum and pitched to a man on the top, who cut the strings and fed in the corn stalks. The straw came out at the front, dropped onto the elevator and was sent onto the straw stack to be formed by two or three men into a stack, so that it could be stored to be used at a later date as winter bedding for the animals in the byres. The threshed corn came out of a chute at the side, and went into corn sacks; these sacks were made of thick hessian, and contained 2¼ hundredweight when full. A man had to change the sacks when full, weigh them, and then move them to one side under a tarpaulin to be stored for transportation using a large sack barrow. The chaff came out of the back, and had to be bagged up, usually by one of the casual boys.

Sometimes this operation went on non-stop for two to three hours. It was very hard, dirty, hot and thirsty work for the men. You could not converse with each other. Sometimes it was so dusty that when you approached the drum you could only see a huge cloud. It was not my favourite time at harvest, and even more so if I was put on the chaff job. Today, as with many other jobs on the farm, these conditions would not be allowed on health grounds.

When it was decided that we should stop work for the day, it would be late evening if it were fine. The horse-boys removed the horses from the shafts, put a corn sack over their backs, and rode them side saddle back to the stables at Church Farm. The horses moved a lot faster going this way. As we had no saddles or control over them, it was a case of hanging on and hoping. The horses knew exactly what the procedures were, and if we tried to get them to do otherwise, they would just look at us and carry on in their own way.

At the stables before we went home, the horses had to be fed, watered and have their harnesses and collars taken off. This last job required the collar to be turned upside-down on the horse's neck. We then reached up to the horse's ears, pulled the head down, and the collar slid down, landing on your shoulders. The horses were then groomed: as we moved from one side to the other, we used to go under the horse's belly, and as there wasn't a great deal of room in the stalls, you had to be careful, as the horses used to lean against us, pushing us into the side of the stall.

At the end of each week we received our pay packet from the farm foreman. I remember that we also received our harvest rations at this time. These consisted of extra cheese, butter, jam and tins of meat or fish. The rations were only issued to the farm workers actually engaged on harvest work. I was very proud when I gave my box of rations to my mother, as food was short at the time.

I also had to take the horses to be shod at the blacksmith's in Main Road, on land opposite the war memorial. There is no trace left of the forge, barns, heaps of old iron, and carts waiting to be repaired, except a mound behind the parish noticeboard. Before the horses were taken to the blacksmith, their hooves and legs had to be cleaned, getting rid of the congealed mud and maggots that lived in the long hair of the lower leg. This was a messy job. At the blacksmith's I often had to pump the bellows of the forge. I used to enjoy taking the horse to the blacksmith.

I assisted in mucking out the cow byres. During winter the cattle were taken in from the fields and put into the byres. Their bedding was the straw from the ricks, which was scattered into the byre throughout the winter. By the end of the winter the yard was a big muckheap. The byres were emptied manually, and the muck was taken by horse and cart to either the fields for spreading before ploughing, or to the muckheap on the middle path. If the yard was wet, this was a heavy, messy job. I remember one year my boots leaked, and my feet got wet. It took me weeks to get my feet clean. Sometimes we delivered a load to the cottages to fertilise the kitchen gardens. This was OK, but if it came from the pig yard, the neighbours were up in arms because of the smell.

The farm workers always wore big flat caps – in fact I can remember my grandfather always putting his cap on to go to the outside toilet. I attended a funeral where the congregation were mostly farm workers, and even at that young age I noticed all the very white heads on top of the very brown weather-beaten faces. When working in the fields, the farm workers always had their flannel shirts buttoned up at the collar and sleeves, with a black waistcoat. The only thing that changed was when it was wet or cold, when they tied sacks around their legs and waists. Also, a corn sack was thrown over their shoulders when it rained.

The hours we worked were long at harvest, but the pace was slow. I never saw anyone run, except the time the horses bolted. In fact the horses determined the pace of work.

I cannot remember any of the farm-hands having pets. All the dogs worked, never entered the house, and were fed on scraps. The cats likewise looked after themselves, and were very rarely fed except for a saucer of milk.

Looking back as I write this, it is very difficult for me to comprehend how tough those times were: not a lot of food, no mains sanitation, no electricity or water in the cottages of the farm workers, hardly any holidays, no free access to medical care. It was a completely different world from Biddenham today. But in spite of the down side, most of the people were cheerful and kind. I do not regret any of the time I spent working on Rawlins' farm.

In 2007 Derek Frossell wrote his memories of the river Ouse as his 'playground' when he was a young boy[2]. Four years later Alan Sims and his wife Rita walked the same stretch of the river with Mary McKeown, and Alan compared the scene in 2011 with Derek Frossell's recollections from the 1940s and Alan's memories from about 10 years later. Alan, the second son of Ernie and Mary Sims, was born in 1943, and grew up in Ford End Cottages, Queen's Park, before the family moved to Biddenham in 1961. Biddenham children played constantly in or near the river, but by the 1980s they were far fewer in number. Now it is doubtful whether any children play there at all:

Derek writes: Last summer on a very warm evening I was walking along the river and I thought how strange it was. It was the lack of people; just a few dog walkers, no children, no boats, no swimmers. You may say 'why strange?' Well, this river was my and many others' playground, and on a summer's evening we would be swimming, boating and playing, whilst our elders would be walking along the bank and putting the world to rights. Alan found the same lack of people in 2011, compared to when he was a boy.

Derek and his friends' playground extended from the twin railway bridges in Queen's Park to Kempston Mill. The twin bridges were the favoured place to go and collect train numbers, and also a place to swim, where the more daring would climb onto the bridge parapet and jump off as the passenger trains roared by. The trouble was that the water wasn't very clean, as it was polluted by the gas works. Alan played there too, and used to cross underneath the old metal bridge to Kempston - hand-over-hand, hanging over the water – the bridge has been demolished and replaced by a wooden structure, but the base plates of the original bridge can still be seen.

Derek continues: Travelling upstream, we come to the Slipe, a small park which had an organised swimming place with a diving board, a wooden landing place both sides of the river, and changing huts on stilts with an attendant in the summer. Only stronger swimmers were allowed to swim here, and also you had to pay; therefore it wasn't so popular with the younger people. Still, in the Slipe there were swings and a roundabout – a great gathering place in the school holidays. Alan found no signs of the diving board or changing rooms in 2011.

Beyond the Slipe was Honeyhill Lido and Foster's boatyard,

where you could hire punts, rowing boats and Canadian canoes. These only became available to the younger lads when they started work. A particular favourite of Derek's was the Canadian canoe. Also at Foster's was a café selling ice cream and teas. In 2011 Alan found nothing now remaining except a clearing under large shady trees, and places on the bank where boats could be moored and boarded. He remembers that Foster's had donkeys, monkeys in cages, a goat, and maybe a parrot too.

Derek described the Paddlers, a few yards upstream - a great favourite with toddlers. The river here was shallow, with a very clean bottom and no mud. He vividly recalls seeing at least 100 children with their parents on a sunny afternoon, all with their picnics, having a marvellous time. Alan thought the Paddlers was still a pleasant shallow area – although when we visited the water didn't look very inviting, since there had been a drought and the flow was sluggish. It was difficult to imagine as many as 100 children playing there, and picnicking with their parents.

75 - The Davis family bathing in the river, 1932. Centre – George Davis, aged 18; left – George's brother and two sons; right – George's sister and two daughters

Carrying on upstream and entering into Biddenham parish, we reach the Ten Foot – as the name indicates, a deeper swimming place with steeper banks. Derek says it was a good place to jump and dive into the river, but only if you could swim. It was quieter here, as it was more remote from Queen's Park – unless you lived in the Honey Hill Road end. Next was the Seaside, another place with a sandy, rocky bottom which made it a favoured place with non-swimmers. Adjacent was the Blacky's, popular with the lads, as there was a large tree with branches hanging over the river to which they attached ropes and gave their impressions of Tarzan. This was Derek's favourite place, as it was here that he started to swim.

Next came Steep-bank, noteworthy because it was the only place where a young lad could cross the river without taking his trousers off - but only when the water was low. Derek says it was here that one winter a large poplar tree fell across the river and formed a bridge, creating a challenge that could not be resisted. On to the field with Honey Hill Farm in the middle, where it is said that the shepherd lived. Derek cannot recall seeing any sheep in Biddenham, nor could any of the farm workers with whom he worked.

The next swimming place was Shepherd's Dip, a place with a shelving bank giving easy access to the water for both swimmers and cattle. Then about 70 yards upstream to the last of the swimming places, called Shepherd's Bush. It was here that the lads and Land Army girls swam one very hot summer's evening after threshing clover, which Derek remembers was the dirtiest job he had ever done.

Alan recognised Shepherd's Bush and Shepherd's Dip. It is now difficult to access the water's edge. However, it is a haven for birds, and on the river in the spring of 2011 Alan saw mallard with ducklings, swans with cygnets and a heron stock-still on the opposite bank. A family of Canada geese, with several goslings, were resting on a grassy ledge by the water.

This part of the river was more remote from where Derek and his friends lived, but they all used to come to the osier beds to cut willow branches to make their implements of war - bows, arrows, darts and catapults.

At this point Alan found many changes in the landscape, especially the huge development of Biddenham Vale, reaching almost to the river's edge in one area. However, he was pleased to see a new patch of young osiers thriving near to where he remembered them in the 1950s.

Finally, Derek reaches a long stretch of the riverbank that was difficult to access, but along this path was a place to gather watercress, the only reason he came this far, because we are now approaching Kempston Mill and its riverbanks, where the lads and lasses of Kempston used to play.
References:

1 *Biddenham Bulletin,* April, May and June 2003.
2 *Biddenham Bulletin,* January 2007.

4 - JONATHAN BEAN - MEMORIES OF A
BIDDENHAM CHILDHOOD IN THE 1950s
(Jonathan was born in 1949, and grew up in Day's Lane)

My family moved to Biddenham – from a mile away – when I was five, in 1954. For 57 years, until she died in December 2011, my mother Joy continued to live in Day's Lane, so I have had happy connections with Biddenham for most of my life.

1950s Biddenham was a village before urbanisation, infill and universal cars and television, before bland golf courses and their designer countryside. It was a village of working farms and hedged fields, a village with a working blacksmith – and a village of clearly defined class lines, of farm workers living in damp, unimproved thatched cottages with vigorous gardens.

I grew up playing in the fields between Day's Lane and the river, days spent spying on walkers and building dens in the copse, bigger then, that still exists behind Vicar's Close.

The smell of Brussels sprouts hovered over fields that actually produced food for local markets, tended by farm workers and rural tradesmen who had spent their lives in Biddenham. I came particularly close to Albert Church, a retired thatcher, who lived next to the village hall and tended a beautiful long cottage garden where the car park now sprawls in black tarmac. I used to visit him, in my teens, on Thursday nights while my mother and his wife Edie were playing whist. He described to me his memories of Biddenham, and a barn that used to stand on the rising field opposite Buttercups, long before the infill of the 1970s. A dewpond still existed – and explains the flooding that still regularly happens there, since the subsequent

76 – Edie Simmons making lace outside Parsonage Cottage, 1961

developers ignored this natural feature. In that cowshed, Albert imagined when he was a boy, Jesus was born. Would I, he asked, sketch it for him if he described it? 'Exactly right!', he judged my drawing, 'Now will you build it as a model and I'll thatch it?' That is the crib that comes out year after year in St James's church.

Looking back without rose-tinted spectacles, I am aware of

the number of elderly spinster women in Biddenham in the 1950s and '60s. Many of the marriageable young men of their generation had been slaughtered in World War I. The Misses Simmons in Church End still wore long black dresses and pulled their hair back into buns as they made Bedfordshire lace

77 – Edie Simmons' lace pillow, 1961

under the rustic porch of their cottage. Bertha, remembered for her warmth towards me as a small boy, accompanied me on the Friday before every Biddenham Show to collect wild flowers for my entry in the children's section. There were more hedges and more flowers then. How pleased she was if I won. There was Miss Robins in Day's Lane, who invited me to an uncomfortable formal tea party every school holiday; an event served by her maid, Olive, with scones in covered silver serving dishes. Miss Mallows, an eccentric thirty years before her time, once, during Bob-a-Job Week (an annual Boy Scouts fund-raising event) asked my brother to clean the engine of her ancient car with paraffin. The Misses Herring, whose brother is listed on the war memorial, lived in Day's Lane. My old friend Miss Scott – Scottie – was of that sad era too.

I watched Len Herbert, the smith, in his tumbledown stone and pantile workshop opposite Lavender Lodge, shoeing horses. I can still smell burning hoof. Sometimes we youngsters were allowed to pump the bellow that flared his forge. Increasingly, as smithying neared its end, he made gates. Nowadays we

Biddenham Dove-cot.

THE Inhabitants of Biddenham Parish—young and old—are invited to the opening of the restored (William and Mary) Dove-cot behind the Manor House, on Monday, 11th July, 1932, at 3.30 p.m. At the suggestion of the Vicar the invitation is extended to descendants who have been baptised in Biddenham Church but who are not lucky enough to reside in the Parish.

Colonel and Mrs. Wingfield have been kind enough to say they will be present.

AGENDA OF VILLAGE PARTY.

I.   1. The Law of Dove-cots.

2. Professor Richardson who has been good enough to superintend the restoration will speak (seven minutes), and tell of the work of Foreman King, Craftsman Poole, and Craftsman Hulett.

3. Appoint Warden, Lady Warden, Sub-Warden of Pigeons.

4. Mrs. Wingfield will name eight pigeons and introduce them in pairs to their new quarters. There is one parlour or living room and 461 Bedrooms.

5. The Vicar will thank Mrs. Wingfield and it is hoped, give good advice to the pigeons as to staying at home and generally (seven minutes).

6. Colonel Wingfield will speak to his people (no time limit).

7. God Save the King.

II.   Sir H. Trustram Eve (Agent of the Biddenham Estate) invites everyone to Mug of Tea and Buns (kindly arranged by his old friend, Miss Tanqueray-Willaume, and her partner, Mrs. Lilley). As there will be no waiters or waitresses perhaps the young will be good enough to give tea to those who know they are old before helping themselves.

III.   On the way home there are 130 pieces of our nice local stone to move from heaps on the Green to positions which will be indicated on the borders of roads and paths on the Green. Stones will be six feet apart.

The Freehold of the Green is vested in the owner of Biddenham Estate and if the inhabitants will place the stones, then the stones will remain to beautify the Green and be duly whitewashed.

NOTE.—There will be nothing to sit on and anyone who wishes can bring camp stool, box, or chair. It is wiser to bring a mackintosh if you sit on the grass.

We shall carry on wet or fine.

No parking place for cars, so please walk as in old days.

D. B. T. R.

Estate Office,
2, St. Paul's Square,
Bedford.
30th June, 1932.

78 – Invitation to opening ceremony of restored dovecote, 11 July 1932

would preserve his smithy as a piece of heritage; in the 1960s we thought wiping it away was progress. Most shameful of all, though, was the razing to the ground of the fine, but increasingly decrepit, timber-framed brick dovecote behind the

Manor House. [In 1932 the dovecote had been restored under the direction of Sir Albert Richardson]. It disappeared one morning, flattened as a 'safety measure', despite the offer by the then chairman of the London Brick Company, Mr Bristow, who lived in Biddenham, to sponsor its restoration. I never fail to walk along the Causeway footpath (from the pond to the church), then a well-kept straight pale gravel path, without picturing the dovecote that I sketched so many times.

Day's Lane was a gravel road full of puddles and potholes. There were large gardens everywhere, long since infilled. There was no Deep Spinney, just the peaceful cornfields that were the gravelly bottom of the old pits behind Day's Lane. There was only the one – rather elite, we always felt – golf course on Bromham Road, where the wealthier residents liberally enjoyed the 19th hole and then drove home. Farm buildings were still leaning things of vernacular blackened boards and weather-stained pantiles before demolition, 'conversion' and gentrification. Darlow Drive and Elger Close were fields, the first to be developed, filling hedged fields between Day's Lane and Biddenham Turn. Great Denham was unimaginable; just Brussels sprouts and cornfields.

79 – May Davis, postmistress, outside the post office

I cried half the night after Mr Letts, the policeman, warned me for riding my bike on the pavement on Bromham Road. The police house was on the corner of Day's Lane and Queen's Close. Mrs Davis (May, still living in Main Road) provided us with Walls ice cream, sweets and essential supplies from her black-boarded shop behind the 'Button A, Button B' telephone box. Going shopping by car was a thing of the future. Shopping was done by bus or bicycle at shops in Bedford town centre. Inspired largely by a desire to win the attendance prize, I went regularly to Sunday school run by Mrs French, the vicar's wife. The vicar held a position of some respect.

80 – Biddenham Show, 1956 or 1957.
Left to right: Eric Green, John Knight, Graham Bean, Ted Brooks.

The first village show I remember was in the mid-1950s, a small affair in the old wooden village hall. Later the show became a large part of my youth, as it grew and grew, a commitment that my mother and father – and I – took on for almost a quarter of a century. In the 1950s it was run by John and Margaret Knight of Lavender Lodge, and was very competitive – many of the old villagers were still keen vegetable gardeners. The biggest onions and marrows, the longest runner beans – all the old classes were fought in bitter rivalry – and invariably won, in my memory, by Ted Brooks.

The village hall was a dingy place, entered through an old dark porch of black boards in the gravelled yard between what were still barns on the main street. Tony Maulden ran a small pig farm in the tumbledown barns round the back. The hall was basic, just the main hall with a high wooden stage at one end. There wasn't much call for a car park: everyone walked. I wasn't allowed in the pub. I remember it, from the plain garden, as a generally male preserve in those days, a rather dark two-roomed place where my father could drink Mr Faulkes' mild and bitter as we prepared for the Show. Food was not an option, beyond crisps with a blue paper salt screw in the bag. The 'gents' was a brick enclosure in the garden. It's still there, but the smell has gone now.

I look at films from the 1950s from Ealing Studios now, quaint nostalgic images of a way of life that has disappeared. That was Biddenham, and every other rural village – for Biddenham felt rural in the 1950s: slower times, country characters, gossip and intrigue, no traffic. I am glad I knew it then. I am glad I still know it. Despite all the changes, it still has a sense of community, fostered now by another generation. Well done, Biddenham!

5 - JONATHAN McKEOWN - MEMORIES OF COARSE FISHING. (Jonathan was born 1957, and lived in Church End from the age of six)

It's hard to identify exactly why fishing was so fascinating to my 11-year-old self. That my parents didn't really approve was certainly part of it – but it was more than that; it held out the prospect of access to a fascinating three-dimensional world of beautiful creatures. Yes, that was the bait – and I was soon hooked.

It started with a session of 'bleak-snatching' with Tony Roberts. We had one rod and reel between us – bearing 6lb line (which most anglers would suggest is better for mooring

81 – Fishing on the river

barges than fishing with), a size 16 hook and a pocketful of
maggots. On the riverbank at Church Farm we simply flicked
a white maggot on a hook into the murky water and watched
for it to 'disappear'. It usually did so, because it was inside
the mouth of a bleak. A quick flick of the rod would bury the
hook in the bleak's mouth, and there was your fish. Bleak
are small, flat-bodied and silver. They grow up to about four
inches long, and shoal in their thousands. Bedford Angling
Club considered them a species of fishy vermin. All kinds of
fish were counted in fishing matches organised by the club –
except pike, bleak and eels.

I think I did much more fishing in my head than actually on
the riverbank. I pestered my parents for a subscription to the
weekly newspaper, the *Angling Times*, and devoured books on
fishing. I could tell you the record weight and catch date of
every species of native freshwater fish.

In the 1960s the river at Church Farm was crossed only by the old

Bromham Bridge. There was no such place as Great Denham, or any road to it. At that time a considerable area of riverside therefore existed that was still fairly 'natural'. Downstream from the bridge there were some three miles of riverbank all the way to Kempston, with no intrusion from roads. From a meander in the river about half a mile downstream from Bromham Bridge was a natural flood defence system in the form of a series of pools. These pools flooded at least once a year, and were naturally restocked with bream, perch, roach, tench – and a few pike. We gave these pools names – each was a different shape and depth, and had different vegetation. Most were surrounded by stands of willow, elm and thickets of blackthorn. There was bream pool, hidden pool and eye-pool – so called because it was eye-shaped and had a perfect growth of reeds on the far side in the shape of an eyelid.

John Sawyer, Martin Simms and I caught perch in these pools. I think perch are the most handsome of our freshwater fish, with smart stripes and sharp, spiky red fins on which we always cut our hands when unhooking them. We also watched adult anglers catch bream and large roach.

Our lack of 'proper' tackle was an abiding theme – fishing is one of those sports (like golf) where there seems to be no end to the kit you can buy. In fact for many, the sport seems to be more about the tackle than what you do with it.

After their annual flooding, the series of pools would gradually lose water to evaporation, and, in the absence of a second flooding, the predators would have eaten everything small enough and start to become desperate. We had watched large pike in the pools as they lay motionless in wait among lilies. Sometimes they would strike at passing fish with such a sudden release of power that we'd almost fall in with alarm. It became a serious ambition to catch a big pike.

One day we saw a pike in the nearest pool to the river. We threw in a dead bleak, and were amazed that the pike was so hungry that it came to within three feet of the bank, and in only two feet of water, to get it. Within minutes we had rigged up a dead bleak on a triple hook, and cast it out. It was so easy – the pike snatched it almost as soon as it hit the water. We landed a pike of some six pounds. The pike record at that time stood at 44 lb-plus – a six-pounder was almost a baby, but bigger than anything we'd ever caught, by a factor of about ten.

We should have put it back in the river, of course. But we were so excited that we had to take it home – and we couldn't transport it alive. So we went home and showed it to everyone. It was a beautiful fish – powerful muscles along its back, and most of its fins way back to offer better acceleration. Its mouth was huge, with a fearsome array of needle-sharp, backward-pointing teeth. Its back was olive green, with dark stripes fading gradually to cream on its belly. I offered to gut the pike if my Mum would cook it. She was obliging way beyond the call of maternal duty, frying it up for us all to try. It made the house stink for a few days afterwards. When it was ready, it was rather like eating boiled mud and tissue paper with a liberal sprinkling of needles.

The following year the river was dredged. This transformed the overgrown banks of alder and blackthorn and the reed beds that grew in the eddies into flat, straight banks of mud. The year after that, the tenant farmer filled in three of the pools with a surplus of potatoes that the then Potato Marketing Board wouldn't buy. This act, though small beer in the grand scheme of ecological and economic idiocy I have witnessed since then, enraged me to insomnia for a few days.

Approaching exams – and the discovery that angling didn't really impress girls – conspired to bring my angling days to an end by the mid-1970s.

Many years later I learned that in the late 1990s the Ouse around Biddenham, Bromham and Oakley was a leading stream for catching prize barbel (*Barbus barbus*) – sometimes up to 20 lb in weight. At that time this stretch of the river had a wide variety of fish of great cleanliness and health. During the 1970s, by contrast, it was regularly dredged in the most eco-unfriendly fashion, polluted and devoid of barbel (a very sensitive fish to pollution). So, ecologically, the health of the river had improved beyond measure over those 20+ years.

[Editors' note: we would not advise readers to attempt to cook or eat pike from the river Ouse.]

6 - SOME MAJOR VILLAGE EVENTS IN THE LATTER HALF OF THE 20TH CENTURY

The Biddenham Show, held every year at the end of August, and since moved to early in September, was a focal point for several village families. Jonathan Bean recalls it as a major event in his family calendar; his father, Graham, took a week of his holiday every year to give to 'show time'. For many years Fin Lawlor organised the side-shows, and later David Slark was a driving force.

Profits from the show are always donated to village organisations, and over the years, the show has re-formed and moved from place to place; now, at the time of writing it has settled on the school field and village hall. In 2005 there was a particularly ambitious programme, on the pavilion field, with a medieval Viking village, Bedford Town Band and a spectacular flypast by the Historic Flight – Lancaster bomber, Spitfire and Hurricane.

The exhibitors of the flowers, vegetables and handicrafts have always shown a competitive streak. The Peacock Spade is as hotly contested as ever.

Jumble sales were organised many years ago by Bill and Yvonne Fowler, and later by Joy Bean and a team of helpers. They were huge events, involving many hours of collecting, sorting and pricing. A long queue snaked around the corner of the village hall, of eager bargain-hunters waiting to get in.

82 – Jumble sale, 1980s

The Street Fair, on Whit Monday in 1964, was organised to raise money for renovating the church organ, and building the vestry. David Palmer was chairman of the organising committee, Leslie Wallace was secretary, and Joyce Ormerod

83 – Jumble sale, 1980s

organised a 'labour force' of about 400 helpers. Main Road closed itself to traffic for the day (without reference to the Police). The event attracted well over 5,000 people to the village, causing huge traffic jams in Bedford as far back as the prison, and in a western direction too. Among the attractions were a little zoo, a penny farthing to ride, a hurdy-gurdy, swing boats, bowling for a pig, a balloon race, children's train rides and a shooting gallery. Outside the Three Tuns you could guess the weight of a huge lump of coal, about six to eight feet long. A mammoth tug of war was held, with 20-30 people on each rope. The day was rounded off with a dance in the village hall.[1]

Dudley Peacock chaired the committee that organised the celebration of the Queen's Silver Jubilee, in June 1977 – comprising a whole day of events, starting with a thanksgiving service in the church, and ending with dancing in the village hall and car park. In between there were children's fancy dress competitions; a treasure hunt; fun, sport and games for the under-13s; swimming fun and games for the 5-12s. Then there was the final of the street tug of war, followed by a village tea in Main Road outside the Three Tuns. This latter event was enlivened by the presence of Ted Pile dressed in drag and serving as a waitress.

The millennium was the focus of a huge series of events, organised by a committee again chaired by Dudley Peacock. Fund-raising events began in 1999, and in December a Time Capsule (filled by the pupils of St James' school) was buried under the foundations of the sundial – which was donated by Richard Wingfield and designed by Jonathan Bean. On the eve of the millennium a party was held in the village hall, and 'a picnic in the pavilion'. At 11.30 pm the village joined together on the pavilion field for the 'big bang' millennium countdown. One of the authors vividly remembers this occasion – holding hands in the field with her 8-year-old grandson as the clock struck twelve, and feeling a tingling sensation as she realised that she and her family were witnessing the very beginning of not only a new century, but a new millennium. The rain came down as we raised our glasses to toast the new millennium.

84 – Millennium celebration, sundial on the Green, 1 January 2000.
Centre - Joy Bean and Dudley Peacock

On New Year's Day the celebrations continued. With Main Road closed, a service was held on the village green, followed by the unveiling of the sundial and the planting of an oak tree. The church bells rang out from 12 noon, and a 'millennium toddy' was served at Biddenham House, where mugs were distributed to all village children aged 14 and under. In the afternoon there was a children's tea party for under-9s, and a senior residents' tea party, and in the evening there was a disco for those aged between 10 and 14.

Later in the year, in May, the special millennium stained glass window in St James's church was dedicated by the Bishop of Bedford, and in June the Biddenham millennium ball was held in the pavilion.

References:

1   *Biddenham Bulletin,* May, 2007, *Bedford Record* 19 May 1964.

CHAPTER 12

EDUCATION - PART 2
ST JAMES' SCHOOL, CONTINUED, 1944 TO 2012,
ST GREGORY'S CATHOLIC MIDDLE SCHOOL
AND
BIDDENHAM INTERNATIONAL SCHOOL AND
SPORTS COLLEGE

As the War was coming to an end, education became an important topic – part of the determination to make this country 'a land fit for heroes'. Sweeping reforms were introduced by the 'Butler' Education Act, which introduced the eleven-plus exam in 1944. This exam was intended to select pupils for one of three different forms of secondary education – grammar school, technical school, or secondary modern school – according to their ability. However, because technical schools didn't materialise in sufficient numbers, the tripartite system, as it was called, came to be characterised by fierce competition for places at grammar schools. The act also reorganised primary education into infants and juniors, made secondary education free for all, and raised the school leaving age to 15.

Mrs Cork, the headteacher of St. James' School, was stung by the report on religious instruction by the diocesan inspector in July 1950 – he criticised her because the pupils gave him only 'a very slight response to questions on the Ten Commandments' – and she replied curtly:

The Ten Commandments were not on the syllabus that I handed to Rev A P Mole. Then why were they (the scholars) examined on work not taught? The response was bound to be slight.

There are 14 scholars on the roll, and 5 of them have not been to school a year yet. When children first come to school they have to be taught how to speak correctly.

The average age of the whole school is <u>6 years</u>.

By present-day standards it certainly seems unreasonable to expect five- and six-year-olds to understand the Ten Commandments.

A different diocesan inspector visited the school three years later, after Mrs Cork's retirement and her daughter Muriel's appointment as headmistress. This inspector was most complimentary about the children's capabilities in religious instruction:

In addition to the Ten Commandments which they repeated faultlessly I understand the children have learnt some of the shorter psalms in addition to the Creed.

This was a most pleasant visit, and encouraging in every way. Miss Cork's work, in spite of the difficulties, leaves little room for suggested improvement, and still less for anything but praise; it is of the highest order.

However, a pupil during the 1950s, after Miss Cork had succeeded her mother in September 1951 and was in charge of approximately 20 children aged from five to 11 years, commented that 'no-one from the school was able to pass the dreaded eleven-plus exam'. He recalled that the first hour of every day was scripture, with once a week a visit from the vicar, the Rev John French. This pupil went on to Robert Bruce school in Kempston, then a secondary modern school, 'a difficult transferral for a village boy into a class of 45 children, far behind academically and the only child from Biddenham.'[1] However, this boy fared very well at his new school – 'After year 1 in the top stream, I was always in the top three in class, and won the prize for science every year until I left in 1966'.

School numbers gradually rose in the 1950s, and in 1952

the county council decided that four-year-olds should not be admitted 'as there would not be room for them'. By 1954 Her Majesty's Inspector of Schools noted that of the 22 children on roll, none was over the age of 10, and 18 were aged between five and eight. In 1953 four pupils took the first part of the eleven-plus exam, with Mrs Cork invigilating, and they all passed, enabling them to take the second part later. For the next 18 years, until comprehensive education was introduced, a few pupils took the eleven-plus exam each year (gradually rising from two to 14), and for much of that time the first part was taken in school, with the teachers invigilating. However, eventually, to facilitate organisation and supervision, both parts of the exam were taken in Bedford.

By the late 1950s the school bell had gone, and flush toilets had been installed – but they were still outside the main building. There were washbasins in the lobby entrance to the school, and the main classroom was heated by an open coal fire surrounded by a large fireguard. The caretaker lit the fire each morning, sometimes as early as 5 am in cold weather. A small tarmac playground adjoined the school, but there was no playing field.[2]

In 1955, with sometimes as many as 29 children on roll, Miss Cork was allowed a clerical assistant, for three hours a week. Her mother, Mrs Cork, was enlisted as an assistant teacher in the mornings, and she was also the invigilator in the school's eleven-plus exams. However, pupil numbers gradually dropped, and with only 19 pupils in 1959, Miss Cork was once again the sole teacher, and the clerical assistance was withdrawn. A second teacher could be recruited if pupil numbers rose to 24, and to justify a clerical assistant, the numbers would have to be about 30. The problem was that many parents in the village did not want their children to attend such a small school, and it needed more children so that extra staff could be provided. Also, many parents withdrew their children at the age of about eight and sent them to private schools, because they were worried whether the school was able to secure eleven-plus passes. At the end of the summer term in 1955 there were 22 pupils on roll, and the diocesan report echoed these concerns when it commented that the average age of the pupils was 7½ years, and 'At the end of the present year only one child will be transferred to a secondary school. The reason for this is that most of the children are withdrawn at nine-plus and attend the preparatory department of one of the Bedford grammar schools'. (By 'grammar schools' he meant 'Harpur Trust schools', as there was no state grammar school in Bedford until 1962).

There was thus a serious danger that the school would close, which would mean that the Biddenham children would have to walk to school over the bridge to Bromham. The vicar, Mr John French, favoured closing the school, but many of the governors, especially Mrs Nancy Allott, supported its continuation. About this time a Parents' Association was formed (later to become the PTA, and now the PSA).[3]

Significant improvements to the school occurred in the 1950s – in 1953 a school wireless and speaker were provided 'and Miss Cork shown how to use it'. This allowed BBC schools broadcasts to be used, such as the *Music and Movement* series. Two years later, in 1955, a telephone was installed, and in 1957 a climbing frame arrived for the playground. However, the county council refused to provide safety features such as a bark pit underneath, or even a large rubber mat - the reason being that the children would take more care not to fall if they feared falling on a hard surface! The old school registers and logbooks, despite being stored in cupboards on the fireplace wall, were in very bad condition – mildewed and disintegrating, or chewed up by mice.[4]

The HMI report in 1954 said:

This is a happy village school attended by 22 children as against 6 in 1948. Many of the children, as in the past, proceed to the Bedford schools at an early age, hence there is no child more than 10 years old in attendance; indeed 18 are between the ages of five and eight. They are very free and natural in speech and behaviour, and they delight in working independently. Such is the thoughtful preparation of the Mistress who took charge in 1951 that each child is given appropriate work in the essential aspects of the curriculum in which progress is generally satisfactory; some training in unhurried speech is desirable.

85 – St James' school photo c 1962.
Back row, left to right: Christine Hall, Miss Copperwheat,
Clive Chapman, William Hall, Michael Seamarks, Mrs Beresford,
Miss Cork, Robert Sims, Susan Church, Celia Cashman.
Centre: Geraldine Green, Chris Lawlor.
Front row: Terry Lawlor, Margaret Lawlor, Michael Lawlor, John Sawyer,
?, ?, Denise Hall, ?, Felicity Collett, ?, Philip Chapman, Donald Muir.

The children's artistic and creative efforts are creditable, as is their singing; their musical education, which is enriched by the school broadcasts, would benefit if percussion instruments were available …

A former pupil in the 1960s recalls that although Miss Cork was quite strict, the children all really liked her. 'Because the school was so small [there were 24 pupils at that time], we got practically one-to-one tuition.'[5] Another pupil from this period remembers being caned across the hand by both Mrs Copperwheat and Miss Cork.[6] (Caning was abolished in state schools in 1987).

The transfer to a bigger school was traumatic for many of the children – in some cases, one class at the new school contained more pupils than the whole of the village school. Another problem was suddenly being separated from your friends – because of the eleven-plus exam, some of the children couldn't understand why their best friends were now going on to a different school from them.[7]

One of the first recommendations the Parents' Association made was that a new boiler should be installed in the school. In the severe winter of 1962/3 one pupil recalls 'eating our frozen school milk out of the bottle with a teaspoon'.[8] This proved to be a turning point for the future of the school. Daphne Lawlor took records of the temperatures outdoors and inside the classrooms, and drew graphs. It was obvious that the heating arrangements with open coal fires were inadequate. A visit by the school doctor reinforced this when she arrived in heavy outer winter clothing, which she was never warm enough to take off. She could not wash her hands before the medical examinations, because the water supply to the washbasins in the lobby was frozen. After a few days the school had to close because the toilets froze. The junior pupils were taken by taxi to Brickhill Junior School every day, and the infants were taught in the mornings at the home of Fin and Daphne Lawlor at 35 Church End. Daphne remembers feeling concerned for the children waiting for the taxis in the snow outside the school buildings in temperatures as low as –10°C. Some of the children were not adequately dressed, for example girls wearing cotton ankle socks and patent leather shoes, and boys in short trousers. The parents persuaded the school governors to invest in and supply mobile oil heaters for when the old school re-opened and until the new school could be built. Since this period lasted from 1963 to 1970, the investment proved very necessary.[9]

The following year the Local Education Authority introduced a policy of encouraging all schools to have an outdoor swimming pool. The Parents' Association set about raising 50% of the cost, and the LEA provided the rest. The PA also raised funds to build a changing shed. The pool was opened in 1965, and 'all the children went in'. The same year the school was invited to take part in Pavenham carnival, but they won so many events that they were asked not to enter again.

The first indication that the diocese might consider rebuilding the school is in their inspection report of July 1964; at the end of the report the inspector says:

..... Numbers are small, but this is the only Aided School within easy reach of Bedford, and an effort to raise money locally (it is not a poor district) to build a modern school might be amply repaid by its increased use by residents and perhaps even from further afield. At present the unattractive exterior may hinder this.

By the summer of 1965 there were 30 pupils, and three members of staff. Miss Cork now only taught the juniors, with the two part-time teachers sharing the infant teaching. Two years later, numbers had risen to 39, and the school was considered to be overcrowded. In fact, numbers steadily rose during the late 1950s through to the mid-1970s, from 16 to 58.

School dinners, sent in containers from Goldington Road School in Bedford, now cost 1s (5p) per day. The children ate their dinners while sitting at their desks. Mrs Mary Sims and Mrs Gladys Church were dinner ladies, and later Mrs Sims was appointed as non-teaching assistant.

In the period from the late 1950s to 1974 many innovations were introduced by the LEA: playground equipment, an electric sewing machine, a television set, VHF radio, football posts, French lessons, regular PE in the village hall, country dancing, music lessons. The children were taking swimming and personal survival tests, and competing in swimming galas. They also played rounders. However, in 1965 the diocesan report was very gloomy: '..... Premises ..... Are outmoded and have serious deficiencies. Neither of the teachers with the infants is qualified or experienced ..... Juniors: ..... The learning opportunities offered are not sufficiently adventurous, stimulating and wide-ranging'.

The LEA introduced a scheme for primary schools to keep pets, and to be aware of their natural surroundings. The school acquired kittens, guinea pigs, gerbils, a pet goat, a bird table and nesting boxes. The police came to talk about road safety, and ran cycle training and proficiency tests.

In addition to medical and dental inspections, the children now had eye tests and hearing tests, and were seen by a speech therapist. An educational psychologist was available to investigate behavioural problems.

In spite of having no playing field, the school managed to teach football, netball, cricket, rounders and swimming. Staff and parents ferried the boys to Kempston for football, and fathers coached them on Saturday mornings. Teams took part in many competitive events both at home and further afield. In 1969 and 1970 the school won the Clifford Barker trophy for swimming, and the years 1971 and 1973 brought success in the Bedford and district swimming gala, when the shield was won by the school, and again in 1975 when the school was runner-up in the same competition.[10]

In 1966 a new red, grey and white uniform was adopted. Mr F W Kuhlicke, curator of Bedford Museum, designed a blazer badge incorporating the scallop shell insignia of St James.

Land behind the school was eventually bought for a playing field, and a celebratory sports day was held there in July 1967. (The last one had been in 1952 in the garden of Buttercups in Main Road).

The Parents' Association, led by Fin Lawlor and Pat McKeown, produced a detailed and cogent report in 1968, recommending that the school should be rebuilt and enlarged, and forecasting a significant increase in pupil numbers. They were strongly supported by the vicar, Mr Eric Gaskell, who was chairman of the managers, and also by Mrs Nancy Allott, a long-standing manager of the school. A decision to go ahead with this plan, at a cost of £30,000, was made by the managers the following year, and building went ahead, the architects being Sir Guy Dawber, Fox and Robinson. The church raised £2,250 towards the cost. The new school site was behind the old school, which was demolished, and the stone sold – some to Mr and Mrs Knight for building work at Lavender Lodge. The swimming pool had to be re-sited to accommodate the new school.

It was decided that the staff could move all the equipment into the new school during the Christmas holidays, and this proved to be a huge undertaking, especially since Mrs Hobson was the only member of staff not suffering from back problems. However, several local teenagers were enlisted to help, and Gareth Williams remembers being delighted to receive a thank-you letter from the Bishop of St Albans.

86 – St James' school, new building, 1970

A 10-year-old pupil at the school wrote of her feelings about moving to the new school:

… We have often been squashed up in the junior room, but it has always been all right in the end. I mean once we didn't have a caretaker, and we had leaking roofs. Then we got a caretaker who lived in Kempston. She usually came every day, but sometimes she couldn't come because her garage door had got stuck so she could not get her car out. This usually happened when we most needed her, and it happened one morning when we needed her quite badly. … At that time we had open fires and usually the caretaker's job was to see to them. She was not there that day and so [the infant teacher] said to Miss Cork 'You light the fires and I'll take the children for class'. So Miss Cork lit the three fires. It took her about one hour to carry in coal and make up the fires. …

Also one day we stuck up the pictures we had painted. They looked beautiful. Next day when we came to school they were all on the floor. You see, they had all fallen off because the plaster had come away from the wall. On several occasions we all had to climb over desks to get to the cupboards, and even the teachers had to in order to get to the telephone. We have not much room now in the classroom as we are very crowded. We have lots of paper and instruments around. Big boxes everywhere, so we are glad really to be moving into a bigger school, although we seem to have found some way out of most things.

Some of the nice things we have had, though, are outings, like visiting Sandy bird gardens, seeing plays and many other things, these are pleasant memories. We have had netball, football and rounders matches. They have been nice because most of us enjoy sport. It was nice making decorations. …

It will be sad to see the old school being knocked down, although we are going into a beautiful new one. So I'm writing about it so as not to forget. … [11]

The new school opened in January 1971, and was dedicated on 25 March by the Bishop of St Albans, the Right Reverend Robert Runcie. By this time there were 59 pupils. The school now consisted of two classrooms, an assembly room, a kitchen, a staff/secretary's room and a medical room. In the same year the school house was sold, for £6,100. As pupil numbers continued to rise during the following years, the assembly room had to double as a third classroom. Mrs Barbara Roberts recalls:

Originally the school was designed to be 'open plan', but when it was agreed that this did not work, sliding doors were fitted. This was even more necessary when pupil numbers increased so that there were three classes. There was a medical room, with a washbasin in a cupboard, and the headmistress and secretary shared this room. It was fitted with a proper desk, a large filing cabinet and a typewriter. The staff room had easy chairs and bookcases. School dinners in the old school were eaten at the children's desks. In the new school, the class in the hall worked on the dining tables. [12]

Just one year after the new school premises opened, reorganisation of the education system in Bedfordshire on comprehensive lines began, with the last eleven-plus exams in the county taking place in the summer of 1972. This meant that in September the whole of the third year of the school, and six pupils from the fourth year, moved to Robert Bruce school (now a comprehensive middle school). Two of the fourth year pupils went on to Harpur Trust schools. The school now accepted children from the age of five to nine.

Music was now a significant part of the curriculum – in addition to recorder, some pupils were having violin lessons with Michael Rose, the head of the County Music Service, who also brought regular staff concerts to the school. A school choir was formed, and entries in music festivals are noted.

The whole school was shocked when the vicar, Mr Eric Gaskell, died suddenly just before the start of the autumn term in 1974, and a short silence was observed during assembly.

Swimming continued to be important during the summer months, and the new vicar, Donald Flatt, who arrived in 1976, became a keen football coach for the boys. A cricket team was also formed.

Pupils applying to be admitted from outside the village now sometimes caused problems because of overcrowding, and the Local Education Authority had to make rulings on their admission. Help was given at county level for pupils with problems – either behavioural or having difficulty learning to read. The police also interacted with the school, regularly showing a film *Never Go with a Stranger*, and taking cycling proficiency classes.

In 1974 Mrs Daphne Davies, who had recently come to live in Church End with her husband and family, joined the teaching staff. Daphne recalls:

There were only two classrooms and a hall for the 5-to-9-year-olds, so the classes were of mixed age groups, and they came not only from the village, but also from Bromham and Queen's Park, which of course was part of the parish of St James. (The parishioners and the children beat the bounds annually on foot).

The school swimming pool was used regularly during the summer months, and because of the legal teacher/pupil ratio, a general assistant or parent would help supervise – in my case it was often Mrs Sally Perry (who lived in Duck End Lane) who helped me, accompanied by her toddler Luke, who happily swam with my 5-to-6-year-olds.

Mrs Thelma Coles taught the 7-9-year-olds. If there was a need for a third class, it would be held in the hall. Mrs Boston usually took Assembly each morning, and I played the piano for the hymns, and for hymn practice and for singing. I taught the recorder at lunch-time for pupils wanting to learn. Mrs Elaine Twigden was the special needs teacher, visiting weekly. Mrs Helen Daniels (who lived in Day's Lane), known as 'Budge', sometimes filled in when teachers were absent, and she taught the older children Ikebana – Japanese flower arranging; Mrs Judy White, of Biddenham Turn, acted as supply teacher too, as well as helping my class with handwork. Mrs Barbara Roberts was school secretary – visitors sometimes mistook her for the head teacher! Mrs Mary Sims, Mrs Gladys Church, Mrs Evelyn Sawyer and Mrs Rhoda Brooks were assistants and dinner ladies. …..

We had an active and very supportive PTA who organised events to purchase extra equipment for the school. There was also great support for our schools from the Education Department at County Hall, headed by Mr Browning, the Chief Education Officer, and Mr David Knowles, the Northern Education Officer.

Mrs Boston retired in 1977, and was succeeded by Mrs Coral King, whose two daughters, Julia and Fiona, attended the school. A year later, I left to take up the headship of Shelton Lower School, after a happy 4½ years.[13]

In a memoir to Mrs Boston on her retirement in 1977, after 26 years of teaching at St James', Mrs Barbara Roberts, who served as school clerical assistant from 1969 to 1981, wrote:

Do you remember the 'office'? A table about the size of the present desk, telephone on the wall, and two cupboards of the row at the end of the classroom. A box file ... was on the desk, and the other files were collecting mould in the dampness of the cupboards. But I was lucky in that I was near one of the oil heaters. You sat at the other end of the classroom, your desk across the corner of the room, your back to the door into the Infant Room, and Drummer [Mrs Boston's dog] lying quietly under the desk. To your right were two cupboards, the taller containing exercise books and paper, and the smaller having an ancient tin tray on top of which stood the small metal teapot, jar of sugar and bottle of milk and kettle for the staff tea. Our mugs hung on hooks on the wall. ... We could only see the tops of the trees through the high windows, which had a small pane at the top which was opened by a long cord. In the summer we opened both cloakroom doors and tied back the handle of the classroom door to the piano leg to keep it open, and let a little air into the room.

My duties in those days were slight. ... On Mondays I arrived after Mr Gaskell had finished Assembly and Scripture, and I took the dinner money. ... When it balanced, I handed it to you in a 'Quality Street' chocolate tin, to be handed on to Mrs Boon, who took it into town to purchase a postal order, and posted it to county hall. The origins of this performance are lost in the mists of antiquity. Each Monday I had to telephone the dinner numbers to Priory Street School kitchen, and the meals arrived in containers which were placed on a large trolley which almost filled the lobby, with the rows of coat hooks on one side and four washbasins on the other. When Mrs Sims and Mrs Church arrived, they spread the desks with seersucker tablecloths and cutlery before serving and supervising the meals. Attempts were made to hire the village hall for the serving of meals, but the management committee of that time were unco-operative, so in bad weather the only breaks the children had from the classrooms were trips to the outside toilets, which, being north-facing, froze up each winter.

The laundry parcel, containing the dinner ladies' caps and aprons, was made up on Tuesday afternoons, and on Friday afternoons the attendance details were entered in the summary book, and those wretched percentages worked out. The milk form was also made up for the week from the book which the milk monitors kept. I filled in all the other odd times with filing – our incoming mail being about a tenth of that which we now receive. Letters were hand-written, as were all the requisitions, which were sent in each May for the whole year.

In order to raise some money for the School Fund – then kept in a tin in the cupboard – we had a wool collection one year. … It must have been about then that I discovered that, the school fund being so small, the teachers were buying the prizes from their own pockets, so the Parents' Association agreed to a termly donation of 2s per family – an amount which has remained the same to this day, although some parents send extra.[14]

Barbara Roberts calculated that 407 children had been admitted during Mrs Boston's 26 years as headmistress of the school. At one point there were only 7 pupils on roll, but in the year before Mrs Boston retired there were 73.[15]

Mrs Boston retired in April 1977, and Carol King took charge in September that year. During her five years with the school, numbers dropped overall from 57 to 36. A colour TV was added to the amenities, and an overhead projector, a copier, a duplicator, and a set of *Encyclopaedia Britannica* – some partly funded by the Parents' Association (which changed its name to Parent Teacher Association) and the Managers. The police continued their involvement, adding road safety to their concerns, and the swimming tests now included survival training. Mrs King had to compile job descriptions for all the non-teaching staff. The vicar continued to coach the boys' football, and some mothers began taking classes in art and craft.

From this time, the pupils had more contact with other schools, including visits to Robert Bruce Middle School before they were due to be transferred there. A library scheme had now been initiated in the county, with 200 books being changed regularly by the County Library Service. In 1981 school meals were no longer cooked on site, because only 16 pupils were taking them – they were sent from Edith Cavell School.

Mrs Mary Draper took over as headmistress in January 1982, when there were 40 pupils on roll. In June that year the school celebrated its 150th anniversary with a pageant, re-dedication service conducted by the Bishop of St Albans (at which Ted Pile, the oldest ex-pupil, read the lesson), and a tea party. An exhibition was staged, showing the development of school life over 150 years. In one instance at least, the wheel had turned full circle, as some of the girls were now learning lacemaking. Many past pupils, parents and staff attended.[16]

At the end of the year when Mr and Mrs Flatt left, they presented a sundial to the school. Six months later the new vicar, Neville Jacobs, was introduced. Developments over the next few years included computer courses for staff, and the governing body was expanded to include a teacher (elected by the staff) and a parent. Dance and drama classes were introduced, and regular PE classes. At Christmas all the children sang at the monthly coffee shop in the village hall, and some of the boys gave a demonstration of handbell ringing, which they had recently begun to learn. Football coaching was now regularly undertaken by senior boys from Bedford School or Bedford Modern School, and Ralph West (a former pupil) took classes in handbell ringing.

After five years, Mrs Draper resigned. The number on roll had fluctuated between 49 and 38 during her time as headteacher. Mrs Lesley C Ely was appointed in 1987.

The logbook now began to change in tone, becoming more of an informal journal, with amusing comments such as 'yet another batch of baby gerbils taken to pet shop and exchanged for food', and 'ducks seen feeding in swimming pool; pool checked urgently!' The children attended entertainments at both St Gregory's and Biddenham Upper School, and an annual school book fair, lasting for one week, began. Bedford Modern School boys were taking a chess club, and Bedford School boys coached rugby. Police talks now embraced 'water safety'. Science, technology and IT courses were undertaken by staff, and the headteacher attended a course on 'awareness of child abuse'. A few children were transferred from Queen's Park Lower School, and a special meeting of the governors was called to discuss admissions policy. In 1989 the first phase of the National Curriculum began.[17] The following three quotations from the logbook show how the school was maturing:

18 July: Mrs Kay Thuryeson (School Liaison Officer/Education Liaison Officer) came to talk to Class 3 about gypsies. She was somewhat surprised by the thoughtful responses she got to the issue of racism, as the children already take this in their stride as part of personal and social education.

19 July: an end of term leavers' service was held in church at 2.30 pm. The leavers read from their recently published poetry anthology on the theme of 'home'.

20 July: term ended. Fourth years performed a play they had written, choreographed and costumed, for the rest of the school.

By the beginning of the 1990s the school was becoming overcrowded again, with over 60 on roll, and the governors, hoping to receive a grant for an extra classroom, formed a building sub-committee.

Boys from Bedford School and Bedford Modern School now added reading to their help with football and chess, and pupils from Biddenham and Sharnbrook Upper Schools and students from Bedford College also helped. The school started a nursery class, the library was enlarged, and a second computer system installed.

In April 1992, after five years with the school, Mrs Ely left, and the keeping of a logbook was discontinued after an uninterrupted period of 119 years. Work began on the new classroom, and the following spring it was ready for occupation by Class 3, thus freeing the hall for PE and other activities.

In 1993 Mrs Vicki Burrows began as the new headteacher. An article featuring the school in the Biddenham Bulletin notes that the policy of the school, as stated in the school handbook, was 'to help our children to learn in a happy, caring and stimulating environment'. The children in Class 3 interpreted this policy in the following rules:
1 Consider the rights of others.
2 No fighting, bullying or busybodying.
3 Don't disturb others during working time.
4 Say kind words that won't offend.

5 Keep the classroom neat and tidy.
6 Don't waste time.[18]

In addition to diocesan inspections every three years, the school now had OFSTED inspections.[19] The first, in 1996, was very successful.

In four years the number of pupils had risen from 65 to 87. However, a cut in the budget of 20% (in real terms) was causing problems. The admissions policy had now become a formal document, listing the order in which children were to be offered places if the school should be over-subscribed. In this year 15 pupils were identified as having 'special needs'. Two years later an after school club was started, offering art and craft, cricket, tennis, indoor games, computer use, videos and TV, and once a week a French club. Teachers attended a workshop on the misuse of drugs.

From 1999 pupils could start at age 4, and if the parents wished, for half days to begin with. A second OFSTED inspection in 1999 was summarised by the headteacher in the Biddenham Bulletin:

Attainment in English & maths well above national average and in comparison with similar schools.
Attainment in science above national average.
By the time pupils leave the school, standards in IT are above what is normally found for pupils of this age.
Every day pupils are challenged in their work in the classroom. There are strengths in art, geography and singing.
Standards achieved by children under 5 exceed those levels recommended in the Desirable Learning Outcomes for children of this age.
Inspection evidence supports the overall picture of high attainment in the school.

Teachers' expectations of what the pupils can and should do are high.

The non-teaching assistants provide good support.

The provision for pupils' spiritual development is good and the school provides good opportunities for pupils to extend their cultural awareness.[20]

By the year 2000 a temporary classroom had become necessary, so that four classes could be accommodated. In the governors' annual report Mrs Burrows outlined in detail the educational aims of the school. Another OFSTED inspection was carried out this year. A sign of the times was that four governors attended a course on 'Marketing your School'.

In 2001 the school was awarded 'Beacon school' status, becoming one of only 38 schools in the country identified as part of the newly-created network of 'writing' beacon schools. These schools demonstrate a particular excellence in the development and teaching of writing.[21] With 95 pupils, the school was now over-subscribed, and had a waiting list. Travelling theatres visited, and both staff and governors attended a variety of courses. Sex education was added to the curriculum.

The following year a major project was embarked on – to build a new hall, at an estimated cost of £340,000, of which the school would be required to fund 10%, ie £34,000. The work was expected to take 30 weeks, starting in November. The school now had disabled access, including a toilet, and 18 pupils with special needs. Staff were provided with personal panic alarms, and the fire service and the police came to talk to the children about 'matters of safety'.

About this time the swimming pool was removed. It had become too expensive to operate, and as with many other primary schools, it was decided not to keep it.

In 2003 there were 105 pupils on roll, and the school was oversubscribed for 2004. Including non-teaching staff, there were now 18 on the staff.

The school retained its 'Beacon' status for three years (after which the project finished). The cost of the new hall rose to £480,000, making the school contribution £48,000. When the hall was finished, it was named 'Nancy Allott Hall', and dedicated to the memory of this devoted member of the board of governors, who had died in 2003, and had worked so tirelessly for the benefit of the school.

Mrs Burrows resigned in 2004, and a new headteacher, Mrs Karen Luscombe, was appointed. The diocesan inspection in 2006 described the school as 'having many strengths and good features, with a strong commitment to the Christian ethos, and the school was judged to provide a caring environment inspired by Christian principles.[22]

87 – St James' school – some of the pupils in 2008

In the autumn term of 2008 the school underwent a further OFSTED inspection. Among comments in the report were that the school was 'a good school that enables pupils to leave well prepared for the next challenges in their lives', and where 'teachers go the extra mile in making lessons interesting and fun' for pupils who are 'enthusiastic learners who want to do well'.[23]

A new classroom was added to the school in 2009, and two years later a fifth classroom was built. In 2012 a breakfast club was introduced.

The most recent OFSTED report was in March 2012. These inspections are now made after only two days' notice. The three-yearly diocesan inspection was carried out shortly after, and the school was declared 'outstanding'. It was noted that the school was smaller than the average lower school, and that the proportions of pupils known to be eligible for free school meals and those with special educational needs were low. There was a broadly average representation of minority ethnic backgrounds, but no pupils were at the early stages of learning English. The strong leadership of the headteacher was noted, enabling the children to demonstrate qualities of respect, compassion and responsibility well beyond their years.[24]

We conclude our history of St James' school in the year 2012, 180 years after its foundation. Over that period education in the UK has changed tremendously, the children being encouraged to care about the environment, other parts of the world and people of other faiths. They help to organise the school assembly and sometimes services in St James's church. The regular visits of the doctor, dentist and nurse have been discontinued, except for the children in the reception class who are examined by a school nurse soon after they arrive. Punishment is in the form of 'sanctions' - for the first 'offence', the child is asked to re-focus on how he or she *should* be behaving, and moved to a different part of the classroom. For the second 'offence' the child is moved to a different classroom. If this has no effect, the parents are told, and finally (but this is very rare) the headteacher is involved. The vicar visits the school once a week, and all pupils, of whatever faith, join in assembly, grace at lunchtime, and a prayer at the end of the school day.

There are now 116 pupils on roll, and the school building comprises five classrooms, a hall, a library area, an office for the secretary and an office for the headteacher. In addition to children who live in the parish of Biddenham, pupils come from Queen's Park and other areas close to the village, in accordance with strict rules enforced by the borough council. At present Great Denham is part of the catchment area, but now its new lower school has opened in September 2012 the catchment area for St James' School will have to be redrawn.

There are two more schools, on the edge of the village – St Gregory's Catholic Middle School and Biddenham International School and Sports College.

St Gregory's Catholic Middle School

In 1959 St Gregory's Catholic Secondary School opened in Biddenham Turn. Technically, the school lies in the Borough of Bedford, and the land (and the adjacent land later occupied by John Howard School – see below) had been bought by the Bedfordshire County Council from the Wingfield Estate. The school, like all Catholic schools, had no specific catchment area, but drew pupils from all areas. It was built to provide secondary education for Catholic children in Bedford.

Following the 1967 Plowden Report, Bedfordshire LEA implemented the three-tier education system of lower, middle and upper schools across the county. In the mid-1970s, St Gregory's was re-designated as a comprehensive Catholic middle school. St Thomas More Catholic Upper School was built on the north side of Bedford, and opened in 1978, completing the pyramid of schools. In 2012 St Gregory's School had 360 pupils on roll.

Biddenham International School and Sports College

Biddenham Upper School (now Biddenham International School and Sports College), a co-educational state comprehensive school for 13-19-year-olds, was formed from the merger in 1988 of John Howard and Pilgrim Upper Schools. This school, like St Gregory's, is situated in Biddenham Turn. There are about 1,100 pupils, including 18 from the village of Biddenham in 2012 - the school serves Biddenham village as well as the Brickhill, Harpur and Queen's Park areas of Bedford. Originally named John Howard Upper School, it was built following the comprehensive reorganisation of education in England and Wales in the 1970s. Due to falling pupil numbers, however, it was decided to close Pilgrim Upper School – built as the first state grammar school in Bedford in 1962 and becoming a comprehensive upper school in the mid-1970s - and merge it with John Howard School, on the Biddenham campus. This merger took place in 1988, and the school was re-named Biddenham Upper School. Since 2003 the school has been a specialist Sports College, allowing greater investment in physical education resources. The pupils form a rich ethnic mixture, and in 2008 the British Council awarded 'international school status' to the school, which led to the new name of Biddenham International School and Sports College.

References:
Information on St Gregory's and Biddenham Upper School was drawn up with the co-operation of the headteachers.

Unless otherwise stated, sources are:

The St James' school logbooks and register at the Bedfordshire and Luton

Archives and Records Service (BLARS), reference nos. SD Biddenham 1/1, 1/2, 1/3 and 1/4 (logbooks), and SD Biddenham 2/1 (admission register), and the two later school logbooks which are held by the headteacher at the school. These logbooks cover the period from 1873 to 1992, when they were discontinued.

Governors' Annual Reports from 1990 onwards, held by the headteacher at St James' school.

Diocese of St Albans inspection reports held by the headteacher at St James' school.

1   Dennis Green, letter to authors 2010.
2   Mrs Daphne Lawlor, memoir, 2010.
3   Ibid.
4   Ibid.
5   Celia Cashman, letter to authors, 2010.
6   Margaret Lawlor, letter to authors, 2010.
7   Ibid.
8   Celia Cashman, op. cit.
9   Mrs Daphne Lawlor, op. cit.
10 Mrs Boston's *Book of Memories*, presented to her by the school on her retirement.
11 From a school essay written by Clare Ellis in December 1970.
12 Mrs Barbara Roberts, information provided in a letter to the authors, 10 January 2009.
13 Mrs Daphne Davies, memoir, 2010.
14 Mrs Barbara Roberts, memoir to Mrs Boston, 1977.
15 Ibid.
16 *Biddenham Bulletin,* August/September 1982. Note: St James' School has an interesting folder recording the exhibition, containing copies of photographs of the staff and pupils in 1881, 1890, 1896, 1905, 1908, 1913, 1920 and the 1930s.
17 The National Curriculum was introduced by the Education Reform Act of 1988, along with extensive testing in schools and the publication of league tables.
18 *Biddenham Bulletin,* April 1995.
19 The Office for Standards in Education was part of the major overhaul and centralisation of the school system initiated by the Education Reform Act of 1988. Schools were to be inspected in a four-yearly cycle.
20 *Biddenham Bulletin,* December 1999.

21 *Biddenham Bulletin,* May 2001.

22 *Biddenham Bulletin,* February, 2006.

23 *Biddenham Bulletin,* October, 2008.

24 Diocese of St Albans inspection, 27 April 2012.

CHAPTER 13

RECOLLECTIONS OF CHILDHOOD IN BIDDENHAM, 1920s TO 1990

We asked as many people as we could contact who had grown up in Biddenham to tell us about their childhood here. Out of about 250 contacted, we received over 120 replies, mostly from people born in the 1950s and 1960s, but the earliest were from a man born in 1921 and a woman born in 1927.

About half those who replied were educated at private schools (either in Bedford or away at boarding schools), a quarter at state schools, and a quarter at both private and state schools.

Born in the 1920s and 1930s

From those born in the 1920s and 1930s (a total of nine replies), a picture of Biddenham as a rural farming village with a definite social class division emerges. The woman who was born in 1927 attended the village school (which she remembers as Biddenham Junior School), leaving when she was 14 years old. She went straight from there to work at Allen's in Queen's Park, where she remained for the rest of her working life. The man, born in 1921, remembers the three farms still operating in the village. His holiday job was driving a horse and cart to fetch sheaves of corn to be threshed at Home Farm. Twice a year, when the cattle, which were kept at Church Farm, were moved through the village, you had to shut all gates quickly, or you would find them making free with your front garden. He enjoyed skating (equipped with proper boots and skates) on frozen ponds in winter. In summer he and his friends would picnic on an island reached by a plank in the river Ouse.

These children mostly walked or cycled to school, or took the bus if they were at school in Bedford. It was rare to be taken in a parent's car – and, of course, in those days very few people owned cars.

John Rawlins (the son of the farmer at Church Farm) recalls that there was a strict class system in the village, and he didn't play with the 'village children' – in fact he only came into contact with them at Sunday school. He remembers that at Sunday school the vicar had a 'brick wall' for the mission to China – you paid 2d for a 'brick'. Only half of our respondents said they attended, but Alan Evans says, 'We all went to Sunday School':

None of us were what you would call religious, and found it rather a bore. The only relief was the musical content. The Rev Douglas Carey used to sing (if that is the word for it) whilst walking up and down the aisle, while Mrs Carey played a small organ. It was a terrible noise, and it took us all our time not to fold up with laughter, which of course would not have done.[1]

All these respondents had freedom to roam in the village and further afield, and both boys and girls built dens in all the thickets and copses round the village, climbed trees and made camps, and had campfires too. Some of the boys swam in the river, and John Rawlins and David Hebblethwaite had RAF pilots' rubber dinghies (probably government surplus) that they bought at Hamley's in London for about £5 each. They played in the backwaters of the river, building dams, and also canoed on the river. The pond behind the Manor was a great attraction for fishing in summer and skating in winter. Here is Alan Evans' memory of life in the village during World War II:

The main thing I remember is that we were never 'in'. After school, at weekends and in school holidays, we were out as soon as we could be. You could be out in those days without any worry to anyone, except for the odd air raid! You learnt from your peers – things like blowing birds' eggs, finding the best mushrooms and blackberries, where you could find the different newts in the three ponds in the village. You learnt the names of all the wild flowers, and in winter tracked the animal footmarks in the snow, knowing which each was. You shared fields with cows and horses, each ignoring the other. You called in on Len Herbert, the blacksmith, a man who never showed that we must have been 'a bit of a pain' with our questions.[2]

Alan Evans also remembers that in 1941 he and an evacuee girl called Shirley buried a cigar box in the Causeway, thinking that someone would dig it up one day in the distant future (long before the days of 'time capsules'). In it they placed the *Beano* comic and the *Sunny Stories* of the week (an Enid Blyton publication), some coloured glass beads, different sized buttons and a Player's cigarette packet. He comments 'we (at 11) did not think of the box disintegrating after a time, so the point of the exercise was lost'. Alan also recalls an escapade involving the local policeman, PC Wells, who lived in the Police House in Bromham:

Biddenham was part of his beat, and he patrolled it on a bicycle. He was a nice, upright man, but I clashed with him twice, both times with John Church of Quenby's mill. The first time was on the path between Biddenham Church and Bromham Road, when we jumped out of the hedge at him, firing our cap guns. This did not go down at all well with him. The second time was when John and I broke approximately thirty-six small panes of glass at Bromham Mill, and he came and saw my Dad. I got told off, and I think Dad had to pay half the cost of the repairs – or he may have supplied the new glass, as this was his line of business.[3]

Alan's family, like most country people during World War II, kept chickens in the garden, and he recalls that 'at the age of 10 my friend and I used to sit in the chicken house and smoke cigarettes. We used to smoke two or three in a very short time, with a "puff and blow" motion'.[4]

David Hebblethwaite remembers another local policeman, Sergeant Kirby, who was 'fearsome' – he once threatened to take some boys to court for throwing another boy's cap around; he said it was 'stealing'. The boys were very respectful of the law.

Once when David Hebblethwaite canoed from the weir past Bromham Hall, the man who lived at the Hall, known to be irascible, hailed him, and said he would shoot him if he didn't leave, as he 'owned the river' there; apparently he was protecting the heronry. Another time David and the two Cooper boys canoed from Honeyhill lido to Kempston Mill, where they encountered two large hostile Kempston boys who chased them. David ran away, with Gerry, but Richard turned and thumped one of them – David was very impressed. They fished in the river for chub and bream, but never caught a pike, which was their ambition. As long as David was home to dinner, his parents didn't mind where he was. There were some especially good pools and backwaters in the river for swimming – he had learned to swim at Bedford Modern School. One particularly good pool, known as the 'carrot-washing pool', had a gravelly bottom, and was surrounded by kingcups. He and his friends played bows and arrows, and when they were older they had air guns, with which they shot rooks (rook pie was made in the village). Pigeons were too difficult to shoot with an air gun, as were rabbits. The farm labourers took the rabbits, he believes. The boys also had catapults, with tin cans as targets. Once when David was on the island on the loop of the river, he looked at the brown earth, the river, the trees and the sky, and thought 'this is heaven'.

The girls played tennis, hoops, tops, skipping, marbles and hopscotch, and climbed trees, and the boys played cricket and football. For the boys, mischief mostly involved playing around the dovecote; and 'smoking in a chicken house'. They also scrumped for apples. The girls scrumped for apples too, and sometimes indulged in midnight feasts.

As far as work for the boys was concerned, Alan Evans had a milk round from the age of 10, which paid for riding lessons. He also carried water daily from the garden tap to Mrs Shorley in the cottage on the Green, on his way to the bus to school in Bedford. His first real wages were at the age of 17, when he worked on Mr Rawlins' farm for five months. During this time he received the extra rations to which farm workers were entitled. John Rawlins worked on his father's farm for wages from the age of 14½, and David Hebblethwaite also worked on this farm in the school holidays. He remembers during the harvest the horse-drawn binders - as they went round the field in an ever-decreasing circle, farmers and other men came with their shotguns, and boys came with dogs and sticks. The boys and dogs were in the inner circle, and had first try at catching the rabbits that ran out. Then in an outer circle, and facing outwards to avoid shooting each other, were the men with guns, looking back over their shoulders to see what was coming. They shot the rabbits. David used to help carting hay and making hayricks in Church Farm yard. The ricks were close together, and thatched with hay. Sharp sticks were used to hold the thatch down. Vertical slices of hay were cut with a very sharp knife. The boys used to make dens in the empty bit of the rick, and 'thatch' a roof with straw and sticks.

Only one of the girls from this period had a job while still at school – in the holidays she worked in her father's office from the age of 13, but wasn't paid. She also picked and sold primroses for threepence a bunch, and sold raspberries from the family garden.

Born in the 1940s

We received 16 replies from people born in the 1940s. Only one travelled to school by car – the others went by bike or by bus – or they walked. One boy said he usually ran to school, and another – who went to school in Bedford – walked a great deal 'to save my bus fare, which was 1½ d. I would save it up for a couple of days to buy the *Beezer* from Mr Collins, the newsagent on Bromham Road, or penny chews from Mrs Crummie nearer town'. Almost all the girls attended Sunday school, and also Guides. One became a Sunday school teacher, and one took up bell-ringing.

One girl says she roamed the village from the age of five, and cycled to Box End to visit her grandparents from the age of 10. All the girls had a great deal of freedom, and one was riding her pony over Bromham bridge to Stagsden woods or Bromham moors from the age of seven. The girls enjoyed horse riding, tennis, hide-and-seek, playing in friends' gardens, climbing trees, collecting tadpoles from the Manor House pond, ball games, netball and make-believe houses. Visiting the blacksmith and watching him work was also a popular pastime.

There were no Cubs or Scouts for the boys in the village during this period, nor was there a youth club. However, most of the boys attended Sunday school – one remembers 'our parents were uncompromising in making us attend, in our best Sunday coats'. Another only went because of a desire to win the attendance prize. Dennis Green started Sunday school when he was two years old:

Mrs French was in charge, with help from two young girls, Flora (Flossy) Goldsmith and Sylvia Eyre. Sylvia played the harmonium. I attended every week until confirmation at 11 years old. My parents were not religious, but insisted that my brother and I should attend church until our middle 'teens. I have always loved the Bible stories, and grew to love the poetry and music of the litany; I regard it as a rich cultural heritage, but no more than that. I was taught to ring the church bells at the age of eight years by the tower captain, Evelyn Steel.

The village was still divided into two 'classes', and the boys who went on at age 11 from the village school to Kempston Secondary Modern School had virtually no contact with those who attended Harpur Trust schools – except later in life if they took up bell-ringing.

Alan Sims remembers cycling to Sandy, and swimming in Honey Hill Lido, on the river, run by Bill Norris, who also had donkeys. Alan also did some coarse fishing. Barry Green recalls sledging in the deep hollows in the meadow below Church Farm in winter. He also fished the whole length of the river from Queen's Park through Kempston to Bromham bridge (where he fished for sticklebacks).

As far as mischief was concerned, one girl recalls clambering over the outside of the dovecote, and crawling through bale stacks. One swam in the river during a particularly hot summer – which her parents had forbidden. Some of the girls also cooked food out-of-doors.

For the boys, mischief included scrumping for apples, other fruit and cob nuts, fights with other boys on the way home from school – a sort of 'class war', 'back-chatting miserable old pensioners', and 'risky behaviour on icy ponds and haystacks'. Three children got into extreme danger after accidentally setting fire to a straw stack while 'camping' inside, narrowly escaping with their lives. The boys from this period – maybe due to the after-effects of the war, and the many war comics that were available in the 1950s – seem to have been particularly belligerent, fighting with air rifles, bows and arrows and stones, often between Biddenham and Queen's Park scholars. A Biddenham gang and a Queen's Park gang would fight in the spinney behind Vicar's Close, but they were not so keen after a man had been found hanging there. One boy recalls being sent out of church for firing lighted matches from a toy cannon during a service. A group of boys from this period used to fly home-made kites with long tails, which they trailed in cowpats, and then tried to hit each other with the tails. Dennis Green recalls playing in the farm buildings at Church Farm, Manor Farm and Grove Farm (all now converted to dwellings), which were 'all rabbit warrens of yards and buildings, often still containing machines and processes from a bygone age. As boys we loved to find our way around those lofts and mills, etc, playing cowboys and Indians. The risk of being caught was always an extra thrill'.

88 – Frank Green with his grandsons Dennis and Barry Green, c 1954

Playing football (with adult handed-down footballs) in the meadows was popular with the boys, using jumpers or cowpats for goalposts. They also had a cricket pitch marked out in the Causeway field, playing with adult handed-down cricket bats and balls, and sometimes played rounders. Making dens, climbing trees and fishing in the ponds were also enjoyed. Most of the boys had some form of four-wheeled cart, and spent many long days 'just messing around on them'. Barry Green recalls being a bell-ringer, taught by Miss Evelyn Steel, who was

… Famous for her bell-ringing background, and was in her early eighties when she taught us to ring bells. We were pleased to earn around 10 shillings for a wedding ringing session. She expected us to attend church in return for teaching us to ring, and we had our own pew. Around Christmas we practised handbell ringing, and toured the village to collect money for good causes.

However, some of these boys were also really interested in the natural world, and learned the names of wild plants, birds and fish. Dennis Green recalls his childhood in the village thus:

Adult supervision was non-existent. However, there were six other Green households in the village (grandparents, uncles, aunts), and everyone from the village community (mostly the agricultural community) knew us, so any transgressions were quickly reported to my father over dominoes at the Three Tuns later that evening. There were very few other children in the village (better off people sent their children to schools in Bedford, and there was very little contact, if any). My friend Edwin Walters and I ranged over the village ponds (there were at least six ponds then), and under the bridge at Bromham collecting caddis larvae and pond beetles, etc, and small fish. We had knowledge of most of the wildlife (birds' nests, rabbit warrens, hares' forms, etc) from the Baulk in the north, Kempston Plank in the south and the river bank from Bromham through Kempston to Queen's Park. We took a scientific approach, observing and recording, but not touching. Edwin had a microscope, which we put to good use identifying pond insects. By the time I was seven or eight years old, I was fully mobile on my bike. My best friend, my cousin Nick, moved into Bedford, not far from Bedford Park. We lived on bikes, and by eight years old I was a confident rider in Bedford traffic. The swimming pool at Newnham, Long Holme boating lake, Russell Park, Bedford Park, the Lido at Queen's Park, Honey Hills, were the favourite spots beyond the village, although I recall one time riding out to Olney. Apart from that, we took every opportunity to be on Fred Rawlins' farm, getting rides on tractors and trailers (also shire horses at harvest time) and helping where we could. At eight, I and my cousin Nick (who was a little older) could drive a tractor using both feet to operate the clutch. This freed the farm labourers to load bags of potatoes or sprouts, etc, onto the trailer as we drove up and down the rows. We loved it, but had to make ourselves scarce if Fred Rawlins was around.

I remember the legal age for working was 13 years old, but I started much younger than that by sub-contracting to my older brother. He sometimes overslept, or the papers were late at the railway station, and I would be called for assistance. The round was big, and started at St Mary's House in Biddenham Turn and finished at the church. There were many long drives to deliver, and it took typically two hours to complete. We used carrier bikes with large bags of papers, and then picked up more papers at the Green. Later I took over from my brother seven days a week, including collecting money on Saturday mornings. I seem to remember earning about £2 a week, which wasn't bad in the early 60s, for roughly 16 hours' work.

During hay time and harvest time, my brother and I worked at every opportunity on the farm. Fred Rawlins employed about a dozen piece workers, who were paid by the quantity of work they did, for instance picking up potatoes. There were also a similar number of hourly-paid workers, tractor driving and other things that needed doing around the farm. For instance, tools would be mended or sharpened by the farm's own blacksmith in the smithy at Manor Farm. Shire horses were looked after at Church Farm, and stock brought in every evening at Manor and Church Farms. I was hourly paid, and was involved in most aspects of farm work at that time. We would have worked for nothing – we liked it so much. We worked in school holidays, but we were officially on the pay roll from time to time. During harvest, we often worked from 7 am to 10 pm if the light held. I still have some of my pay packets, and note that pay was about half-a-crown (12½ p) per hour. This totalled about £5 or £6 per week.

Alan Sims recalls harvest time thus:

We would make our way to the current field being harvested. I remember the one at the end of Church Lane where I was later to live, in No 45. The Dutch barn along that cartway was a place of real interest, with the buildings, mangers, cattle feeding troughs replenished with a ballcock valve – we didn't even have those valves in our homes, as we weren't on the water main at Old Ford End – we drew our water from a well, which changed levels in line with the river.

Many of the boys helped on Church Farm, especially at harvest time, which they loved. One boy was potato picking from the age of nine for four to five hours per week, and being paid two shillings per one-hundredweight sack; another boy stacked potato boxes and weeded, for 10 shillings per week. Other boys did paper rounds. Alan Sims bought a blue *Dansette* record player for about £20 with his farm pay, and also saved for foreign trips with his school (this was between 1955 and 1960). Another source of work, at Christmas time, was with the post office.

Several boys mention keeping pets – including raising baby pigeons and orphaned baby birds and wild baby rabbits. Barry Green collected a baby rock dove from a hollow tree and tamed it. 'It would attack the family cat and chase it indoors and up the stairs'. At various times Barry also had a crow, a jackdaw, a grass snake, a small pike in a tank and a little grebe. This latter:

… Was an amazing find on my paper round in Vicar's Close, in a rut in the snow-covered road. It enjoyed the family bath, where I fed it sprats from the fishmonger's. I was cross when my brother returned it to the river, but it was probably for the best.

A considerable amount of fear of adults was generated among the boys: one says he was afraid of the vicar, Mr French, and another was 'afraid of Mr Rawlins, Romola Russell and Mrs Carpenter-Holland-Griffith'. Some of them were also very conscious of letting down parents or Miss Cork, their teacher, if they got into trouble. Barry Green says:

I believe we were very intimidated by authority. The village policeman was respected and was evident on his bike around the village, and when he appeared we always felt guilty about something – probably having crossed someone's private land. At age 11 I recall feeling a little oppressed by the village school regime and more than ready for new challenges.

Holiday jobs were not so usual for the girls of this decade – only half of those who responded did any paid work, and then not until they were 17 or 18 years old. One girl worked in a shop in Bedford, one in the Three Tuns, and another delivered Christmas mail for the post office.

Born in the 1950s

40 people born in the 1950s replied – 20 men and 20 women. One tells of his shock when he left the small, friendly village school and started at middle school, which was so much

bigger. Another recalls ruefully, 'Lessons were interludes between sporting encounters. I had no concept that intellectual competence might somehow be useful – until too late'. There were now more children living in the village, following the development of new housing in Darlow Drive and Elger Close around 1960.

Until 1962 the nearest state grammar school to Bedford was Stratton School in Biggleswade. A significant change came about in that year for children born in the early 1950s, when Pilgrim School (a state grammar school) was built in Brickhill Drive, Bedford, and opened its doors to all pupils who passed the eleven-plus exam (introduced in 1944). If their parents wanted to apply for places for them at the Harpur Trust Schools (Bedford School, Bedford High School, Bedford Modern School and Dame Alice Harpur School) on the basis of this exam, they could obtain a place if their score was high enough.

About half those who responded had joined the village hall youth club, which started in 1971, after 60 young people had indicated their keenness to start one in the village - too late for those born towards the beginning of the 1950s, one of whom says 'the nearest approach to a youth club was the army barracks at Kempston; they allowed young people to meet there'. Most went to Cubs, Scouts, Brownies or Guides, and nearly all attended Sunday school, some of the girls going on to teach there. Several others (both girls and boys) later took up bell-ringing and handbell ringing, or sang in the church choir.

One boy recalls:

Bell-ringing was brilliant, and we had some fantastic parties at the leader's house, particularly on Christmas Eve after handbell ringing around the village. There was a need to get out of the house, and the bell-ringing was part of that, particularly as it was a very young bunch that took part, and it gave us the perfect excuse for the real aim – to get into the Three Tuns and have a few drinks. The ones legally old enough to drink would swear blind that the rest of us were too, and we would play skittles in the public bar, often beating people who had every right to drink there – unlike us.

Handbell ringing was something that took place at Christmas, and in mid-December we would do a bit of practice. Two bells each, and the carols such as *Good King Wenceslas* would be learned by rote, in much the same way as times tables. Then, approaching Christmas, we would tread the same path as the carol singers, but perhaps with a slightly more original offering, around the doors of the village. We were rarely refused a donation, and sometimes we were invited in for a sherry or something better. At the end of handbell ringing on the final night, Christmas Eve, we would finish at the Three Tuns and hope for a drink 'on the house'. Thereafter we went to the tower captain's home for a party, which often went on well into Christmas morning, and was really the highlight of the Christmas season for me – much better than what happened at home.

In Mr French's time as vicar, Mrs French ran the Sunday school, and one girl remembers marching round the church singing 'Onward, Christian Soldiers', and sitting on little chairs near the piano. A boy remembers trying to keep the sixpence that he was supposed to put in the collection, and a girl says she always went to Sunday school, in best clothes 'and called in to auntie Sisi on the way home for sweets [Bertha and Edie Simmons in Church End] – I think my parents just wanted us out of the way!' Several people wrote praising Eric Gaskell, who became vicar in 1966. One girl says 'he was an extremely kind, generous man, with a wonderful sense of humour, and PATIENCE!'

At this time the village hall youth club had about 50 members, and in addition to discos, they played table football. A founder member recalls 'dancing madly to *Brown Sugar* by the Rolling Stones, and being jealous of another boy's excellent impression of Mick Jagger dancing'. One girl recalls the youth club being run by Jim Lloyd and:

… A man called Steve [Martin], who didn't live in the village. We had a disco on alternate weeks, with 'Cloud Nine', which was great. People came from far and wide to the discos, but had to be signed in by a member. Sometimes a fight would break out between the 'greasers' and the 'smoothies' [others referred to them as 'skinheads']. I would walk to and from the youth club, and after the discos my ears would be ringing from the volume. There was no bar or alcohol, but we had cans of soft drinks.

Another girl says, 'We were keen on just listening and dancing to music. We did put on a revue [*Just Us*]; the girls did a couple of dance routines in leotards and boots – a good job there are no photos of the occasion. There were a few bands, and comedy mini-plays'.

About half sometimes travelled to school by car, but mostly the children walked, bicycled or took the bus – there was free school bus travel for state school pupils now. The girls had considerable freedom, some being allowed to play out all day, just coming home for meals, and others only allowed to play in the village and surrounding fields. Some of the girls rode ponies on the footpaths and bridleways, and one remembers cycling to Carlton. One girl, who from the age of five or six was free to roam the fields up to a couple of miles away from home, mentions an 'unpleasant incident which affected three or four of us, which I won't go into. After that we stayed a bit nearer the village till we were older.' Another girl recalls twice seeing a 'flasher' when out on her own.

The boys played in the village and as far as the river, and some were allowed to roam anywhere on foot or on bicycles. One boy was cycling to Bedford at the age of 12, and another once cycled to Newport Pagnell with a friend – 'A meticulously planned and pre-approved expedition, with sandwiches and a flask of orange squash'. Some of the boys canoed on the river, and some played in the dovecote, which by then was dirty and full of pigeon droppings. One boy describes his adventures in the village thus:

There were one or two favourite haunts, the 'copse' being the closest to Darlow Drive, where I lived. The copse was exactly that, a small patch of trees on the southern side of the village, right next to one of the main footpaths to the river. It had a narrow entrance at the path end, with a hump and two trees on either side, like a gateway to another realm. Once inside, there was a loop-shaped track that led around the edges, with a screen of low undergrowth from which you could observe any comings and goings. There were two small clearings where you could all sit down and plot. It was like having our very own castle. Here we made spears, bows and arrows, and later even slings, with which we tried to knock over tin cans. We designed snares that never caught anything; we defended our kingdom from hosts of imaginary enemies (how could you stop a Dalek?), and we happily whiled away many hours of school holidays.

Then there was the 'dip', a great steep-sided, semi-circular arena in the riverbank, down which we rode our bikes. It was a terrifying plunge, almost out of control, desperately holding the handlebars straight against the harsh bumps until it pulled out at the bottom, and you turned to catch the narrow footpath along the river's edge to see how far you could go without pedalling. The furthest distance won. If you got it wrong, there was always the risk of a hideous crash on the way down, or a soaking at the bottom.

My enterprising brother built a large hot-air balloon one year, out of tissue, glued together with flour-and-water paste. At the bottom he attached four 'golden rains' to a light frame of balsa wood. Underneath, suspended from two cross wires, was a meths-fuelled burner. On the night, I was sent up to the top of a stepladder to hold the top, while he filled the balloon, using a hairdryer. This was a welcome innovation for me, as one prototype had rapidly gone up in flames during a test inflation with the burner instead. When it was ready, my brother lit the meths, the lengthened fuses, and off it went. It was most spectacular - the 'golden rains' lasted over at least four gardens. However, we did have some anxiety about the balloon landing on a thatched roof somewhere.

Favourite occupations for the girls included 'hanging around the bus shelter, the war memorial and the bench at the bottom of Day's Lane', horse-riding, making dens, building rafts, playing imaginative games, tree-climbing, hide-and-seek, ball games, tennis, go-karts, cycling, camping in the garden and in the fields, playing in hay barns and grain silos, playing in the dovecote when it was falling down (but one girl was afraid of the dovecote because its walls were unsafe), playing 'horses', and digging a hole in the garden to find Roman ruins, and then deepening the hole in the hope of reaching Australia. Some of the girls were fascinated by the wells, although scared of them too, and used to drop things into them to hear the splash. Others mentioned French skipping, hula-hoops, water fights, space-hopper races, badminton, roller-skating, canoeing (one girl remembers being bitten by leeches), swimming in the river, and trying to make perfume by grinding up flowers. A girl says she found reading the headstones in the churchyard was 'a fascinating pastime'. In winter they skated on the pond, and sledged on tin trays in the old gravel pits on Mr Rawlins' land the other side of the bridle path, but he was cross if he caught them at it. One girl wrote:

We had old pram wheels for making go-karts, and played with them. I was horse mad, and followed the horse-owning groups around for rides and mucking out. We played in the hay barns and grain silos on Pile's and Rawlins' farms and the village hall farm, and when the hay barn was built at the top of Duck End Lane. We played on the logs in the pond at the back of Duck End Lane. We had bonfire nights at the top of Duck End fields with wood from the dismantling of the Three Tuns outbuildings.

A girl recalls being a member of the Royal Observer Corps and spending several weekends underground, simulating a nuclear explosion and subsequent fallout.

Different areas of the village had a distinct character as far as the children were concerned. Church End, for example, to one girl who lived there, seemed 'the noisiest road in the village, where the children stayed together and played together'.

When Celia Cashman was playing in the fields or gardens near her home in Church End, her father used to call her in for tea by blowing a hunting horn out of an upstairs window.

Mrs Shurety's house in Church End was popular for buying sixpenny bottles of pop, and the village post office was a source of sweets and ice creams.

The boys rode bikes, made dens, canoed, built 'houses' out of straw bales in the barn along the track north of Church End, played in the dovecote and in the burnt-out Honey Hill Farm, hid in haylofts and collected conkers. They also played 'kickstone one-two-three', a form of hide-and-seek when you had to return to base without being caught. This game was very similar to one that Albert Church records, called 'Hi Hackey', which also involved shouting 'one, two, three'.[5] Other activities included wide-ranging hide-and-seek, football, swimming in the school pool, improvised cricket, fishing in the pond and in the river, playing with air rifles, flying kites and making model boats and planes. A group of boys in and around Church End formed a six-a-side football team, 'Church End United'. One boy built a 'car' from an old sidecar given to him by the blacksmith, mounting it on pram wheels. Watching the blacksmith shoe horses was a favourite pastime – he seems to have been a very patient man. They also played cowboys and Indians and 'Blytonesque games', and one boy went horse riding at Box End, and had tennis lessons in the village. A group of boys played in the post office field when a pond had been filled in, and there was 'a great big mound of earth that was to be used to fill the pond. We would be either side and throw mud balls at each other'. Coarse fishing in the river was popular with some of the boys.[6]

The girls of this period do not recall much mischief, apart from birds' nesting, apple scrumping, and one or two of them smoked, or went to the pub when under age (but local people knew how old they were, so this wasn't very successful). Together with boys, some girls bought split packets of cigarettes at 'a little shop in Kempston – three or four cigarettes, a few matches and a striker in a paper bag'. One girl says she fell in the pond, getting wet socks and shoes, daily, and another girl went out at night for a midnight feast with friends, and also had a scary experience playing with a Ouija board, when they thought they had conjured up the spirit of the farmer's son who had recently died in a tragic accident at Church Farm. Another girl says she used to drink vodka and lime in the Three Tuns when under age – 'it was the place to meet friends'.

The boys appear to have been more mischievous than the girls – again perhaps due to the popularity of war comics and cowboy films on television. There were 'skirmishes between groups of boys who went to different schools – throwing stones and using catapults'. Fireworks were also a source of dangerous escapades, and smoking in a hayloft. One group (of boys and a girl) recall taking it in turns to hyperventilate, then someone would grip them round the waist until they passed out. Under-age drinking in the Three Tuns was again popular, as was trying to buy cigarettes from Mrs Davis at the village shop. Other pranks included turning round the 'No Through Road' sign in Church End, stealing signs, and 'rearranging gnomes in gardens'. One boy tried (unsuccessfully) to snare rabbits with old guitar strings – perhaps after hearing how his grandfather had had to do this (but not with guitar strings) to supplement his family's food during World War I. Another boy 'sneaked the odd bit of parents' alcohol'.

Most of the girls of this decade had some sort of work before leaving school – voluntary work at Bromham hospital, paper rounds, potato picking and pea picking (from age 11) – for the potato picking, the pay was one shilling per row. One girl worked on Saturdays at a kennels, for £1 per day. From the age of about 14, girls baby-sat, and when they were a bit older some obtained Saturday jobs as shop assistants in Bedford – Marks & Spencer, Safeway, Canvin's, Debenhams, Dollies clothes shop, Lee's sweet shop, Timothy Whites. One girl saved up her pay so that she could have contact lenses – her father having agreed to match whatever she could save towards them – and one started teaching swimming when aged 16, and saved up to buy a Volkswagen car. Another girl worked for the post office in the Christmas holidays, and another did housework for people in the village and at the Three Tuns. Another girl worked in Peacock's auction yard on Saturdays.

For the boys, working on the farms was still popular, and vegetable picking. One boy could earn £11 per week. Or they would drive the tractors while potato setting, and later, when picking the potatoes, chasing the rabbits that were disturbed by the tractor. Another boy counted sheep for the farmer, night and morning. He also worked for a wholesale newsagent, travelling overnight to and from St Pancras station, and throwing the bales of newspapers out at intermediate stations, snatching sleep on the train in a sleeping bag. Now that the village school had an outdoor swimming pool, there were opportunities to earn money looking after it in the school holidays. The pay for a 'swimming pool operator' was 67p per hour in 1976. Paper rounds were now paying about 75p for two/three hours per week. One boy says:

I did a paper round firstly for Bert Redman, and then for Jeff Burden, for about seven years. It took in Church End, Gold Lane and Duck End Lane. I had a push-bike with a basket on the front. When Jeff Burden asked if I would deliver his papers for him in the same round, it meant I had to have a basket on the back of the bike as well.

The pay for delivering Christmas mail for the post office seemed like a fortune. One boy recalls delivering mail to the thatched cottages in Main Road, and 'one of the dear little old ladies was standing outside. I said to her, "No post for you today I'm afraid" and she replied, "Them mouldy buggers!"' Another boy sold Corona soft drinks all day on Saturdays from a van in Queen's Park, for £2.50, and a couple of boys worked for a week in the run-up to Christmas on a Walls' van delivering pies and cooked meats to shops and supermarkets, being paid £7 each for the week's work. One of these boys recalls, 'We had to organise the orders into trays as the van was moving, and nearly puked into the sausages a few times. We started at about 6.30 am in the freezing cold. It was easily the worst job I have ever had.' In those days the borough council was willing to employ schoolboys in the holidays – one found himself counting street furniture [equipment such as lights, road signs and telephone boxes], for about £12 per week. ManPower was a source of employment for some of the boys – working in a DIY warehouse, drilling fenders for harbours at Cardington, serving in a café at Luton Airport. A milk round (8 hours over two days), working in Bedford market on Saturdays, 'bob-a-jobbing' for the Scouts and doing odd jobs for parents complete the picture of boys' employment during this period.

On 28 July 1971 the Williams family, who lived opposite the church, were seriously affected by the tragic death of Mr Cook's son James, aged 17, when he fell from the top of the trailer while tying the twine on the straw bales, and broke his neck. Mr Cook ran to the Williams' house, where only Gwynneth was at home, and she dialled 999 to call an ambulance – but nothing could be done, and he rushed back to tell Gwynneth that the boy was dead; all due to a snapped rope.

During this period (the 1960s and 1970s) there were problems with gangs in the village. Celia Cashman says:

There was a 'gang' – an older group of boys who didn't go to the village school. They would hang around by the war memorial from time to time. If word came that they were there (whoever left [St James] school first would run back and tell the others), we would all walk home together in a big group. Sometimes we walked a long way round – perhaps by Day's Lane or Honey Hills fields instead – to avoid them. As far as I know, they never hurt anybody, but they were reputed to carry knives!

A boy recalls: there was a gang of boys who were a real terror for me. I was often scared to walk home from the bus stop at the village green for fear of being beaten up by one particular boy. On more than one occasion I remember deliberately missing the bus, and then calling my mother from a phone box to ask her to come and pick me up.

Mo-peds and motor bikes were now creeping in as alternative forms of transport to bicycles. For a few, there was the opportunity, after the age of 17, for driving and passing the driving test, enabling them to borrow their parents' cars occasionally. In this way, some young people's horizons were significantly widened.

Born in the 1960s

We received replies from 36 people born in the 1960s: 19 girls and 17 boys. Children born in the early 1960s would have been the first to be affected by the abolition of the eleven-plus exam in 1972, and the full implementation of the comprehensive re-organisation of education in Bedfordshire.

Nearly all the girls went to Sunday school, Brownies and Guides, and over half the boys went to Sunday school and Cubs or Scouts. Seven girls and seven boys said that they attended a youth club. By early 1980 the village hall youth club was offering table tennis, darts, table football, records, swing skittles, chess, opportunities to take part in football, cross-country, weekend residential courses, swimming, canoeing, etc. They ran occasional discos, and also offered various adventure holidays, at prices from £28 inclusive. However, even with all these attractions, this youth club was in temporary suspension later in the year, and closed a couple of years later.[7] The youth club run by St James's church was popular at this time, however, with three boys and three girls saying they attended. One girl remembers making many friends there from other schools, and with whom she has remained in contact. Several boys and girls reported singing in the church choir, and becoming bell-ringers. Four girls became teachers in Sunday school (held in the village school until the church barn opened in 1981).

Cars now featured more prominently in transport to school, although many children were also going by bus or bike – one boy on his motor bike. Those who were taken to school by car usually travelled home by bus. One girl who was at the village school with her brother recalls that 'Granddad used to sit in the Three Tuns and walk home with us for dinner when we came out of school'.

Most of these children – both boys and girls – had considerable freedom to roam the village and further afield. However, the new farmer at Church Farm, Mr Cook, was more diligent in preventing trespassers than Mr Rawlins had been, and often walked around the fields carrying his shotgun; so the area between his farm and the river was now virtually out of bounds. But nearly all the boys and girls were free to roam the village, and many of them considerably further. Girls who had ponies rode as far as Bromham, one girl canoed on the river, and another had a fishing licence. Some went to Allen Park in Queen's Park to play. Bikes were prominent in children's freedom to roam – some boys going as far as Kempston, Wootton, Kempston Hardwick (to fish in the pits there), Turvey and Odell when they were older. One was a train-spotter who sometimes went to Bletchley by train.

89 – Derelict farm buildings, Manor Farm, 1977

One boy canoed on the river, and another swam and fished in the weir above Bromham Bridge. Skateboarding now appears as a new form of recreation – Ison Close providing a good smooth slope – and sailing toy boats on Manor Pond. One boy spent hours fishing for newts and frogs in various ponds in the village.

Many children still made dens (in hedges, in the spinney behind the village school, in cornfields), tree houses and camps – especially in the spinney at the end of Vicar's Close – and played in the (by now derelict) barns in Church End. Go-karts were also popular. One boy remembers building camps in the old barns in Duck End, where he and a friend imploded an old TV tube with a brick, digging a big hole in a field, and playing with walkie-talkies. Girls camped overnight in the garden, had water fights, and went bird-watching by the pond. However, the most popular occupations were hide-and-seek (for the boys sometimes all over the village and surrounding fields), 'cops and robbers', cricket, tennis, badminton, French cricket, rounders, croquet, roller-skating, kickstone one-two-three, catching tadpoles in the village pond, and swimming in the village school pool in the summer holidays. Some of the girls also played on stilts and pogo sticks, with go-karts, and (at school) group skipping. Girls also enjoyed dressing up and role play. They often gathered in a group at the war memorial, and when they were older, went shopping in Bedford. One girl remembers, 'I would visit a lady [Pearl Forrest in Main Road] who kept a pony in the field behind her bungalow (now sadly all built on) and cycle round the village with her when she took him out for a ride; very Enid Blyton!'

The mischief this group indulged in included: for the girls, scrumping for apples, playing 'ring and run', 'trick or treat', hiding in haystacks, playing in the crops and hay barns, smoking in the fields, 'rendezvous-ing in the bus shelter for illicit cigarettes', going out to the Manor pond bird-watching at 6 am before their parents were awake – one group of girls got covered in mud there, and went to the village hall toilets to clean up before daring to go home. However, they somehow got locked in. Two girls recall riding their ponies over the farmer's land. Another girl remembers:

I used to sneak out to Stapleton's grocery van, which came really late, about 10 pm sometimes, to buy sweets. This involved creeping down the stairs, leaning against the door jamb of the sitting room with my left hand, while taking a big step over the last two treads, which creaked dreadfully. Then I had to do the same in reverse, with the loot! I did confess this to my parents, but not until I was quite grown up.

The Three Tuns featured in another girl's memory of mischief:

A group of my friends used to meet up at the semi-circular seat at the bottom of Day's Lane, club together a few pennies, and send the oldest-looking one down to the Three Tuns for two litres of cider, which we shared between about 12 of us, and enjoyed the whole clandestine experience – pretending to be drunk – until it was time to go home, which in summer time was usually when it got dark.

Another girl recalls family gatherings in the Three Tuns:

The Three Tuns featured largely in all our lives – it was such a wonderful true village pub, and we spent many happy lunches in the garden, or evenings with friends and family. My brother and I went to a fancy dress party one New Year's Eve there. Unfortunately we were the only ones to turn up in fancy dress – a bit unfortunate, as I was sporting a suit of armour which was really uncomfortable!

The boys were, again, more mischievous than the girls: one recalls breaking into the old wheelwright's hut in Duck End and 'purloining various items, including mantraps and old tools'; letting off fire crackers and throwing them over friends' garden fences; playing the fruit machines at the Three Tuns; trying to shoot pigeons with air rifles; going for bike rides at 2 am; sneaking into Santa Pod to watch the drag racing; and scrumping for apples.

The girls took on a variety of paid work when they were older, and one worked voluntarily at St Etheldreda's children's home in Bedford. Baby-sitting was popular for earning pocket money, as were paper rounds and working at the Three Tuns. One girl had a regular weekday baby-sitting booking, for 75p. Some girls worked in Bedford: Beavis's china shop, Argos, the baker in the Arcade (9-5 on Saturdays, £10 age 16), Bedford Sports (£5 for a whole Saturday, age 16), the Health Food shop, a hairdresser, (8 hours for £3, age 14), Marks & Spencer. Other girls worked at Mike Pile's farm shop and picking strawberries, or at Unilever in Sharnbrook.

90 – The wheelwright's shop
in Duck End Lane,
crumbling into oblivion, late 1970s

Paper rounds were poorly paid at this time, but ten of the boys reported taking up this work – one recalls 'working for one hour a day, seven days a week, and the pay was in coins, so can't have been as much as £1!'

This boy also sang in the church choir at weddings, for which he was paid 50p or £1. Another boy worked 45 minutes a day on a paper round, for £1.50 per week, and one worked two or three hours a week at the age of 15 for about £1.50 per week. Two boys undertook milk rounds, bringing in £2 to £4 per week. A boy worked on Michael Pile's farm, and another worked on one of the farms for 40 hours per week, from the age of 11 to 18, in school holidays, for which he was paid about 50p per hour. Other jobs undertaken by these boys were working in a café in Bedford, at a newsagent's on Saturday afternoons, in the Bedford Iron Foundry kitchen, at a filling station in Bedford (age 13) for two or three evenings, and (having access to a car) working on Bedfordia farms at Milton Ernest, 'managing 100 hours per week during harvest'. One boy delivered groceries on his bike on Saturdays, and another delivered Christmas post for the post office.

A boy comments:

We had plenty of freedom and no real concerns about security, except riding bikes at night through the unlit village with the inadequate lights and dynamos of the time. I accessed most of my teenage entertainment by bike in Bedford, mainly just eating sleeping and doing homework in Biddenham. It was pretty, but not a whole lot going on!

Born in the 1970s

Five girls and seven boys replied to our questionnaire. They travelled to school by car, bike, or walked or took the school bus. One boy recalls the shock he felt when he transferred from the village school, where there were 45 pupils, to Robert Bruce in Kempston. He found life rather lonely there, because his friends lived too far away for playing together after school or in the holidays.

Two girls went to the church youth club, all five were Brownies and/or Guides, and they all attended Sunday school, one going on to teach there, and another becoming a bell-ringer. They played in the village, and also further afield, as far as Bromham. One belonged to a gang, and so did her brother. Popular games were: rounders, sardines, army games (with older brother), tennis, skating round the house, games of ball against a wall, make-believe, hide-and-seek, plays, making dens, fishing for tadpoles, horse petting and dog walking. One girl flew her kite in the paddock on the south side of Church End, and was praised by the farmer for helping to scare the birds away from the crops.

91 – The Church Sunday school and youth club, 1981. Second row from back, left hand side – Anne Mellor and Dorothy Richards; right hand side – Karen Hurn, Laurie Hurn and Hilary Hurn.

One of the boys attended 'Sundays at Seven' held fortnightly in the church barn. (This group, for 11- to 18-year-olds, originated in the home of Jim Pringle in 1983, and from 1987 was run by Mrs Hilary Hurn, assisted by other teachers.

About 30 children attended at any one time). Another boy attended the Saturday evening youth club in the church barn, run by Laurie Hurn, which was intended for all children, not just those who came to church. This youth club, for 12- to 17-year-olds, ran from 1981 to 1986, with about 15 members, and offered darts, snooker, netball, and five-a-side football for the boys. One boy praised the vicar, Donald Flatt, for playing cricket with the boys, and starting a youth club for them, and also praised Mr and Mrs Hurn for their work with children in the village. Three boys were Cubs/Scouts, and four attended Sunday school. They played in the village and the fields as far as the river. They spent much of their time on bikes in the village, and also played tennis, football and cricket, and swam in the school pool. One group of boys, including several from outside the village, built a huge den near the heronry in the Baulk. Den building seems to be a universal urge in children – one boy made one in the village hall newspaper store. Two boys had a motorised go-kart powered by a lawn mower engine, which prompted complaints from neighbours because of the noise it made. They also had a motor scooter which they once accidentally rode into the river.

The mischief the boys mention includes: 'knock down ginger', garden hopping (having to get from a garden near the bottom of Day's Lane to one near the top, via the back gardens and climbing the intervening fences), swimming in the village school pool after dark, playing cards in the tennis hut, creeping into people's gardens on night manoeuvres, and illicitly smoking cigarettes. One boy remembers, with a friend, riffling through the skips that were placed around the village for people to put their large-size rubbish in. Another group of boys played strip poker in the newspaper store, and engaged in fights between boys from different streets in the village, 'but all was friendly afterwards and at school'. This fighting was probably set off by the tug-of-war between Duck End and Day's Lane at the 1977 Jubilee celebrations in the village.

The girls' mischief consisted mainly of 'dares' in neighbours' gardens, sneaking out of the house a couple of times and going to night clubs while saying they were staying at a friend's house, and playing near the river and the pond.

One girl worked long hours in the holidays at the Swan hotel in Bedford, and another worked as a waitress in a hotel in town – up to 30 hours per week in the holidays, at nearly £3 per hour. Other jobs were paper rounds, cleaning cars, baby-sitting – at age 16 one girl earned £3.50 per hour for five hours, which was a good wage.

Cleaning cars from the age of about 10 was the work undertaken by one boy, and another collected eggs at Stagsden egg farm from the age of about 14, being paid sevenpence per tray of 24 eggs. Helping the milkman during the school holidays and at weekends brought in about 20-50p per round for one boy, from the age of about 10. He spent two to three hours at weekends, and 15-20 hours a week during school holidays. One brother and sister used to potato-pick on Church Farm, and also did 'rogue-ing' – picking out the wild oats from the wheat.

Born in the 1980s

A total of eleven people responded who were born in the 1980s – seven girls and four boys. Three boys and two girls attended the youth club, and one boy and five girls went to Sunday school, and another boy to the youth club run for the church by Michael Hurford. Three boys went to Cubs/Scouts, and four girls to Brownies/Guides. By this time they were almost all going to school by car – otherwise by bike or on the bus.

While these children were growing up, the new development of housing in Deep Spinney was completed, and thus a large swathe of land for roaming was denied them. However, the new houses meant there were now more children in the village, and the provision of the playing field, tennis courts, children's playground and the pavilion were a huge bonus to the village in general.

These children mostly played in the village or in Great Denham, which was now under construction. However, the same games and activities took place as in earlier times – building dens, riding bikes; playing tennis, rugby, cricket and football on the pavilion playing field. There was also now a playground for young children next to the pavilion, with swings and other equipment.

One girl writes at length about how being at school in Bedford affected her life in relation to the village:

At weekends, until I was about 10 years old, I went to a gymnastics class in Bedford on Saturday mornings. In my spare time I would sometimes play in the road with the kids who also lived here. We would cycle and rollerblade up and down Hampden Court. We all went to different schools, and were different ages, but we played in the road after school and some weekends. Our meetings were never organised, and we rarely did much apart from rollerblading or skating in the road, or going to the pavilion park.

After the age of about 10, I stopped playing out in the village, and had more sporting commitments, like hockey, swimming, tennis and gymnastics. These would occupy me a lot, and I would not have either the time or the energy to play in the road. Of course, all these activities would be outside the village, either at school or in another part of Bedford.

We didn't really get up to much mischief; I suppose I sound a bit boring, but there was always something occupying my time. I didn't belong to the youth club or go to Sunday school, but I did go to Rainbows, then Brownies. I then quit Brownies, as it became too much to do, along with all my sports. Whilst writing this, I've realised that I actually didn't have much to

324

do with Biddenham when I was growing up, apart from living here. I suppose it's because I didn't go to school in the village. School, which was a huge part of my life, was in Bedford; so it almost seemed that Biddenham was just my base.

Touch rugby was played by boys and girls together, and one girl practised 'Crufts' agility' with dogs. Rollerblading was still popular, and one of the boys went into Bedford to skateboard, and to Bromham to play basketball. One group of boys had a very secret hideout in the village, where they used to play with small guns that fired plastic pellets. One day, one of these boys accidentally set alight a patch of grass. 'When we realised how dry it all was one of us had to run to the nearest house and get them to call the fire brigade. We must have only burnt a small area, but I remember they made us wait in the house, telling us it wasn't safe outside (when we knew it was) and then the police arrived and took us home to our parents!'

The mischief owned up to by the boys included playing in the half-built houses in Great Denham, knocking on doors and running away (a perennial!), 'trying to buy beer from the Three Tuns when obviously 12 years old', and 'misplacing the odd road sign'. The pavilion area became a meeting place for a group of boys:

We used to sit at the park and thought it was cool to sit at the top of the swing frame on the big swings. There were a few houses that would call people from the council when we were sitting at the park playing, and tell them there was a group of kids hanging around up to no good, etc. So sometimes we played knock-a-door run, especially to people in the village who we thought called the parish council or came down to check up on us while we were hanging around the park. We used to go over to the phone box outside the village hall, and make prank phone calls to free numbers. We would all listen and rate each other's story made up to the people at the other end of the phone.

One of the girls admitted having parties at home when her parents were out; one remembers scrumping for apples (another perennial). Two more misdemeanours were throwing balls at cars at night, and exploring the Great Denham building site. Another girl says she remembers 'singing "Jerusalem" in the middle of the village after a night out with the lads, picking lilac out of people's gardens to give to my grandma, and saving up my church collection money so I could buy *Horse and Hound* instead'.

Paper rounds featured yet again in the paid work of these children – now the pay was a lot better, one boy receiving £17.50 per week for five hours' work, and another boy worked in a newsagent's shop in Bromham in the holidays, aged 14, for 20 hours per week, receiving the minimum wage. Car washing was also a useful source of pocket money.

For the girls there were more opportunities – working in Boots' on Saturdays, Sainsbury's for 15 hours per week in the holidays, waitressing at Astwood for £6 per hour at weekends, serving drinks at the Three Tuns for £5 per hour. Girls also did: dog walking (£4 per hour), dog-sitting, baby-sitting (£3 to £4.50 per hour), cleaning at Manor hospital (£4.80 per hour), teaching tennis to children on Saturday mornings, from age 13 to 16, for £5 per morning at first, rising to £20, life-guarding at swimming pools for £5 per hour. One girl worked in her father's office during the summer holidays from the age of 16, for about £5 per hour. Another girl writes at length about what earning money meant to her:

I started work for money at the age 13, teaching tennis at my old school, Polam. I would teach on Saturday mornings, provided it didn't clash with a hockey match, and my starting pay was £5 for a morning's work. Since I wasn't qualified, and was only 13 years old, that money was like winning the Lottery.

Many of these contributors have added to their questionnaire a few lines to say how they loved growing up in Biddenham. One girl says, 'I really enjoyed growing up in Biddenham – a very safe environment. The only downside was reliance on a car for transport – once we started going into town at the weekend; the bus service was very poor and often didn't turn up'. A third girl says, 'Not being interested in church, it was hard to meet people, and nowhere official to 'hang out', as the youth club was too church orientated'. [This would be the club that met in the church barn, the village hall youth club having closed down some years previously].

Conclusions

Whilst it is unreliable to draw too many conclusions from a limited survey, it is clear that many aspects of children's behaviour have remained virtually unchanged over the past fifty or so years. They still have a great need to 'escape' from the confines of their homes; they still build dens, play hide-and-seek, scrump for apples, and the boys especially are prone to dangerous activities involving wheels and fire. Over the years children have acquired far more equipment for playing than the hand-me-down bats and balls and home-made carts of the 1940s and 1950s, such as bicycles, pogo sticks, skateboards and rollerblades. However, the lack of a real farm in the village has significantly curtailed their experience of rural life. Rivalry between gangs appears to have waned since the 1950s. The fear of, and respect for, authority, has waned too over the years, partly no doubt because very few of the parents worked in the village after most of the farms were closed, and Church Farm was farmed by farmers who lived elsewhere. Also the local police constable disappeared from the village during this period.

Conditions at the village school improved out of all recognition during the period of this survey. The privations endured by the children in the early part of the 20th century make school life today seem luxurious by comparison.

In the 1930s and 1940s very few girls had holiday jobs, while most of the boys worked on the farms. However, by the 1960s the girls had plenty of opportunities for holiday work in Bedford shops, while the boys were still mostly on the farms. Ten years later, there were more varied opportunities for both girls and boys in the school holidays, but unfortunately, as we conclude this village history in 2012, the availability of Saturday jobs is dwindling.[8]

We hope that children living in Biddenham today will continue to lead adventurous lives in the outdoors, and appreciate the many advantages of growing up in a village. We also hope that when they are old enough they will continue to find paid work in the school holidays, so that they can enjoy the feeling of independence that earning money brings. We also hope they will set down their thoughts later in life, so that future generations can enjoy reading about their childhoods.

References:
All unattributed quotations are from respondents to our questionnaire, who were offered anonymity.
1 *Biddenham Bulletin,* January 2004.
2 *Biddenham Bulletin,* April 2008.
3 *Biddenham Bulletin,* January 2004.
4 *Biddenham Bulletin,* May 2004.
5 Albert Church, *Recollections of My Life in Biddenham* (privately printed).
6 See Jonathan McKeown's memoir, Chapter 11, No 5.
7 *Biddenham Bulletins:* February 1980, April 1980, February 1981.
8 Jeevan Vasagar, Education editor, 'Decline of the Saturday job hits pupils' future work chances' in *The Guardian,* 3 July 2012.

CHAPTER 14
THE BIDDENHAM SOCIETY
This chapter was contributed by Tony Wood, Chairman
of
The Biddenham Society

The Early Years

In 1961 a number of residents who were concerned about a proposed new housing development in the village met and formed The Biddenham Society. Some years later they formalised the arrangement and the society held its first AGM on 11 October 1965 under the chairmanship of Graham Bean. Both he and his wife Joy were destined to be stalwarts of the society for the rest of their lives, and up to her death in 2011 at the age of 94 years Joy still insisted on baking 24 loaves of bread every year for the AGM and ploughman's lunch.

The society was founded with three main purposes: To stimulate interest in, and care for, the beauty, history and character of the village and its surroundings; to encourage the preservation, development and improvement of features of general public amenity and historic interest; and to encourage high standards of architecture and village planning. Consequently the scrutiny of planning applications relating to the village and the immediate surrounding area has always been central to its activities, and the responsibility taken very seriously by successive committees.

A related function which also found much favour with villagers for many years was to follow the AGM with a 'beating the bounds' communal walk. Clad in scarves, woolly hats, gloves, boots, or wet weather gear as appropriate, and accompanied by children of all ages plus a motley selection of dogs, teams of walkers – all well fortified by a hearty lunch - would set off in all directions to cover the many public footpaths in the parish. A variety of circular routes was provided, all of which terminated back in the village hall where tea and cakes awaited. The practice survived for more than thirty years, but gradually lost its appeal when much of the surrounding farmland was developed.

Four years after that first AGM the routine work of the society was disturbed by a matter requiring special attention: a proposal to site the third London airport at Thurleigh. An *Airport Resistance Fund* was quickly formed under Cecil Winnington-Ingram, another tireless worker for the village.

The airport battle was eventually won, but was soon replaced with an application to construct a large housing estate on Deep Spinney Farm - the first of a series of large-scale development proposals which were to span the next 30 years. The next was to create a golf course and up to 2,000 dwellings inside the loop of the Great Ouse, incorporating the first section of a new western bypass for Bedford. Some years later the land north of the A428 Bromham Road was identified for a continuation of the bypass to join the A6 road to Kettering, with a further 1,300 houses in the adjoining areas. It was clear these major developments would, when complete, transform Biddenham from its former peaceful rural setting into a village encircled by housing and busy highways.

With local authorities throughout the country under great pressure to expand their housing stock, it was predictable that much of the land around Biddenham would eventually fall to developers, but during this lengthy period of uncertainty and change the society was far from inactive. Successive committees fought long and hard to ensure the village would not suffer the worst aspects of mass house building, so that as much as possible of the unique character of Biddenham could be retained for present and future generations to enjoy.

Particular mention must be made in this context of my predecessor chairman, Douglas Kitchen, who served for 29 years on the committee, the last 21 as chairman. He was at the forefront of the society's submissions and appeals during this lengthy period, and the powerful evidence he presented in person at planning inquiries was instrumental in preserving many of the views, outlooks and green spaces adjacent to the village boundary which give us pleasure to this day. Without these interventions, much more would have been lost, and Biddenham would now be a pale shadow of its former self.

In 2003 Bedford Borough had published its Local Plan which brought together all the changes mentioned above, setting out the pattern and character for future development across the borough and providing the basis for determining planning applications. With the large housing schemes surrounding the village now settled in principle, the society's work underwent a subtle change in emphasis. Whilst the need for good and appropriate building design remained unchanged, preserving the village's beauty and character now rested to a much higher degree on protecting the remaining unbuilt areas within, and in immediate proximity to, the village boundary, to prevent the processes of infill from causing Biddenham to become a continuous urban sprawl. The society argued that having approved in outline the construction of over three thousand dwellings around the village perimeter, the planning authority had ensured Biddenham would contribute its fair share to the borough's house building targets, so that infilling any remaining green spaces within the village itself could no longer be justified, and proposals seeking to do this should be refused.

However as a result of changes in planning law, which put increased pressure on planning authorities to release more land for building, in 2008 Bedford Borough invited proposals to build on previously protected land, and predictably in Biddenham this produced requests to overturn several of the society's

331

hard-won victories of the past. These included a resubmission to build a giant housing estate on the 63 acres of farmland west of Gold Lane, another to construct a retirement complex on 7 acres of open countryside adjacent to Vicar's Close, and a third to build houses on an ancient orchard alongside the playing fields. A new application sought approval to relocate a Bedford gospel church to a triangular plot of land of 4.67 acres situated between the Bromham bypass and the road leading to the bridge.

All these proposals were potentially very damaging to the village, so the society and the parish council joined forces to rally community opposition, with the result that over 380 households submitted individual letters of objection to complement those submitted by the two bodies. Faced with such a united response, the council withdrew the proposals, although appeals were soon lodged by applicants.

What of the Future?

The Biddenham Society remains an unusual organisation, with few parallels elsewhere. It has held an annual general meeting (now combined with the ploughman's lunch) in the village hall every year since the first in 1965. These have always been well supported, with typically up to a hundred residents in attendance. The AGM is an opportunity to review all planning matters affecting the village, and enables residents to air any matters of concern. In addition, an occasional column in the monthly *Biddenham Bulletin* helps to keep them up to date on current issues and encourage support when it is needed.

Over the years, responses opposing applications have been drafted with great care, resulting in the society being designated a formal consultee of the planning authority, and the planning officers holding its views in good regard.

A section of the older part of the village was designated a conservation area in 1973. Fifty years on, it is clear there are other parts of Biddenham which – by virtue of being visually distinctive and incorporating many mature properties of significance – could now be eligible for designation, thereby helping to stiffen future resistance against unsympathetic development. As a long-term aim, the society will seek to have the Biddenham Conservation Area extended, to help preserve the special ambience of the village.

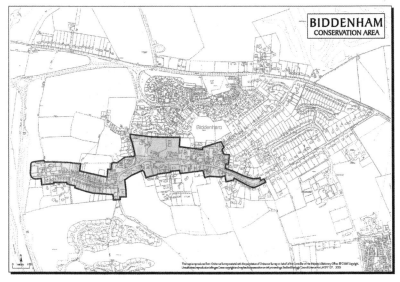

92 – Map of Biddenham Conservation Area

CHAPTER 15
FLORA AND FAUNA OF BIDDENHAM, AND THE VILLAGE POND

Dr David George (Flora)*, Christopher Haydn Jones (Fauna), and Peter Applewhite (Village Pond) contributed to this chapter

Until the middle of the 20th century Biddenham was a small agricultural parish, bounded on the north, south and west by the river Ouse, and the main habitats it contained were the river and its margins, farmland - mainly arable - with neutral grassland on the lower-lying floodplain fields and ponds. There were no woods, but a few small copses were present in the fields, and a much larger copse alongside the northern edge of the Ouse. There were hedges between the fields. The soils are sandy river gravels, except for a small area of Oxford clay on both sides of Bromham Road around Biddenham Turn. The river also has a margin of peaty clay.

Since that time there has been a period of great change in the area, with a conversion of agricultural land to housing - first Deep Spinney and later Great Denham and the golf course; also building development north of Bromham Road. The habitat now includes a significant number of gardens, which have attracted some birds that have not previously frequented areas so close to humans. Gardens have also, because of their enclosed and often tidy nature, deterred hedgehogs.

FLORA

As a consequence of this change of land use, there has been a considerable alteration in the species composition of the Biddenham flora. This is illustrated by two five-yard radius plots by the river just south of the church which were surveyed by John Dony in 1950 - a marshy area and an adjacent meadow area.[1] These plots were re-surveyed in 2004.[2] Dony found 24 species in the first plot and 22 in the second. In the later survey 14 species were found in the first plot with only 6% of species in common with the first survey, and 21 in the second with 9% in common. The main reasons for the difference were the new bypass opened in 2009, and the increased drainage of the marshy areas. More general reasons are eutrophication, the increase in nitrogen content and thus fertility of the soil, by the seepage of artificial fertilizers, and also by air from traffic fumes. This favours the growth of larger plants such as nettles and coarse grasses, which smother more delicate plants.

Within the parish boundaries approximately 320 species of native or naturalised plants growing in the wild have been recorded, although a few have now disappeared. In reality there are probably at least 400 species present. Apart from the usual omnipresent common plants such as dandelions, daisies, stinging nettles and thistles, etc, there are some more botanically interesting areas, for example:

The River and Margins

In the river: yellow water-lily *(Nuphar lutea)*, arrowhead *(Sagittaria sagittifolia)*, common club-rush (*Schoenoplectus lacustris*), used in Pavenham for basket making, and more rarely the beautiful flowering rush *(Butomus umbellatus)*. At the margins: common reed *(Phragmites australis)*, reed sweet-grass *(Glyceria maxima)*, purple loosestrife *(Lythrum salicaria)*, great yellow cress *(Rorippa amphibia)* and marsh woundwort *(Stachys palustris)*.

The Village Pond

Some of the interesting species that grow or have grown in the past are: on or in the water - yellow water-lily *(Nuphar lutea)*, duckweed *(Lemna minor),* celery-leaved buttercup *(Ranunculus sceleratus),* from 1998 a florid growth of the alien small floating fern azolla *(Azolla filiculoides),* which as it matures colours the surface of the pond red. It smothers everything, and is eradicated only with great effort; and at the margins - bulrush *(Typha latifolia)*, greater pond sedge *(Carex riparia)*, purple loosestrife *(Lythrum salicaria)*, great willowherb *(Epilobium hirsutum)*, water mint (*Mentha aquatica)*, marsh marigold *(Caltha palustris) and* water forgetmenot *(Myosotis scorpioides)*.

The Churchyard

Between 90 and 100 species were recorded in the old churchyard. Of interest are the spring flowers: snowdrops *(Galanthus nivalis),* winter aconite *(Eranthis hyemalis)***,** primrose *(Primula vulgaris),* hepatica *(Hepatica nobilis);* also later lady's bedstraw, *(Galium verum),* and star of Bethlehem *(Ornithogalum angustifolium)*. There are two small conservation areas in the old churchyard, and a much larger one in the new churchyard, created in 2009, which is developing.

The Golf Course

The golf course was constructed in 1997/98, and unless one is a golfer the flora cannot be fully surveyed. At first there were some unusual plants, probably brought in with imported soil, such as crimson clover *(Trifolium incarnatum)*. There are water hazards (ponds) which have common reed *(Phragmites australis)* and bulrushes *(Typha latifolia),* and on the muddy banks the very invasive New Zealand pygmy weed *(Crassula helmsii),* a recent arrival from the antipodes first recorded in Bedfordshire in 1998. In one of the boundary hedges of the course there is a planting of sea buckthorn *(Elaeagnus rhamnoides)* with its striking orange berries.

The 'Cowslip Field'

This is the large field below the church and the footpath leading to the bypass. It is being very successfully managed as an unimproved meadow, being cut annually at the end of summer. This enables the seed to ripen for further propagation.

There is a rich diversity of flowering plants. Dominant in spring are cowslips *(Primula veris);* in summer, oxeye daisies *(Leucanthemum vulgare),* hogweed *(Heracleum sphondylium),* hawksbeard *(Crepis vesicaria),* red and white clover *(Trifolium pratense, Trifolium repens),* grass vetchling *(Lathyrus nissolia),* ribwort plantain *(Plantago lanceolata),* and many species of grass. Later on there are knapweed *(Centaurea nigra),* ragwort *(Senecio jacobaea),* wild carrot *(Daucus carota).*and thistles.

Rarities

Some less common plants growing in the parish are wild clary *(Salvia verbenaca),* which has been present for many years in the grass verge of the service road before Bromham bridge, and great dodder *(Cuscuta europaea),* a parasitic plant which grows along the banks of the Ouse, mainly on nettles. Twiggy spurge *(Euphorbia x pseudovirgata)* grows on the banks of the river near Kempston. There are also two garden escape spurges naturalised - cypress spurge *(Euphorbia cyparissias)* by the coffin path and Mediterranean spurge *(Euphorbia characias)* by Footpath 6.

Orchids are often the plant hunter's holy grail. There seems to have been a dearth in Biddenham, as the only verified record is for one pyramidal orchid *(Anacamptis pyramidalis)* in the 'cowslip field' in June 2009, but not seen since.

Agricultural Land

When the land in the Biddenham Loop was farmed it was for mainly cereal crops, and more recently oil-seed rape. Due to the use of chemicals there were few weeds within the crops, apart from wild oats *(Avena fatua)*; other weeds were around the periphery. Nothing uncommon was recorded recently except for Venus's looking-glass *(Legousia hybrida)*. In the absence of chemicals or when the land was left fallow or for set-aside there were beautiful crops of poppies *(Papaver rhoeas)* like Flanders fields.

Hedges

In 1994/95 a survey was made of Biddenham hedges. There were 78, including 18 relict and partial hedges between the fields still being farmed; four hedges were inaccessible. The most common planted species was hawthorn (*Crataegus monogyna),* present in 96% of the hedges. The commonest adventitious non-planted species was elder (*Sambucus nigra),* present in 80%. Altogether 27 woody species were found in one or more hedges.[3] A large number of these hedges have been removed due to new developments.

Trees

Probably the greater proportion of trees, both on public and private land, have been planted. Those most likely to have been self-set are the willows along the banks of the Ouse, which are mainly white willow *(Salix alba),* but also crack willow *(Salix fragilis)* and osier *(Salix viminalis)*. There may be other species of willow and hybrids.

The commonest trees are ash *(Fraxinus excelsior)* and oak *(Quercus robur),* some self-set and some planted. There is a good group of oaks lining Biddenham Turn up to Main Road. There are silver birch *(Betula pendula),* but very few beech *(Fagus sylvatica)* although there is an ancient gnarled specimen by Footpath 7, and there are copper beeches along Main Road. There were many sizeable elms in the village, but these were destroyed by Dutch elm disease during the 1960s and early 1970s. There are plenty of smaller elms *(Ulmus procera)* in the hedgerows which may have developed from suckers of larger trees, but they usually die after attaining approximately five metres in height. The horse chestnuts *(Aesculus hippocastanum)* have also more recently been affected by a disease, this time due to a bacterium and not a fungus, with the result that many splendid trees in Biddenham have been felled - although many survive.

At the bottom of Manor Road adjacent to the start of Footpath 7 there is a copse containing old apple trees *(Malus domestica)* and cherry plums *(Prunus cerasifera)* - a lovely sight when in flower in early spring.

There are good specimen trees in many gardens. Particularly notable are the cedars of Lebanon *(Cedrus libani)* - two in the churchyard and one in the old vicarage - the seeds of which were gathered in Lebanon, and are known to have been planted in 1875. Also in the churchyard are several common lime *(Tilia x europaea),* a hybrid between the large- and small-leafed lime. There are three old yew *(Taxus baccata)* at the back of the church, and a more recently planted one; also a sycamore *(Acer pseudoplatanus),* of which there are many large specimens in the village. In the garden of Biddenham House there is a magnificent hornbeam *(Carpinus betulus),* considered one of the finest in the county. Many of the roads in the village are planted with a variety of spring flowering trees, and maples which produce splendid autumn colours.

Nature does not stand still, and every year there are changes: some plants disappear and new plants arrive. In 2009 a numerous group of salsify *(Tragopogon porrifolius)* was first recorded on the edge of Footpath 6. Like those of the closely related 'Jack-go-to-bed-at-noon' *(Tragopogon pratensis)* the handsome mauve flowers close up at midday. In 2012 the salsify invaded the 'cowslip field', where there are even larger patches. Other new finds in 2012 are yellow rattle *(Rhinanthus minor)* in the 'cowslip field', and the delicate rue-leaved saxifrage *(Saxifraga tridactylites)* and thyme-leaved sandwort *(Arenaria serpyllifolia)* on the churchyard wall.

FAUNA

The small amount of woodland restricts the diversity of wildlife in the parish. However, the river and the pond areas support many species of birds – on the river mallard, mute swans, common terns, common gulls and black-headed gulls from the coast, and herons. There is a heronry on the north-west edge of the parish by the river, with nine nests in 2012. There are also little owls, and barn owls that hunt along the riverbanks and in the meadows. Extensive flocks of lapwings used to rest on the fallow land, also fieldfares and redwings. They are rarely sighted now. However, following the reduction in the use of agricultural chemicals, once again there are otters in the river. Similarly there are losses of mammals associated with farming – harvest mice and dormice. The recent proliferation of scrubland and the introduction of some small new woodlands have allowed those two aliens, the muntjac deer and the grey squirrel, to thrive in Biddenham. Foxes became common in gardens in the late 20th century, but are rarer at the time of writing.

Mammals

The little muntjac deer occasionally seen in the village are descended from animals that escaped from Whipsnade Zoo, and possibly also from the Woburn Abbey estate. Grey squirrels are an 'introduced' species, from North America in 1876. Brown hares have not been sighted in the Church End fields and the Loop for many years now, and the decline of agriculture has meant that harvest mice are no longer seen. However, there are still a few rabbits, house mice, wood mice, long-tailed field mice; bank voles, short-tailed voles and water voles that are probably predated by the American signal crayfish [*Pacifastacus Leniusculus*], a North American species introduced into Europe in the 1960s. There are also common shrews, moles, stoats, weasels, hedgehogs and brown rats. In addition to otters, there are probably mink near the river. To the north of the parish, by the Baulk, there is a badger sett. Bats include pipistrelle, and maybe other species.

Birds

Changes in agricultural practice have considerably reduced

flocks of lapwings and starlings, but wood pigeons have increased in number. Skylarks have become rarer following the housing development in Great Denham, and swallows, swifts and house martins are not so common since the disappearance of the old farmyards and barns. However, more species of birds now frequent gardens and their bird feeders – greater and lesser spotted woodpeckers, green woodpeckers, carrion crows, jackdaws, magpies, wood pigeons, collared doves (which are relative newcomers to the United Kingdom, having first arrived in the 1950s) and long-tailed tits in particular.

Buzzards and red kites are sometimes seen flying over the village. Kestrels and sparrowhawks are relatively common, and kingfishers are seen on the river – and a few years ago one appeared on a ledge above a small garden pond in Church End.

The village pond is regularly visited by mallard and moorhens, which sometimes breed there. Kingfishers also visit, but are hard to spot. Herons were regular visitors too, when there were fish in the pond.

Reptiles

Grass snakes are seen in and around the village pond, but adders do not appear to have made a home in the parish – although a sighting has been reported in 2012 on the golf course..

Amphibians

The village pond is home to a large number of great crested newts, also common (or smooth) newts, common frogs and common toads. An unusual inhabitant of Biddenham (also parts of western Bedford) is the midwife toad (*Alytes obstetricans),* which was accidentally introduced to Bedford from France in 1904 among a consignment of ferns imported by a market gardener. These tiny toads (about 4 to 5 cm long) are more terrestrial than the native species, needing pools only for their tadpole stage. Usually light brown in colour with dark speckles, the adults spend most of their life under stones in gardens, hunting insects at night. The species earned its common name from the way it cares for its eggs, unlike most amphibians who abandon them as soon as they are laid.[4]

The male carries the eggs – from 15 to 30 – behind his back legs, placing them in the water when they are ready to hatch. They grow rapidly for the first six weeks, when their hind legs appear. After this, their development slows down, and they overwinter in water as tadpoles, becoming toads in the following spring. Another characteristic of these toads is their call – a bell-like peep from which the midwife toad gets its other common name – the bell frog. Both sexes call, and they are at their most vocal at night, between April and October, especially in warm weather. New residents in the village are often puzzled by these intriguing sounds.

Fish

There have been no fish in the village pond since it dried out completely in autumn 2011, following two years of exceptionally dry weather. In the river there are eels, bleak, pike, bream, perch, roach, tench and barbel.[5]

95 - The village pond, 2011

Insects

There are legions of insects in the village. Among the more interesting are the occasional stag beetle found in rotting timber, and dragonflies hunting in the evenings.

THE VILLAGE POND

Victorian surveys of the village reproduced on early Ordnance Survey maps in the 1880s show a number of ponds. The two largest still exist – the manor pond behind what is now the Manor Hospital, created around 1700 as a carp pond to supply fish to Biddenham Manor, and in time becoming known as the village pond, and the smaller Ramsmead pond in Church End.

96 – The village pond sign

Over the years, the village pond fell into disuse and became overgrown. In 1986 a group of villagers, led by the late Dorothy Richards, began a project to restore the pond and maintain it as a nature conservation area and an amenity for the village. The Friends of the Biddenham Village Pond was formed soon after, to help financially and practically with the continuing conservation work, and the management of the pond site and the triangle of land between the pond and Gold Lane.

The way to the pond, down the Causeway, is directed by a painted metal signpost on Gold Lane in the form of a fish with a kingfisher perched on top, made by Don Sherwood in 1991. Edwin Lambert provided the wildlife drawings for the information board that was placed by the pond in 2003.

Shortage of water was a serious problem in 1989, when the pond was topped up via a chain of irrigation pipes all the way from the river. On two subsequent dry occasions, the fire brigade stepped in to help. Most recently the pond dried up completely, for the first time in living memory, in 2011. In the general economic circumstances of the time, the Friends pond management team decided that nature should be allowed to take its course. And of course once a drought order had been imposed in early 2012 by Anglian Water, the rains returned and water returned to the pond.

In the meantime the pond team had removed some of the accumulated silt from the bottom of the pond, and vegetation from around it, to improve its capacity, reduce take-up of water from it, and improve water quality by reducing leaf fall into it. The team is also trying to find new ways of introducing water into the pond, as regular adequate rainfall is becoming increasingly unreliable. The wet and warmer weather conditions of 2012 also heralded, unfortunately, the large-scale return of azolla, and the team is looking at options for its more sustainable removal.

The strength of the Friends is crucial to the continuing success of the pond as a peaceful place for villagers and visitors, and a haven for wildlife.

* - The illustration at the head of this chapter, by Val Fitzhugh, contains all but one of the flowers mentioned by David George.

References:

1 J G Dony, *The Flora of Bedfordshire 1953* (Bedfordshire Natural History Society, 1953).
2 C R Boon and Alan R Outen, *The Flora of Bedfordshire 2011* (Bedfordshire Natural History Society, 2011).
3 D M George, *Biddenham Hedge Survey 1994/1995.*
4 Helen Muir-Howie, Have you heard the Midwife Toads? In *Friends of the Biddenham Village Pond Spring/Summer 2000 Newsletter.*
5 The list of fish was kindly supplied by Ken Gates of Luton Angling Club.

Footpath No 6 runs from the top of Manor Road, west between the golf course and the gardens and paddock of Church End.

Footpath No 7 starts at the river near the old settlement of Honey Hill, and runs north-east across the golf course to the end of Manor Road, where it meets Footpath No 6.

For further reading: C R Boon, J P Knowles and B S Nau, *Bedfordshire Wildlife* (The Book Castle, 1987), ISBN 9780948555053.

CONCLUSION

On 26 March 2012 Ernie Sims died aged 100. At his funeral on 5 April, Alan, the second of his four sons, read some lovely memories of his father, which the family then sent to the *Biddenham Bulletin,* where they were published in June 2012. Ernie was the last Biddenham resident to have spent most of his working life on the land. He worked for the Davidson family of Great Barford and Fred Rawlins of Biddenham, amongst others. Alan said:

My strongest early recollections of Dad were of him coming home after cycling from Biddenham to Great Barford in the pouring rain, some 10 to 12 miles, after a cold day in the fields picking Brussels sprouts. Dad's hands were red raw and his legs were soaked through – even through the leggings and newspaper he wore: a hard life, pedalling all that way, to come home to a house with no indoor running water or electricity.

Towards the end of his working life, Ernie was with the local council, repairing roads. Alan commented, 'He'd never had it so easy, with late starts and early finishes, lots of tea – plus a pension!' Ernie and his wife, Mary, found time for village activities when they moved to Church End. Alan said 'Dad had his allotment and skittles; Mum was involved with the school.'

Biddenham has lost its agricultural character, and its residents no longer work on the land, but the Diamond Jubilee celebrations in June 2012 showed a high level of community spirit, as well as a desire to commemorate national events. On Friday 1 June the 'First Friday' lunch team organised a special lunch in the village hall. Liz Watson and Judith O'Quinn started the lunches in 2006, and they have been a successful way of bringing people together, enabling them to meet their friends over lunch on the first Friday of each month. The Diamond Jubilee lunch was a splendid occasion: the hall was decorated with bunting, the helpers who served home-made soup, delicious sandwiches and a wonderful array of puddings were dressed in red, white and blue, and guests were greeted with a glass of sparkling wine to toast the Queen. The village hall was full, and there was a convivial, festive atmosphere.

97 – Ernie Sims' 98th birthday celebration with his family, August 2009

At 2 pm Richard O'Quinn, village hall committee secretary, accompanied Graham Bates, who unveiled the commemorative weather vane at the village hall. Graham, who has given long service to Bedford and to Biddenham (he was Mayor of the Borough of Bedford from 1973 to 1974), had just become chairman of Biddenham parish council once again, after an earlier period in office from 2005 to 2009. Some of the staff and pupils of St James School were invited to the unveiling. Graham has been a governor of the school since 2003, and it was fitting that he should address the children, who are the future of the village.

Some of the activities planned for Sunday 3 June had to be cancelled or rearranged, because of the weather. Many had signed up to attend the 'big lunch' on the pavilion field, but the cold weather and constant rain prevented this. However, many residents still enjoyed their picnics with friends and families in each others' homes. Some of the children's activities still went ahead. Kate Jones, Val Fitzhugh and Chris Gleave had the difficult task of picking the winner for the children's crown competition held in the village hall. The 'Rolling Stones' part of the live music that had been scheduled for the pavilion field went ahead, with 'Mick' strutting about on the stage and the audience sheltering under umbrellas outside the pavilion.

At 5 pm on Sunday 3 June the Bedford concert brass band played in the church, accompanying a well-attended thanksgiving service. Part of the Diamond Jubilee exhibition of memorabilia from the early years of Queen Elizabeth's reign was staged at the back of the church. The exhibition was organised by Jane George, Katherine Fricker, Hugh Clifton and Peter Squire, and many villagers generously contributed memorabilia. Visitors had the opportunity to buy the Diamond Jubilee recipe book, containing recipes from the village collected by Fran Moxon and Rosemary Harris. Visitors could also contribute to Hugh Clifton's collection of 'tweets' – short memories of what Biddenham's over 60s were doing on the day of the Queen's coronation on 2 June 1953. (Later published in the *Biddenham Bulletin* for July/August 2012). May Davis remembered that 'In Biddenham there was a parade through the village and tea in the hall. There was a sports day in the field opposite Day's Lane. In the evening there was a dance and slim ankle competition'.

The Diamond Jubilee celebrations showed that Biddenham is thriving as a village, and that the residents are prepared to come together to organise and attend festivities whatever the weather. We still have our parish church, supported by the Friends of St James, with regular services, bell-ringing, a children's choir and 'young explorers' group. The village school is thriving, and its field is the venue for the village show each September. The Three Tuns is still at the heart of the village, although it is now noted for its food, and not just for its beer. The village hall provides a useful meeting place for the Guides, the Biddenham under-5s group, whist drives, the Tuesday coffee shop (started by Maudie Winnington-Ingram), the 'First Friday' lunches and the well-attended Gardeners' Association. These activities all help to bring the residents of the village together. The church barn is another valuable facility for meetings: the 'Biddenham Women's Group', led by Val Fitzhugh, arranges monthly talks and activities, art classes are held there, and the handbell ringers practise regularly. The Friends of the Village Pond hold their 'splash out' to review progress. The pavilion field is used by the Biddenham cricket club, which has four adult and three junior teams. With Sport England Clubmark accreditation, they have good opportunities for encouraging younger players. The tennis club, which is entirely self-financing, uses the three tennis courts. They coach the pupils of St James' school, and hold 'sports camps' on the courts at half-terms. They are now part of the borough council Re-Active 8 Gold programme, for bringing sport to the over-50s. The pavilion is a venue for parish council meetings. In December each year the Biddenham Society holds its AGM in the village hall. The high level of support shows that the residents of Biddenham are as concerned in 2012 as they were in 1965 in their commitment to the continued preservation of the beauty, history and character of the village.

98 – Grace Harral (3rd from right) with Audrey Cooper and
Winifred Fowler who in 1971/2 was the first lady Mayor of Bedford

In the 1965 Women's Institute scrapbook, Grace Harral wrote
to the residents of Biddenham in 2015 from those of 1965.
Her words are a fitting legacy to us in 2012, and hopefully will
be for the Biddenham residents of 2065:

So, here we are, set in our time and place,
And bound within the homely framework of our days,
Too rarely do we pause and step aside
To see the larger vision of our life and ways.

What will be left to link you with the past?
What will you think of us whose happy tenancy
Of this fair plot is ours to cherish now,
And minister with thoughtful care, your legacy?

The River Ouse will still wind on its way
And willows lean to dip their branches in the flow;
But will the fertile fields be set with homes?
Our quiet, narrow paths be roads with lights aglow?

New skills must alter things in ways we cannot see;
The pattern of your lives may be entirely new
But as we depend upon each other
For kindly help and cheerful friendship, so will you.

The sturdy Norman church stands for us all –
A silent witness of man's need for more than bread
And so, across the intervening years
We wish you peace and joy upon the path ahead.

The Queen's Diamond Jubilee
June 2012

(Rosemary Harris)

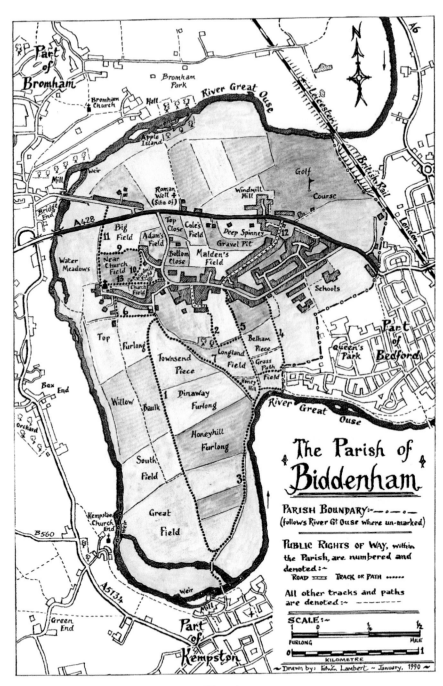

The Parish of

Biddenham

PARISH BOUNDARY:— —o—o—
(follows River G. Ouse where un-marked)

PUBLIC RIGHTS OF WAY, within
the Parish, are numbered and
denoted :—
ROAD ⨯⨯⨯   TRACK OR PATH ......

All other tracks and paths
are denoted :— ———

SCALE :—

~ Drawn by: Edwin Lambert ~ January, 1990 ~

Plate 1

Plate 2 – Detail of Kempe (east) window

Plate 3 – Millennium west window

Plate 4 – Main Road and the war memorial

Plate 5 – Village sign and Dawn Cottage

Plate 6 – The bypass (A428 The Branston Way),
from the church tower, 2012

Plate 7 – The river in winter, 2001

A Walk Round
Biddenham Village

(photography by Roger Day)

To see most of the architectural and historic buildings and sites of interest in the village, start at the Three Tuns car park. The walk is divided into two parts.
PART I

No 1 THE THREE TUNS PUBLIC HOUSE

17th or 18th century coursed limestone rubble with thatch. 19th century extension to west in brick and tile. At the back of the building is a timber building, re-thatched in 1990, used formerly as a morgue, the first village hall and the changing room for Biddenham United football club. Listed Grade II.

THE WAR MEMORIAL

Walk across the road and look left from the war memorial to take in the spacious open green and the variety of trees and shrubs that border the area. The memorial was designed and sited by Frederick Landseer Griggs ARA, RA, after World War I, with three names added after World War II. It was unveiled by Mrs Wingfield on 18 May 1922.

No 2 42 Main Road, LAVENDER LODGE

The oldest house (as opposed to cottage) in Main Road. This was the farmhouse to Clay Farm. It was built in the early 18th century, and named after a Huguenot family, the Lavenders, who came to this country in 1700, some of whom are buried in the churchyard.
Conservation Area.

No 3 63 Main Road, THE FORGE

Cross over the road to The Forge, which

was the former blacksmith's cottage. 17th century, restored. Black and white colourwashed over limestone, but part wattle and daub, and part lath and plaster. Thatch, with three gabled dormer windows. Modern wing to the east is of brick, rendered, with tiled roof. The forge itself was unceremoniously demolished in the 1970s, and is marked now by the grassy mound. Conservation Area.

No 4 65 Main Road, ROSE COTTAGE

Built at the end of the 19th century for the agent, Harry King, of the Biddenham Estate. The bricks are called light reds, and are laid in an attractive pattern known as rat-trap bond, where headers and stretchers are laid side by side. The headers, or ends, of the bricks have been burnt in firing, thus giving the blue/black pattern work. Conservation Area.

No 5 48-50 Main Road, known as MEADOW END and HORSESHOE COTTAGE.

The latter was home to the Estate Overseer, Harry King, from about 1824 to 1887. 17th century or earlier, mainly colourwashed plaster over wattle and daub, with thatch. In the *AA Book of British Villages* they are described as a 'blue-and-white latticed-windowed creation, which looks just like a Wendy House grown up'. Listed Grade II.

No 6   52 Main Road, ABBOTSBURY

The house was built for Mr and Mrs Maurice Stanton in 1935 by Sidney Smith of Queen's Park.   The plot had been purchased the year before from the Biddenham Estate on condition that a 'bungalow with a roof of thatch is erected in keeping with the adjoining cottages at a minimum cost of £550'. The Estate later made two concessions – ridge tiles were allowed instead   of thatch, and bedrooms could be inserted in the roof. Mr Stanton was Biddenham's first commuter, who cycled daily to Bedford station with rolled umbrella and bowler hat. Conservation Area.

No 7   67 Main Road, THE OLD VICARAGE

This was the vicarage from 1762 to 1935. Limestone rubble, hipped slate roof. Two storeys. Front elevation has three windows on each floor, re-fenestrated mid-19th century. To the east is an 1808 two-storey block in limestone with slate roof. The cedar of Lebanon, planted in 1875, gives a distinctive flavour to the centre of the village. The other, smaller, Atlas cedar was planted by the then owner, David Palmer, to mark the landing of a man on the moon in 1969. Listed Grade II.

No 8   1-3 Gold Lane, DAWN COTTAGE

17th   century,   modernised. Originally two or three cottages - a dairy, and workplace for a cobbler and a costumier. Coursed limestone rubble, part colourwashed plaster. Thatched roof, three-room   plan. The rating valuer of 1925 reported that there were two dwellings. Listed Grade II.

No 9 **67a Main Road,
GROOM'S COTTAGE**
Late 17th century carriage
house, stables and tack
room of the Old Vicarage,
sympathetically restored in
1985-6 and reed thatched.
Old timbers have been re-
used.

**Now turn left into
CHURCH END.**

No 10 **Church End, THE MANOR HOSPITAL** The Manor was a private house
until 1966, when it was sold, and is now a private hospital. Coursed limestone

rubble, old clay tiled roof. Two
storeys. Front elevation has two
projecting gabled wings either
side of a central porch. Gabled
porch has large decorated barge-
boards and central drop finial. A
dovecote, built in 1706, stood in
the field next to the carp pond
behind the Manor, until it was
demolished in 1966. Listed
Grade II.

No 11 **2 Manor Road, WALNUT COTTAGE** Manor Road becomes a track
heading for Bedford across the golf course and the site of the original Biddenham
Manor some two miles distant. 18th or 19th century cottage in two units. The west

side in colourwashed
plaster over a timber
frame, one storey
with thatch, modern
casements and
porch. It was much
altered at the east
end around the turn
of the century, with
a further south
extension since then.
Listed Grade II.

No 12 **17 Church End, THE WHITE COTTAGE**

House built by M H Baillie Scott in 1909 for £450 ('only half the price of a Mercedes, but still expensive for a cottage'). Simplified Tudor style with white roughcast. Two storeys with gables, brick chimneys and a tiled roof. Two storey gabled porch. Listed Grade II.

No 13 **39-41 Church End, PARSONAGE COTTAGE**

Cottages of late 17th or 18th century on corner site. No 39 was the first known church house in Biddenham, where the parson lived. In 1574 (possibly referring to a previous building) a dovecote and warden pear trees were noted. It fronts Church End and is colourwashed over timber frame with thatch and central brick stack. No 41 was where the parson's manservant lived, and is at right angles, end on to Church End, similar construction, one storey, with thatch. It stands on a track leading to the golf course. Listed Grade II.

No 14 **55 Church End, CHURCH COTTAGE**

The remaining one of a row of four 17th century cottages which burnt down in 1959. The other three were wattle and daub, but this cottage has a limestone rubble chimney complex to the east (now rendered and capped) with a limestone inglenook in a single storey extension, and therefore survived. The rest of the cottage is wattle and daub. Two-storey timber framed cottage of two bays in main part. Rendered, painted walls and thatched roof. Stained timber wicket fence. Listed Grade II.

No 15 **CHURCH FARM BARNS**

Now converted into multiple housing. Church End terminates abruptly outside

the church. The barn at the entrance is 17th century with weatherboarding over the carriageway and an old tiled clay roof. The barn immediately to the south has a lower pantiled roof, and originally had stone steps up to the first floor to the west. Listed Grade II.

THE PARISH CHURCH OF ST JAMES

12th century origins or earlier, with later extensions: the lower bell-tower in the 13th century, the chancel in the 14th, the upper bell-tower, south aisle, porch and parvis in the 15th, the north aisle in the 16th and the vestry in the 20th century. Coursed limestone rubble with ashlar dressings and clay tile roofs. The chancel is separated from the nave by a Norman or earlier

chancel arch. There are two squints or hagioscopes. The north aisle is two-bay, the south aisle one-bay. There is a six-bay Jacobean screen enclosing the south aisle. There are two piscinas, one in the chancel and one in the south aisle, both of the 15th century. The font is octagonal 15th century. There is an important early 17th century marble monument to the Boteler family on the north wall of the chancel, and small but early brasses in the north aisle. The south aisle and two-storied porch are castellated; the tower is castellated, with gargoyles on the tower and north aisle. Listed Grade I.

Leave the churchyard by the north gate and turn east along the causeway, leaving the churchyard extension on the left.

THE VILLAGE POND

This is on the Causeway, behind the Manor Hospital, and leads back to the centre of the village, lying more or less parallel to Church End. It was once the Manor carp pond, and was dug out in 1700. It was restored in 1986, and is kept as an amenity for the whole village.

On reaching the Green, beside Dawn Cottage, turn left and left again into Duck End. This lane enjoys extensive views of open pasture and cultivated land.

No 16 **8-10 DUCK END**

No 8   possibly 16th century or earlier, of limestone rubble. One gabled dormer window on front elevation. Main floor 18 to 20 inches below road level. Several floor levels have been removed, in one place revealing the remains of a Roman road. Under a brick-shaped floor there was a shaped tiled floor, and under this, a flagstone floor. Under the top floor level a one halfpenny piece dated 1799 was found embedded. No 10, one elevation, of stone, wattle and daub, blends with No 8 on account of the   elm   timbers used throughout and the thatched roof. Unlisted.

[Nos 2, 4 and 6 Duck End Lane were demolished in 1970 to make way for the retirement flats on the corner].

No 17 **OUSE VALLEY FARMHOUSE**

Originally four cottages. The part furthest west, in stone, is 18th century, and was the old bakehouse and village shop. Main part is 19th century, with applied timber framework and brick infill, part plastered with attractive Dutch hanging, fish scale clay tiles. Front elevation has three gabled dormer windows and a timber framed porch with clay tiled roof. There are two wells to the rear. Unlisted.

Retrace your steps to Gold Lane and cross over.

No 18 **Gold Lane, BIDDENHAM HOUSE**

It is reputed to have once been a hunting lodge of a Duke of Marlborough. It was built in 1766, with 19th century additions on all four sides, with the result that the original Georgian façade has been lost. Coursed limestone with brick colourwashed additions and a tiled roof.   The property, standing in spacious grounds, is well screened by high hedges. The former stable block (No 54 Main Road), converted into a house   about   1975, can be glimpsed up a driveway to the right. Unlisted.

THE GREEN AND VILLAGE SIGN

This is a wide view, dominated by the cedar tree planted by the vicar, Henry Wood, in 1875. The village sign was erected in 1987, to replace former ones to commemorate the Festival of Britain and the Queen's Silver Jubilee. In 1974 the Chief Commons Commissioner confirmed that the Green was owned by the trustees of the Wingfield Estate.

PART II **Walk back along the village green, past the present St James' school opposite the Three Tuns.**

No 19 **38 Main Road, the OLD SCHOOL HOUSE** This was built at the same time as the old village school in 1832, as a residence for the head teacher. Limestone rubble, two storeys. The school was demolished in the 1960s to make way for a new one, but the school house remains as a private residence.

No 20 **THE VILLAGE HALL**
The village hall lies to the right of Nodders Way. It was made from the farm buildings of Clay Farm during World War I, and was first used as an army canteen.

Cross over the road to the left of the Three Tuns.

No 21 **55 Main Road, MARTLETS**
18th century cottage. Colourwashed plaster over limestone rubble; thatch, brick gable end stacks, the northern projecting, the southern integral. Two-room plan. One storey and attics. One eyebrow dormer over central front door, three casements. Listed Grade II.

No 22 **49-53 Main Road**

17th or 18th century, altered and extended limestone rubble. Main house has modern

tiled roof and modern porch. Two old light casements with glazing bars to ground and first floor. Two Victorian privies at the bottom of the garden, and a zinc-lined wash boiler with brick chimney in a barn of limestone rubble with pantile roof. Listed Grade II.

No 23 **49 Main Road, LAVENDER COTTAGE**

Cottage of 17th or 18th century origins. Limestone rubble, thatched, brick extension on road. Gable end has two casements with glazing bars to the first floor, and one large fixed window in a moulded frame at the ground floor. Listed Grade II.

No 24 **37-41 Main Road**

Row of three 18th century cottages, colourwashed over limestone rubble, part timber frame. No 37 is one storey with attics, thatched. Nos 39-41 are taller. Thatch with two eyebrow dormers. (Extra eyebrow dormer added in 1990 when roof re-thatched). Right-hand side set forward with tiled roof, one storey. Listed Grade II.

No 25 **20-28 Main Road, POST OFFICE ROW** Mid-18th century row of timber

framed roughcast cottages known, since the beginning of the 19th century, as Post Office Row. The village post office was in the end cottage. Thatched roofs. One storey with attics. Eight dormer casements on wall plates with thatch cut back. Nos 20 and 22 are taller. Listed Grade II.

No 26 **1-3 Day's Lane, MAGNOLIA COTTAGE**

17th or early 18th century timber framed, colourwashed, with thatch. One storey with attics. Left-hand gable and hipped. Central brick stack. One modern dormer window to front elevation. Modern windows and porch with tiled roof. Listed Grade II.

No 27 **34 Day's Lane, WHITE COTTAGE**

Built by C E Mallows in the early 20th century. Two storeys. White roughcast with tiled roof and brick stacks. Unlisted.

At the end of the lane the Royal Observer Corps building has been converted into multiple housing.

No 28 **35 Main Road (at right angles to Day's Lane)**

18th century cottage. Colourwashed plaster over timber frame. Two-room plan with gable end stacks. Thatch with one central eyebrow dormer and two ground floor casements. The earliest recorded inhabitant was James Smith, 1792. Listed Grade II.

No 29 **18 Main Road, GROVE HOUSE**

Grove farmhouse – originally two 18th century houses abutting each other. 19th

century alterations and extension to rear. Main wing coursed limestone rubble, old clay tiled roofs. Two storeys and attics. Each house has symmetrical front elevation. All main windows have pointed arched glazing bars. A wooden porch with a flat moulded hood on two circular columns. Listed Grade II.

No 30 **23 Main Road, PENNY BLACK**

18th century white colourwashed plaster over part limestone rubble, part wattle and daub, with thatch and gable end stack. Originally there were no casements to the upper floor, to maintain the privacy of Grove Farm House opposite. It was used as a post office until 1954. The wooden building next door was the last post office, which closed in 1966. Listed Grade II.

No 31 **19 Main Road, BUTTERCUPS**

17th century cottage with modern two-storey cross wing extension. Colourwashed

plaster over limestone with thatch. Original part one storey and attics, three-room plan, central double-sided chimney. One eyebrow dormer, two ground floor casements, dormers in rear slope. In 1912 the name was Murree Cottage. Since 1945 it has been known as Buttercups. Listed Grade II.

No 32 **11 Main Road, KING'S CLOSE**

Built by M H Baillie Scott in 1907 for a Mr Salmon. Tudor style, white roughcast and red tile roof. Two storeys; entrance front has two gables between which is timber framing with double entrance doors and mullion windows with leaded lights. The gable to the left has mullion windows in two floors, and to the right has a roughcast chimney. Listed Grade II.

No 33 **9 Main Road, KING'S CORNER**

Built by C E Mallows in 1899 for John White. Handmade red brick with red tiled roof, upper storey roughcast, two storeys and attics. Many mullion windows on all floors. Unlisted.

No 34 **17 Biddenham Turn**

Known as Three Gables, and then Barringer, designed and built by C E Mallows in 1900 for his father-in-law Mr H J Peacock. It was the first house in Biddenham Turn, then known as New Road. C E Mallows lived at the house with his wife Sybil, née Peacock. Two-storey building, brick with a tiled roof. It was one of the first houses in the Arts and Crafts movement where the garden was designed to be integrated with the house. In the 1980s the kitchen garden was sold off as a building plot, but the tennis lawn, spinney and rose beds with holly hedges remain as designed. Unlisted.

The last two houses can more conveniently be reached by car.

No 35 **Windmill Hill, WINDMILL HOUSE**

Windmill Hill was first mentioned in a lease of 1602. The windmill must have been pulled down before 1794, it was not shown on a map of that year. The present Windmill House, which stands at the furthest end from Bromham Road, was built by H J Randall, and designed by E H C Inskip. Originally it was set,

with the lodge and its stables on the main road, in five acres, which included a bowling green and two tennis courts. Today it stands solidly with its two gables and a wooden balcony, looking out on the other properties which have been built towards the main road since 1960.

No 36 **66 Bromham Road, THE BAULK HOUSE** House in cottage orné style

with gable end date stone 1869. Timber frame construction with patterned red brick infill. Large steep sloped roof with bands of fish scale clay tiles. Large central brick stack. Rectangular plan; two storeys. Elevation to road has large gabled

dormer with four-light casement over ground floor bay. West gable end has first floor jetty with four-light casement over ground floor bay. East elevation has small porch with bracketed sloping head and two-light casement to each floor. Two dormers in rear roof slope. Main windows have diamond leaded lights. Listed Grade II

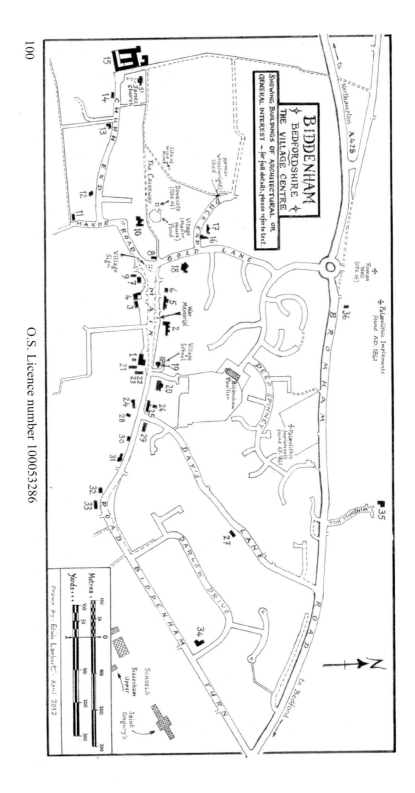

O.S. Licence number 100053286

371

101 –
The Three Tuns

102 –
Dawn Cottage and
Manning's Farm

103 –
Former cottages
in Church End

104 –
Post Office Row

APPENDIX I

GRAVEL PITS IN THE BIDDENHAM AREA (BASED ON BEDFORDSHIRE HISTORIC ENVIRONMENT RECORDS)

HER 13654 Box End Park (on the other side of the river)
Sand and gravel TL501490 248625
HER31737 Biddenham Gravel Pits
Close to the A428 TL501780 250500
HER 31738 Biddenham Gravel Pits
Close to the A428 TL501830 250550
HER 31739 Biddenham Gravel Pits
Close to the A428 TL502060 250500
HER 31740 Biddenham Gravel Pits
Close to river near Queen's Park TL502505 249185
HER 31747 Church End
Old limestone pits. Large worked area TL501300 249775
HER 31748 Church End
Old limestone pits. Large worked area TL501380 249470
HER 55483 Deep Spinney
Sand and gravel TL502385 250346
HER 55484 Biddenham
Sand and gravel TL502674 250275

APPENDIX II

WILLS OF NICHOLAS SKIPWYTH MA AND JOAN POLEY

The will of Nicholas Skipwyth MA – see Chapter 4

To master Gerald his Bible; the proceeds (*proventus*) of his house in Bedford to the painting of the tabernacles of the saints Jas and Jn in the chancel for 10 years; to make a common highway from the house which Jn Hyne inhabits to the gates of the testator's close belonging to the rectory 'de le Peblys' and not otherwise 40s or more if necessary; for the repair of Biddenham bridge 20s; to his sister Isabel his silvered (*deargentatum*) green girdle; to Wm Tychemersshe his best gown, to br Gerald his second best and to testator's sister Margt Cocke his third best and to each of his godsons the issue (*proventum*) of one cow from the hour of his death until they come to marriageable years; all his holy wax to his priests celebrating for him to pray for him; his houses and lands at Biddenham to the chantry at Capleton at Riccall near York; to cousin Gerald 10 marks also the reversion of 'le Cocke' at Waltham with 'Yongis' there for the maintenance of a fellow (*socii in aula*) of Pembroke if it is possible but if it is not, to King's College there for find a fellow (*socio*); Jo his br late of Skipwith is indebted to him for sheep and wool as is stated in an indenture made thereof for more than 20 nobles and Jn his s and his exor had of testator 1 ac of meadow at Riccall for 24 years and further 3s pa and 9 measures (*lagunculas*) of honey; to the chantry of Riccall [omission] with 2 copper pans, the one large and the other small.

The will of Joan Poley – see Chapter 4

To s Jo Poley the best bowl and saltcellar, 2 little crucifixes, her rings, and all her utensils, not otherwise bequeathed, that he and his children want; to the w of son Jo a black belt, 2 feather beds, a kerchief and 'lehangynges de Reed saye'; to Joan Erneys her best gown; to Thos Poley a mazer, a coverlet and a pair of sheets; to Margt Poley of Chicksands a coverlet, a pair of sheets, and 2 silver spoons; to Joan Poley a pair of sheets and 2 silver spoons; to Jn Poley the ender s of testator's s Jn, the best coverlet, a pair of sheets and 2 silver spoons; to Robr Poley a pair of sheets and 2 silver spoons; to Jn Poley the younger s of testator's s Jn, a cow and 2 silver spoons; to sir Wm Atmere 3s 4d; to Joan Eyre one furred gown and one sleeveless gown; to Felicia Eycr a gown; to the wife of Wm Trowghton a gown; to the w of Peter Goody a kerchief; to each of her son's servants 12d; residue to s Jn for charitable purposes.

APPENDIX III

INCUMBENTS OF THE CHURCH OF ST JAMES, BIDDENHAM
(Compiled from the Episcopal Registers, Lincoln, and Public Records)

RECTORS

THE ADVOWSON
The right to present a
clergyman to a benefice

	RECTORS		THE ADVOWSON
	Gilbert Passelewe	1252	William Passelewe
1231	M Richard de S Cruce	1258	Ralph Passelewe
1235	William Tricket	1278	John de Kirkeby,
*1247	M Alexander de Elnestowe		who became Bishop of
*1273	M Richard Neven (Hexon)		Ely and died in 1290
1293	Gilbert de Fulmer	1290	Sir William de Kyrkeby,
1301	Jan 22 M John de Osevyle		who died in 1302
*1301	Nov 16 Gilbert de Fulmer	1302	Mabel Grimbaud
*1330	Jacobus de Bodekesham	1314	William de Kyrkeby's
*1349	William de Wykewane		widow Christina
	(dies of plague)	1315	The Abbess of Waterbeach
1384	John Cope (Tape)	1349	The Countess of Pembroke
1385	M John Rudeby (Buddleby)		moved the nuns from
*1398	Richard Kymeston		Waterbeach to Denny, who
1412	May 25 John Clench		held the advowson at
*1412	Jul 8 Thom. Moriell		Biddenham until the
	(Moysel) dictus Lavenham		dissolution of the monasteries
1435	Sep 16 M Robert Ayscogh		
14--	M John Sperhawke		
1453	May 7 John Aylyff		
147-	D Robert Skypwith		
1493	M Robert Halytreholm		

Vicars and Chaplains

1527	D John Lee (chaplain)	1539	After the dissolution, the
1536	Thomas Cowper (chaplain)		living and rectory were
1537	D William Stoddard (chaplain)		given to Edward Elryngton,
1538	D Richard Holden (alias Wright)		who sold them almost
1545	Henry Franklyn		immediately to
1547	Richard Howden		Sir William Gostwick
1550	Richard Wright	1540	Sir William sold them to
1552	Henry Atkinson		William Boteler, who
1571	Thomas Negus		acquired the Manor at
1602	John Johnson		Biddenham at the same time,
1605	William Gower MA (curate)		but died in 1564.
1607	Robert Marrit		
*1617	John Malcote (Threlcott) (curate)		

1618   Robert Gifford
1627   Daniel Gardener
1629   William Lucas
1636   William Gwynne
*16--   David Faldo
168-   Joseph Hanmer
1692   John Nodes
1708   Andrew Moore (curate)
1717   John Teap
1730   Thomas Tipping (curate)
        (buried at Biddenham)
1758   William Fleming (curate)
        vicar of Clapham
*1761   Thomas Richards MA
        (curate) vicar of Bromham
        and Stagsden
1799   John Jones MA
*1808   Thomas Grimshawe MA
        (buried at Biddenham)
1850   Henry Rice BA
1856   Boteler Chernocke Smith BA
1865   Henry Wood MA
*1890   William E B Norman MA
        (buried at Biddenham)
1936   Douglas F Carey DSO MA
        (buried at Biddenham)
1946   John French d 1973 (buried
        at Biddenham)
*1966   Eric A Gaskell d 1974
        (buried at Biddenham)
1975   Donald Clifford Flatt
1983   Neville E Jacobs ALCD
1989   John M Schofield MA

Priest in Charge
1995   Richard R Sutton MA
2005 - Stephen L Huckle MA
        * – Died at Biddenham   M – magister   D - dominus

1712   The estate passed to Thomas,
        Lord Trevor of Bromham
        (who bought the Manor at
        Ford End in 1703, and
        Bromham Hall in 1708).
1758   It passed to his half brother
        Robert, Lord Trevor, and was
        attached to the Bromham
        Estates. Robert took the title
        Viscount Hampden.
1776   His son, John Trevor
        Hampden, left the villages of
        Bromham, Biddenham and
        Stagsden, one to each of his
        three daughters.
1848   Lt Edward Folliott Wingfield
        married Frances Emily Rice
        Trevor of Bromham Hall.
        The Wingfield family from
        then on owned much of the
        land in Biddenham.
1934   Lt Col Mervyn
        E G R Wingfield.
1966   It passed from
        Lt Col Wingfield to the
        Bishop of St Albans
        (*London Gazette,*
        23 September 1966).

Parish registers were first established by Lord Cromwell in 1538. Biddenham has four ancient registers:

1 1602-1732
2 1732-1806 marriages only until 1754
3 1754-1812 marriages only
4 1732-1812 baptisms and burials

The above list is inevitably incomplete, and in particular (1643-1662) clergymen who fill in when the incumbent is ill or has been given leave of absence are not always noted.

As early as 1375 William Stanford and John Harwolde sign 'chaplains of Biddenham' as witnesses to a will.

The aptly named Rev John Missing, who died in 1840, must have ministered concurrently with the Rev Thomas Grimshawe (1808-1850).

In the 18th century there was overlapping of vicars in the adjacent parishes of Bromham, Stagsden, Clapham and Kempston. Between about 1719 and 1754 the Biddenham marriages include the great majority of those for Stagsden (a parish two miles to the west), chiefly because the two vicars of Stagsden during this period were also curates of Biddenham. The later one, Thomas Tipping, apparently lived at Biddenham, for he baptized his children, and he himself was buried, there. The former, John Teap, was also vicar of Clapham (1709-1723). William Fleming, vicar of Clapham (1753-1794) was also curate-in-charge of Biddenham, and - a particularly bad case of plurality - Thomas Richards, vicar of Bromham and Stagsden was also perpetual curate of Biddenham.

CURATES (ASSISTANT)

1991-1998	David Mason
1998-2001	Dennis Mihill
2001-2002	Dr Paul Andrews
2002-2007	Geoffrey Smith
2005-2008	Gillian Webb
2008-2011	Jane Nash

CHAPLAINS OF THE CHANTRY OF BIDDENHAM BRIDGE

1324-	Simon Wolston or Wulstan	1398-1450	{ John Cook / Robert Baldock
1324-1339	John de Oseberton	1450-1456	John T............
1340-1347	John Becke	1471-1479	Nicholas Skypwith *
1347-1360	{ Richard de Wombewell / Pbr John Wrabet de Naresby	1480-1494	Robert Halytreholm *
		c1507	Thomas Ibbott
		c1530	Pbr Henry Atkinson
		1536	Henry Boswell
1363-1397	{ Pbr John Wrughte / Robert Burgh	1539-1548	Peter Weyver

* Also Vicar of Biddenham

APPENDIX IV

FAMILY TREE OF THE BOTELERS

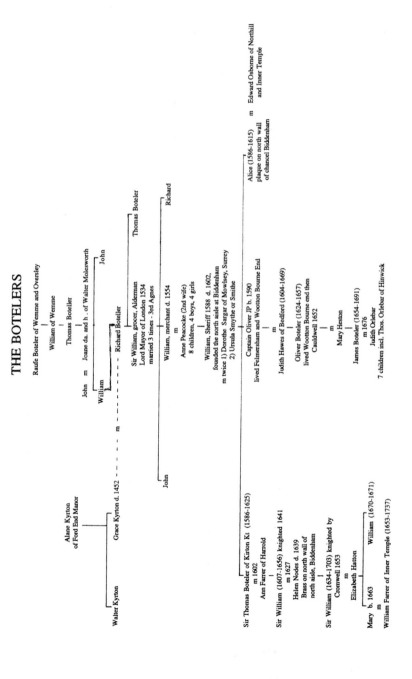

THE BOTELERS

Raufe Boteler of Wemme and Oversley

William of Wemne

Thomas Boteler

John m Joane da. and h . of Walter Molesworth

John

Richard Boteler — — — — m — — — — — William

Thomas Boteler

Sir William, grocer, Alderman Lord Mayor of London 1534 married 3 times - 3rd Agnes

John

Richard

William, merchant d. 1554
m
Anne Peacocke (2nd wife)
8 children, 4 boys, 4 girls

William, Sheriff 1588 d. 1602, founded the north aisle at Biddenham m twice 1) Dorothe Sargar of Mowlsey, Surrey 2) Ursula Smythe or Smithe

Alice (1586-1615)   m   Edward Osborne of Northill plaque on north wall of chancel Biddenham and Inner Temple

Alane Kyrton of Ford End Manor

Walter Kyrton   Grace Kyrton d. 1452 - - - - m - - - - -

Sir Thomas Boteler of Kirton Kt (1586-1625)
m 1602
Ann Farrer of Harrold

Captain Oliver JP b. 1590 lived Felmersham and Wootton Bourne End
m
Judith Hawes of Bedford (1604-1669)

Sir William (1607-1656) knighted 1641
m 1627
Helen Nodes d. 1639
Brass on north wall of north aisle, Biddenham

Oliver Boteler (1624-1657) lived Wootton Bourne end and then Cauldwell 1652
m
Mary Heston

Sir William (1634-1703) knighted by Cromwell 1653
m
Elizabeth Hatton

James Boteler (1654-1691)
m 1676
Judith Orlebar
7 children incl. Thos. Orlebar of Hinwick

Mary b. 1663   William (1670-1671)
m
William Farrer of Inner Temple (1653-1737)

378

APPENDIX V

BIDDENHAM DIRECTORY

LAY READERS
2001   Christopher Dawe   2012   Paul Fricker

CHURCHWARDENS (from 1960)

	Vicar's Warden	People's Warden
1960-1963	Sir John Howard	Captain Carter
1963-1970	Sir John Howard	Les Wallace
1971-1982	Sir John Howard	Peter King
1982-1983	Sir John Howard	Cecil Winnington-Ingram
1983-1984	Sir John Howard	Barry Fielden, John Miller
1984-1986	Cecil Winnington-Ingram	John Miller
1986-1991	Joy Bean (first woman churchwarden)	John Miller
1991	Joy Bean	John Miller
2001	Chris Haydn Jones	Madeleine Fone
2003	Chris Haydn Jones	Anne Church
2007	Ann Morrish	Anne Church
2008-	Ann Morrish	Laurie Hurn

ORGANISTS (from 1941)

1941-1981	Eric Hill
1981-1987	David Wells
1987-1991	Adrian Quarry
1992	Paul Edwards
1992-1994	Adrian Quarry
1994-2007	David Williams
2008-2012	Paul Edwards
2012-	Graham Weeks

TOWER CAPTAINS (from 1941)

1941-1958	Miss Evelyn Steel (President Bedfordshire Bell Ringers Association)
1959-1981	David Eyre
1981-1989	Ralph West
1989-1990	Don Sherwood
1990-1998	Ralph West
1998-	Brian Toyn

EDITORS OF THE PARISH MAGAZINE/ BIDDENHAM BULLETIN

1966-1968	The Rev Eric Gaskell
1968-1983	John Miller
1983-1988	The Rev Neville Jacobs and Meg Ratcliffe
1988-1993	Chris and Jan Haydn Jones

(In 1991 the name was changed to *Biddenham Bulletin*)

1993-1994	Margaret Benson and Gladys Wellesley-Harding
1994-1996	Margaret Benson (Diana Toyn)
1996-2001	Christopher Dawe and Diana Toyn
2001-2002	Laurie Hurn and Diana Toyn
2002-2005	Debbi Clifton (Laurie Hurn)
2005-	Rosemary Harris (Debbi Clifton)

BIDDENHAM INTERNATIONAL SCHOOL AND SPORTS COLLEGE - HEADTEACHERS

(John Howard Upper School)

1979-1988	G R (Roy) Grace

(Biddenham Upper School)

1988-1996	G J (Garry) Fitzhugh
1996-1997	J R (Rob) Jackson – acting headteacher
1997-2010	M G (Mike) Berrill (who in 2011 became executive principal)
2011-	David Bailey

ST GREGORY'S SCHOOL - HEADTEACHERS

1959-1964	Jock Campbell	1991-1994	Betty MacDougall
1964-1973	Peter Robinson	1997-2006	Paddy Boylan
1974-1975	Aidan Mackey	2006-2007	Paul Gardiner
1975-1982	Jack Robbins	2007-2010	Robert Mundy
1984-1986	John Day	2011-	Frances Topa
1987-1991	Frank McMahon		

(Gaps in continuity were covered by temporary teachers)

ST JAMES' SCHOOL - HEADTEACHERS

1832-1847			
1934-1951	Mrs Ruth Cork		
1847-1875	Miss Mary Nichols	1951-1977	Miss Muriel Cork
1875-1876	Miss H Felts	(later Mrs Boston)	
1876-1881	Mrs H M Bloomfield	1977-1982	Mrs Coral C King
1881-1895	Miss Adelaide Osborne	1982-1987	Mrs Mary Draper
1895-1916	Miss E M Goodwin	1987-1992	Mrs Lesley C Ely
1916-1923	Miss I Chitham	1993-2004	Mrs Vicki S Burrows
(Temporary heads to 1925)		2004-	Mrs Karen Luscombe
1925-1933	Miss H M Haffenden		
(Temporary heads to 1934)			

BIDDENHAM SHOW - CHAIRMEN

1965-1967	Arthur Reed	1991-1993	David Palmer
1968-1969	F C Cox	1994-1998	Barry Truscott
1969-1977	E J Cooper	1999-2000	David Slark
1978-1981	Mike Baber	2001-2005	Paul Sanderson
1982-1990	Bill Fowler	2006-	Simon Smith

BIDDENHAM SOCIETY - CHAIRMEN

1963-1965	V Brackenbury	1986-2007	Douglas Kitchen
1965-1981	Graham Bean	2007-	Tony Wood
1981-1986	Arthur Willett		

GARDENERS' ASSOCIATION - CHAIRMEN

1990-1992	Ted Kendrick	2005-2007	Peter Carter
1992-1997	Derrick Day	2007-2012	Mary Johnston
1997-1999	Alan Macpherson	2012-	Jeremy Arthern
1999-2005	Cynthia Lilley		

INDEX

Biddenham Green, 86

Biddenham House, 84, 116, 124, 126, 155, 209, 212, 266, 339/40

Biddenham International School and Sports College, (formerly John Howard School and Biddenham Upper School), 283, 290

Biddenham Loop, 4, 5, 6, 10, 12, 243, 338

Biddenham Manor, 16, 106, 142, 155, 344

Biddenham pits, 3, 4, 94

Biddenham Show, 119, 165, 253, 255, 258, 263, 349

Biddenham Society, 329, 350

Biddenham Turn, 124, 126, 135, 156, 161, 339

Biddenham United Football Team, 122-3

Biddenham Vale, 253

Biddenham Women's Group, 351

Biddenham, origin of name, 11

Biggs, John, 89

Bishop and Son, 57

Bishop of St Albans, 275, 277, 282

Black Death, 19, 24

Blacksmith, 114

Bonney, Archdeacon, 41

Boon, Mr, 243

Boston, Mrs Muriel, 164, 268, 269, 270, 272, 273, 276, 279, 280, 281, 304

Boteler Charities, 80, 116

Boteler Estate, 83

Boteler family, 33, 79, 80, 88, 93

Boteler Manor, 16

Boteler monument, 48, 49

Boteler pew, 43

Boteler, Anne, 77

Boteler, Elizabeth, 40, 85, 91

Boteler, Helen, 50

Boteler, Mary, 77

Boteler, Oliver, 48, 49

Boteler, Richard, 32, 70

Boteler, Thomas, 70, 74

Boteler, Ursula, 48

Boteler, William, 25, 27, 30, 31, 34, 40, 59

Boteler, William and Agnes, 71

Boteler, William and Anne, 71

Boteler, William and Elizabeth, 77, 79

Boteler, William and Ursula, 73/4

Bovis Homes, 5

Box End, 298, 311

Boy Scouts – see Scouts

Bracket, James, 96

Branson, E, 143

Bristow, James, 257

Britannia Works, 103

British Museum, 4, 10, 59

British Red Cross, 143, 144, 145, 146, 148, 149

Brittain, Vera, 136

Broadwood Piano Co, 58

Brockett, Mrs, 112

Brodrick, Ann, 199/200

Bromham, 14, 26, 83, 92, 95-98, 99, 107, 126, 152

Bromham bridge, 31, 80, 94, 95, 216, 219

Bromham Estate, 83, 87

Bromham Hall, 10, 83, 85, 296

Bromham Manor, 83

Bromham Mill, 295

Bromham Road, 3, 93, 334

Bromham School, 119, 179, 184

Bronze Age, 4, 7

Brooks, Captain John, 37, 44

Brooks, Edward, 143, 150

Brooks, Mrs Rhoda, 43, 279

Brooks, Ted, 240, 259

Brytte, Bartholamewe, 40

Bucklow Hundred, 14

Bucknall, Mr and Mrs, 116

Burden, Jeff, 313

Burdett, Mrs, 213
Burrows, Vicki, 284, 286, 287
Burton, Arthur, 109, 141, 142, 163, 203
Burton, Biscay, 123
Burton, Harry, 150
Burton, John, 89
Bury St Edmunds, 15
Butler Education Act, 1944, 267
Butler/causeway money, 116
Buttercups, 147, 160, 275

Calendar of Fines, 32
Campbell, Mr, 124, 209
Campbell, the Misses, 116
Campling, John, 189/90
Campling, Peggy & Monica, 189, 196
Campling, Percy, 189
Camulodenum, 8
Caractacus, 7
Carey, the Rev Douglas, 164, 185, 228/9, 294
Carey, Mrs, 165, 225, 294
Carey, Peter, 206
Carpenter, Mrs, 143
Carpenter-Holland-Griffith, Mrs F, 166, 213, 304
Carrier, Georgina, 120
Carrier, Joseph, 119, 120
Carrier, Sarah, 91
Cartwright, Bobby, 240
Cartwright, Queenie, 240
Cashman, Celia, 310
Catevallauni, 7
Cauldwell, prior of, 28
Causeway, the, 93, 154, 257, 295, 345
Census 1801, 8
Census 1811, 83
Census 1821, 83, 89
Census, 1831, 83, 89
Census 1841, 83, 89, 174

Census 1851, 83, 112, 113, 115
Census 1891, 113
Census, 1901, 126
Census, 1911, 126
Chantry chapel, 30, 71
Charles Wells Brewery, 110
Chibnall, Bernard, 240
Chibnall, Hilda, 143/4
Chibnall, Mr. A, 108, 143, 144, 149, 150, 154, 240
Chibnall's Farm, 240
Chitham, Miss I, 181, 184
choirs, 165, 166, 349
Church – apotropaic marks, 26
Church – aumbry, 56
Church – bell tower, 43
Church – bell peal boards, 46
Church – bells, 37
Church – Boteler arms, 26
Church – Boteler pew 53
Church – chest, 24, 25
Church – clarinet, 56
Church – clock, 37, 58
Church – coronation tapestry, 56
Church – Flemish tapestry, 59
Church – font, 25
Church – gargoyles, 57/8
Church – gates, 36, 39
Church – laudian, 56
Church – lectern, 55
Church – lectionary (part), 59
Church – mass dial, 26
Church – organ, 56, 57
Church – parclose screen, 64, 65
Church – parvis, 26, 36, 65
Church – plate, 52, 53
Church – porch, 26, 36
Church – restoration, 58
Church – ringing chamber, 45, 46
Church – sedilia, 24
Church – squints, 27
Church – tapestry, 56, 59
Church – tombstones, 37, 38, 57

Dillingham, Mr, 211

Dionysus, 10

Dobbs, Mrs, 164

Domesday Book, 11, 12, 13

Dony, John, 335

dovecote, 85, 86, 256, 296, 299, 308, 309, 310

Dowler family, 155

Dowler, A, 209

Dowler, Don, 209, 243, 244

Dowler, Ernest, 143

Dowler, Mrs A, 168

Dowler, Nobby, 243

Dowler, Willie, 138, 143

Draper, Mrs Mary, 282, 283

Duck End Lane, 86, 114, 137, 279, 310, 317, 319

Dudley family, 135

Dudley, Alfred, 135, 151

Dudley, Arthur, 150

Dudley, Mr & Mrs William, 135

Duigan, Edith, 38

Dynevor of Bromham, Lord, 202

Dynevor, 3rd Baron, 102

Dynevor, George Rice (4th Baron Dynevor), 102

Dyve family, 70, 72

Dyve, John, 73, 74

Dyve, Sir Lewis, 72/3, 75/77, 85

Dyves of Bromham, 27

Eaglet, 221

Ednie, Mr, 127

Education Act, 1870, 118, 176

Education Act, 1880, 176

Edward the Confessor, 15

Edwards, Ethelbert, 114

Eleven-plus exam, 278, 315

Elger Close, 257, 305

Ely, Mrs Lesley, 283

emigration to Australia, 91

Emmerton, William, 37, 43, 44

Empire Day, 183

Enclosure Act, Biddenham, 88, 89

enclosure, 86, 87

Ermine Street, 8

Ernwin the priest, 16

eutrophication, 335

Evacuees Reunion Association, 204

evacuees, 203/7

Evans, Alan, 156, 159, 160, 161, 162, 163, 164, 166, 230, 294, 297, 303

Evans, Rita 'Peg', 161

Everett, Douglas, 189

Everett, Bennett & Lily, 189

Everett, Lilian, 189

exemption certificate - see Labour certificate

Eyre, Sylvia, 298

Eyre, W, 209

Factory Act, 1833, 174

Fairmead, 136

Faldo family brasses, 28

Faldo, Agnes, 28

Faldo, Joan, 79

Faldo, John, 28

Faldo, William, 28

Farrer, Dennis, 94

Faulkener, Mrs, 207

Faulkener, Sydney, 55

Faulkes, Mr, 259

Favell, Mr, 201

Felmersham village school, 182

Felts, James, 89

Felts, John, 89, 114

Felts, Miss H, 177

fires, 116, 155

Fire Service, 211, 212

First Friday lunches, 348

Firth, Major Denys, 139, 140

Fitzhugh, Val, 345, 348, 350

Flag Fen, Cambridgeshire, 7

Flatt, the Rev Donald, 278, 282, 322

Fleming Close, 3

Ford End – see Kirtons
Ford End Cottages – see Kirtons
Ford End Manor – see Kirtons
Ford End Road, 124
forge, 78
Forrest, Pearl, 317
Forster Act. See Education Act 1870
Foster's boatyard, 250
Fowler, Bill & Yvonne, 264
freemen, 16
French, Mrs, 258, 298, 306
French, the Rev John, 268, 270, 304
Fricker, Katherine, 349
Fricker, Paul, 66
Friends of St James, 58, 59, 66, 349
Friends of the Village Pond, 344, 350
Frossell, Charles, 114
Frossell, Derek, 220, 230, 242, 249
Frossell, Sheila, 242
Frossell, Theed, 201, 242
Frossell's Farm, 201
Frost, James, 89
Fuller, William, 89

Galley, Richard, 147
Gallows, 95
Gallows Field, 146
Gammons, Miss D, 213
Gardeners' Association, 350
Gardner, Admiral, 126
Garratt, William, 98
Gaskell, the Rev Eric, 43, 57, 59, 275, 278, 306
George V, King, 146, 147
George V's Silver Jubilee, 1935, 168
George VI, King, Coronation 1937, 168
George, Dr David, 334
George, Jane, 349
Girl Guides, 349
Girls' Friendly Society, 121, 164
Glass, Mr, 242

Gleave, Chris, 348
Glynne, Sir Stephen, 42
Godber, Joyce, 87
Goddard, Robert, 99
Godwin, burgess, 16
Gold Lane, 114, 147, 332, 345
Golding, Charles, 89, 93
Golding, Miller, 89
Golding, Miss, 178
Golding, William, 93
Goldsmith, Flora, 298
golf course, 243, 330, 336
Goodwin, Miss E M, 178, 179, 180, 181
Goss, Mrs William, 113
Goss, William, 106, 107
Gostwick, John, 30, 71
Graham-White, Claude, 125, 167
gravel pits, 86, 103, 157, 158, 160, 257
Gray, Captain Harry P T, 138, 139
Gray, Mrs, 138
Great Denham, 5, 66, 243, 258, 289, 324, 325, 334, 341
Green Farm – see Mannings Farm
Green, Barry, 300, 301, 304
Green, Dennis, 220, 300, 301
Green, Eric, 220
Green, Frank, 143, 300
Green, Herbert, 142, 168, 221
Green, Nick, 302
Green, Samuel, 114
Greetham, Mr, 114, 202
Griggs, Frederick Landseer, 38, 151
Grimshawe, Charles, 62
Grimshawe, John, 62
Grimshawe, Mrs, 60, 175, 178
Grimshawe, the Rev Shuttleworth, 42, 60/62, 88, 173, 174, 175
Grocers' Company, 31, 34, 71
Groom's Cottage, 78
Groot, H, 209

Peacock, Dudley, 112, 238, 265
Peacock, H, 168, 212
Peacock, H J, 127
Peacock, Harry, 112
peasants, 17, 18
Penny Black Cottage, 161
Perry, Mrs Sally, 279
Pile family, 36, 235, 236
Pile, Michael, 319, 320
Pile, Mrs, 144
Pile, Ted, 108, 109, 110, 111, 112,
116, 121, 123, 124, 125, 157, 163,
166, 179, 235, 265, 282
Pilgrim School, 290
Pipe Roll 1224, 32
plague, 80
Plain, George, 135
Plain, James, 135, 151
Plain, Mary, 135
Plowden Report, 289
Pole, Capt., 114
Poley, Joan, 33, 78, 80
Poley, John, 32
Policeman, village, 304
pond – manor (see village pond)
pond – Ramsmead, 344
pond – village, 317, 336, 343, 344/5
Poor Law Act, 79, 90
population, 89, 90, 107, 126
Post office, 115, 126, 161
Pringle, Jim, 321
prisoners of war, 223
prizefighting, 99, 100
Profser, Humphrey, 98
Prudden, John, 89
Pyghtle Works, see White and Son,
J P

Quarry, Leonie, 199
Queen's Park Lower School, 283,
289
R101 airship, 167
Randall, Major, 121

Ratsey, Gamaliel, 80
Rattenbury, Mr, 204, 205, 206
Rawlins, Fred, 158, 199, 216, 217,
222, 243, 245, 297, 302, 304, 310,
347
Rawlins, John, 168, 213, 294
Rawlins, Marjorie, 200
Red Cross, 213
Redman, Bert, 313
Reeve, Francis, 54
Reformation, 30
Rice Trevor family, 119, 175
Rice Trevor, Miss, 112
Rice-Trevor, Frances Emily, 102
Rice-Trevor, George Rice, 83, 88,
89, 91, 102
Rice-Trevor, the Hon Miss, 120
Richards, Dorothy, 78, 92, 143, 212,
344
Robinson, Chris, 89
Riddy, Celia, 134
Riddy, Monica, 134
Riddy, Nancy, 134
Riddy, Thomas, 134, 151
Robert Bruce School, Kempston,
268, 278, 280, 282, 320
Roberts, Arthur, 142
Roberts, George, 124
Roberts, Mr L, 211, 212
Roberts, Mrs Barbara, 279, 280/1
Roberts, Tony, 259
Robertson, Ian, 192/5
Robertson, Pat, 193
Robins, Miss, 255
Roll of Honour (St James's Church),
134
Roman invasion, 8
Roman well, 8, 9
Romano-British period, 4, 8
Ronn, Penelope & Phoebe, 196
Ros, Ralph and Serlo de, 16
Rose Cottage, 152, 153, 154
Rose, Michael, 278

Rose, William, 96
rotation of crops, 17
Rowney, Emily, 138
Rowney, Thomas & Kate, 138
Rowney, Walter, 138, 151
Royal British Legion, 229
Royal Observer Corps, 207, 219, 310
Russell, The Hon Romola, 156, 304
Russell, Thomas, 79, 92

Saint James, 52
Salmon, M R, 95
Salmon, Mr, 128
Salmons, F, 209
Salpho, Dom John, 29
Sampson, Richard, 78
Samson, William, 32
Sanders, Mr, 127
Sandon's Act, 176
Sandy, 8
Sargent, Alfred, 150
Sargent, Mr & Mrs, 155
Sargent, Tommy, 240
Sargent, Willie, 143
Sawyer, John, 261
Sawyer, Mrs Evelyn, 279
Schools Attendance Officer, 178
Scott, Miss, 255
Scottish Regiment (Seaforth
Highlanders), 144, 145, 147, 148,
150
Scouts, 121
Sharnbrook Upper School, 284
Sharpe, Mrs, 161
Shaw, Annie C (née Strong), 138
Shaw, Giles Havergal, 135, 151
Shaw, Greville, 138, 151
Shaw, P, 209
Shaw, the Rev & Mrs William H,
135, 138
Shaw, Robert & Alice, 142, 150
Shaw, Ruth, 240
Shelton, John, 89

Sherwood, Don, 58, 345
Shorley family, 106, 107
Shorley, Mr & Mrs, 107, 297
Shurety, Percy, 124, 160, 243
Shurety, Mrs, 310
Silver Jubilee 1977, 265
Simmons, Bertha, 133, 255, 306
Simmons, Edie, 133, 254, 255, 306
Simmons, Fred, 133
Simms, Martin, 261
Simpson, M L, 157, 158, 160, 161,
162
Sims, Alan, 42, 249, 299, 347
Sims, Ernie, 347
Sims, Mrs Mary, 274, 279, 347
Sims, Rita, 249
Skipwyth, Nicholas, 33
Slark, Anthea, 48
Slark, David, 263
Slaughter, Mrs, 166
slaves, 15
Slipe, the, 250
Smallholders, 15
Smith, Ernest, 141
Smith, G, 178
Smith, Mr, 243
Smith, the Rev Chernocke, 62
Smithy – see blacksmith
Smyth, Geoffrey le, 31
Speke, William, 15, 16
Sports, 121-123
Squire, Peter, 349
St Aubyn's, 127
St Gregory's Roman Catholic
Secondary Modern School, 283, 289
St James's infants school, 173
St James's church, 16, 21, 22, 120,
254
St James' school, 63, 66, 173, 226,
276, 287, 299, 306, 348
St James' school photo c 1930, 63
St Mary's House, 302
St Paul's church, Bedford, 15

West family, 36, 46, 116

West, Billy, 242

West, C, 178

West, James, 46, 57, 88, 121

West, Percy, 63

West, Ralph, 46, 48, 283

West, Reginald, 46

West, William, 46, 165

Westaway, Miss Kate, 196, 199, 219

western bypass, 330

wheelwright - see Hebbes, Alfred

wheelwright's shop, 319

whist drives, 163, 349

White and Son, J P, 55, 123, 127, 128, 141, 203

White Cottage, 127

White Cottage, the, 128, 129

White House, The, 127

White, Charlie, 123

White, Miss E, 213

White, John, 90, 127

White, Mrs Judy, 279

Whiteley, Dr M, 1

Whittaker, Christopher, 10

Whitworth, Joseph, 96

Whitworth, Maria, 55

Whitworth, Matilda 89

Whitworth, Mr, 135, 166

Whitworth, Mrs, 111

Whitworth, Robert, 108, 110, 114

Whitworth's Farm, 110, 111

William I (the Conqueror), 12, 13, 15, 16

Williams family, 314

Williams, Bill, 237

Williams, Gareth, 275

Williams, Gladys, 240

Williams, Gwynneth, 314

Williams, L, 209

Williams, William, 150

Williamson, Steve, 96, 97

Wing, Mr, 41

Wingfield Estate, 108, 152, 154, 168, 243, 289

Wingfield family, 102, 152, 153, 239

Wingfield, E R, 36

Wingfield, Edward Ffolliett, 102

Wingfield, Lady, 152

Winnington-Ingram, Cecil, 44, 330

Winnington-Ingram, Maudie, 349

Wolston, Simon de, 31

Women's Institute, 164, 165, 222, 225

Women's Institute scrapbook 1956, 78, 79, 111, 113, 117, 118, 120, 125, 141, 155, 164, 350

Women's Land Army, 143, 198, 199, 244, 245, 246

Wood, Miss, 178

Wood, the Rev Henry, 36, 62, 115, 126, 177

Wood, Tony, 329

Woodward, Henry, 79

Woodward, Mary, 91

World War 1, 109, 129

Wright, Frederick & Eliza, 137

Wright, Richard, 137, 151

Wright, Thomas, 40

Wulfmer, burgess, 16

Wykewane, William de, 19

Young Explorers, 349

Youth club – early, 164

Youth club – church, 315, 321, 327

Youth club – village hall, 315, 327